DE·ROMA

EXCERPTS FROM ANCIENT WRITERS ABOUT ROME

SECOND EDITION

Table of Contents

Sources

	LATIN WRITERS	**GREEK WRITERS**

Middle Republic

PLAUTUS—T. Maccius Plautus (254–184 BCE) was a Roman practitioner of the Greek New Comedy, and one of the earliest surviving playwrights in Latin.

POLYBIUS—Polybius of Megalopolis (200–118 BCE) was a Greek historian who lived in Rome and moved in its elite circles. His important *World History* attempts to explain the rise of Rome down to 146 BCE.

Late Republic

CATULLUS—C. Valerius Catullus (84–54 BCE) was an influential poet whose works were unusual for celebrating the personal rather than the public.

CICERO—M. Tullius Cicero (106–43 BCE, consul 63 BCE) was a Roman philosopher, statesman, lawyer, and political theorist. He came from a wealthy Italian family of the equestrian order, and is generally considered one of Rome's greatest orators and writers.

CORNELIUS NEPOS—Cornelius Nepos, who probably lived from around 100 to 24 BCE, is our first surviving Latin biographer. Nepos among other works wrote at least 16 books of *On Famous Men* and *On Eminent Foreign Leaders*. The last survives and fragments of others remain.

SALLUST—C. Sallustius Crispus (86–34 BCE) was a Roman historian who belonged to a well-known plebeian family. Sallust's writings, including a *History* (which we have only in fragments) and surviving accounts of the Jugurthine War and the Catiline Conspiracy reflect his opposition to Pompey's party and to the old aristocracy of Rome.

DIONYSIUS OF HALICAR-NASSUS—Dionysius (c. 60 BCE–after 7 BCE) of Halicarnassus was a Greek historian and teacher of rhetoric whose history of Rome is, with Livy's, the most valuable source from early Roman history. This work, called *Roman Antiquities* (c. 20 BCE), treats Rome from its origins to the First Punic War.

Julio-Claudian Principate

ASCONIUS—Q. Asconius Pedianus's only surviving work is part of a commentary (54–57 CE) on Cicero's speeches, apparently much abbreviated.

AUGUSTUS—C. Iulius Caesar Octavianus, emperor 27 BCE–14 CE.

CLAUDIUS—Ti. Claudius Caesar Germanicus, emperor 41–54 CE.

HORACE—Q. Horatius Flaccus (65–8 BCE) was a clerk in a public office who attracted the attention of arts patron Mæcenas, henceforth devoting himself to literary pursuits. The first book of *Satires* was soon published in 35 BCE.

LIVY—T. Livius (59 BCE–17 CE) was the author of the authorized version of the history of the Roman republic (27–25 BCE), of which several chapters survive.

PLINY THE ELDER—C. Plinius Secundus (23–79 CE) was a Roman officer and encyclopedist and author of the *Natural History* (77-79 CE).

SENECA—L. Annaeus Seneca, or Seneca the Younger (c. 1 BCE–65 CE), was a Roman Stoic philosopher, statesman, dramatist, and humorist. He was tutor and later advisor to the emperor Nero.

VELLEIUS PATERCULUS—Velleius Paterculus (c. 20 BCE–after 30 CE) was a Roman officer, senator, and scholar, and author of a brief *Roman History* (30 CE).

STRABO—Strabo (63/64 BCE–ca. 24 CE) was a Greek historian, geographer and philosopher, most famous for his 17-volume work *Geographica* (7 BCE), a descriptive history of people and places from different regions of the world known to his era.

	LATIN WRITERS	**GREEK WRITERS**
Flavian Principate	MARTIAL—M. Valerius Martialis (38–104 CE) was a Latin poet and epigrammist from Roman Hispania whose *Elegies* famously satirized Roman life. PLINY THE YOUNGER—C. Plinius Caecilius Secundus (62–c. 115 CE) was a Roman senator and nephew of Pliny the Elder. He was governor of Bithynia–Pontus (109–111) and author of a famous collection of letters.	JOSEPHUS—Josephus, a law-observant and Hellenized Jew, recounted the Jewish revolt against Roman occupation (66–70 CE), in which he had fought as the Jewish military commander in Galilee. After the war he went to Rome, attached to the entourage of the future emperor Titus, and became a Roman citizen.
Middle Principate	SUETONIUS—C. Suetonius Tranquillus (c.71–c.135 CE) was a Roman scholar and official, best-known as the author of the *Lives of the Twelve Caesars* (121 CE). TACITUS—(c.55–c.120 CE) was a Roman historian, author of the *Histories* (105 CE) and the *Annals* (117 CE), which survive but with substantial sections missing, among other works	APPIAN—Appian of Alexandria (c.95–c.165 CE) was a valuable Greek historian, author of a *Roman History* (c. 165 CE). The part on the Civil Wars survives. HERODIAN—Herodianus of Syria (c. 170–240 CE) was a minor Roman civil servant who wrote a colorful history in Greek titled *History of the Empire from the Death of Marcus* (240 CE) in eight books covering the years 180 to 238. PLUTARCH—Plutarch of Chaeronea (46–c.122 CE) was influential Greek philosopher and author, well known for his biographies (including the *Parallel Lives*, written in the late first century) and his moral treatises.
Late Principate	AMMIANUS MARCELLINUS—The last great historian to write in Latin, Ammianus Marcellinus (325/330–after 391 CE) was born in Syrian Antioch. He served in the Roman army in Gaul and against the Persians, and was an officer in the Praetorian Guard. His *History* runs through 378. CONSTANTINE—Flavius Valerius Aurelius Constantinus Augustus, emperor 306–337. JORDANES—Roman bureaucrat and clergyman in the eastern empire who, in his retirement (mid-6th century), wrote a history of Rome and another of the Goths (from which the excerpt on the Battle of Chalôns comes). PRUDENTIUS—Aurelius Prudentius Clemens (348–413 CE) was a Latin poet living in northern Spain, a provincial governor and courtier who later devoted himself to asceticism and Christian poetry. RUTILIUS NAMATIANUS—Rutilius Claudius Namatianus was a 5th century Roman poet whose surviving work elegantly describes a coastal voyage from Rome to Gaul. VOPISCUS—one of the credited authors of the problematic *Historia Augusta* (late 4th century).	EUSEBIUS—Eusebius (263–339 CE) studied under Pamphilius, a Christian scholar and presbyter in the church at Caesarea. His major work was his *History of the Church* (c. 326 CE), a massive piece of research that preserves quotations from many older writers that would otherwise have been lost. JULIAN—Flavius Claudius Julianus Augustus, emperor 355–363. He was known as Julian the Apostate because he attempted to return the Roman Empire to pagan rule, reversing the promotion of Christianity begun by Constantine (his father-in-law and cousin). OXYRHYNCHUS PAPYRI—A large cache of thousands of papyri manuscripts discovered in the 19th century at an ancient Egyptian rubbish dump. SOZOMEN—Salminius Hermias Sozomen was one of the famous historians of the early Church. He was born in Palestine, in the last quarter of the fourth century CE, and died probably in 447 or 448.
Byzantine		PROCOPIUS—Procopius of Caesarea (500–565 CE), a scholar who accompanied Justinian's armies, has been called the last major ancient historian. ZOSIMUS—Zosimus (fl. 490s–510s CE) was a Byzantine historian, who lived in Constantinople during the reign of the Byzantine Emperor Anastasius I (491–518) and was one of its officials.

DIONYSIUS OF HALICARNASSUS

On the Subject of Roman History

Source: Dion. Hal. RA 1.1-8. Translated by Earnest Cary. In The Roman Antiquities of Dionysius of Halicarnassus. Loeb classical library. Cambridge, Mass: Harvard University Press, 1937.

Dionysius began his history of Rome with an assertion that such an endeavor was a worthy one.

Although it is much against my will to indulge in the explanatory statements usually given in the prefaces to histories, yet I am obliged to prefix to this work some remarks concerning myself. In doing this it is neither my intention to dwell too long on my own praise, which I know would be distasteful to the reader, nor have I the purpose of censuring other historians, as Anaximenes and Theopompus[1] did in the prefaces to their histories, but I shall only show the reasons that induced me to undertake this work and give an accounting of the sources from which I gained the knowledge of the things that I am going to relate.

For I am convinced that all who propose to leave such monuments of their minds to posterity as time shall not involve in one common ruin with their bodies, and particularly those who write histories, in which we have the right to assume that Truth, the source of both prudence and wisdom, is enshrined, ought, first of all, to make choice of noble and lofty subjects and such as will be of great utility to their readers, and then, with great care and pains, to provide themselves with the proper equipment for the treatment of their subject.

For those who base historical works upon deeds inglorious or evil or unworthy of serious study, either because they crave to come to the knowledge of men and to get a name of some sort or other, or because they desire to display the wealth of their rhetoric, are neither admired by posterity for their fame nor praised for their eloquence; rather, they leave this opinion in the minds of all who take up their histories, that they themselves admired lives which were of a piece with the writings they published, since it is a just and a general opinion that a man's words are the images of his mind.

Those, on the other hand, who, while making choice of the best subjects, are careless and indolent in compiling their narratives out of such reports as chance to come to their ears gain no praise by reason of that choice; for we do not deem it fitting that the histories of renowned cities and of men who have held supreme power should be written in an offhand or negligent manner. As I believe these considerations to be

necessary and of the first importance to historians and as I have taken great care to observe them both, I have felt unwilling either to omit mention of them or to give it any other place than in the preface to my work.

That I have indeed made choice of a subject noble, lofty and useful to many will not, I think, require any lengthy argument, at least for those who are not utterly unacquainted with universal history. For if anyone turns his attention to the successive supremacies both of cities and of nations, as accounts of them have been handed down from times past, and then, surveying them severally and comparing them together, wishes to determine which of them obtained the widest dominion and both in peace and war performed the most brilliant achievements, he will find that the supremacy of the Romans has far surpassed all those that are recorded from earlier times, not only in the extent of its dominion and in the splendor of its achievements—which no account has as yet worthily celebrated—but also in the length of time during which it has endured down to our day.

For the empire of the Assyrians, ancient as it was and running back to legendary times, held sway over only a small part of Asia. That of the Medes, after overthrowing the Assyrian empire and obtaining a still wider dominion, did not hold it long, but was overthrown in the fourth generation.[2] The Persians, who conquered the Medes, did, indeed, finally become masters of almost all Asia; but when they attacked the nations of Europe also, they did not reduce many of them to submission, and they continued in power not much above two hundred years.[3]

The Macedonian dominion, which overthrew the might of the Persians, did, in the extent of its sway, exceed all its predecessors, yet even it did not flourish long, but after Alexander's death began to decline; for it was immediately partitioned among many commanders from the time of the Diadochi,[4] and although after their time it was able to go on to the second or third generation, yet it was weakened by its own dissensions and at the last destroyed by the Romans.[5]

But even the Macedonian power did not subjugate every country and every sea; for it neither conquered Libya, with the exception of the small portion bordering on Egypt, nor subdued all Europe, but in the North advanced only as far as Thrace and in the West down to the Adriatic Sea.

Thus we see that the most famous of the earlier supremacies of which history has given us any account, after attaining to so great vigor and might, were

---

[1] Anaximenes of Lampsacus wrote a history of Greece (down to the battle of Mantinea) and a history of Philip of Macedon; also an epic on Alexander. Theopompus in his *Hellenica* continued the history of Thucydides from 411 down to the battle of Cnidus in 394; his *Philippica*, in 58 books, treated not only of Philip but of contemporary events elsewhere.

[2] In 550 BCE, in the reign of Astyages, the fourth Median king.
[3] 550⧄330 BCE.
[4] I.e. "Successors," the term applied to the generals of Alexander who divided his empire among themselves after his death.
[5] By the overthrow of Perseus in 168, or possibly by the defeat of Philip V in 197, followed by that of Antiochus in 190.

overthrown. As for the Greek powers, it is not fitting to compare them to those just mentioned, since they gained neither magnitude of empire nor duration of eminence equal to theirs.

For the Athenians ruled only the sea coast, during the space of sixty-eight years,[6] nor did their sway extend even over all that, but only to the part between the Euxine and the Pamphylian seas, when their naval supremacy was at its height. The Lacedaemonians, when masters of the Peloponnesus and the rest of Greece, advanced their rule as far as Macedonia, but were checked by the Thebans before they had held it quite thirty years.[7]

But Rome rules every country that is not inaccessible or uninhabited, and she is mistress of every sea, not only of that which lies inside the Pillars of Hercules but also of the Ocean, except that part of it which is not navigable;[8] she is the first and the only State recorded in all time that ever made the risings and the settings of the sun the boundaries of her dominion. Nor has her supremacy been of short duration, but more lasting than that of any other commonwealth or kingdom.

For from the very beginning, immediately after her founding, she began to draw to herself the neighboring nations, which were both numerous and warlike, and continually advanced, subjugating every rival. And it is now seven hundred and forty-five years from her foundation down to the consulship of Claudius Nero, consul for the second time, and of Calpurnius Piso, who were chosen in the one hundred and ninety-third Olympiad.[9]

From the time that she mastered the whole of Italy she was emboldened to aspire to govern all mankind, and after driving from off the sea the Carthaginians, whose maritime strength was superior to that of all others, and subduing Macedonia, which until then was reputed to be the most powerful nation on land, she no longer had as rival any nation either barbarian or Greek; and it is now in my day already the seventh generation[10] that she has continued to hold sway over every region of the world, and there is no nation, as I may saw, that disputes her universal dominion or protests against being ruled by her.

However, to prove my statement that I have neither made choice of the most trivial of subjects nor proposed to treat of mean and insignificant deeds, but am undertaking to write not only about the most illustrious city but also about brilliant achievements to whose like no man could point, I know not what more I need say.

DIONYSIUS OF HALICARNASSUS

Early Rules for Clients and Patrons

Source: Dion. Hal. *RA* 2.10-11. Translated by Earnest Cary. In *The Roman Antiquities of Dionysius of Halicarnassus*. Loeb classical library. Cambridge, Mass: Harvard University Press, 1937.

Dionysius is extolling the justice by which Romulus placed the plebeians in the hands of the patricians, creating a set of mutual obligations.

The regulations which he [Romulus] then instituted concerning patronage and which long continued in use among the Romans were as follows: It was the duty of the patricians to explain to their clients the laws, of which they were ignorant; to take the same care of them when absent as present, doing everything for them that fathers do for their sons with regard both to money and to the contracts that related to money; to bring suit on behalf of their clients when they were wronged in connection with contracts, and to defend them against any who brought charges against them; and, to put the matter briefly, to secure for them both in private and in public affairs all that tranquility of which they particularly stood in need.

It was the duty of the clients to assist their patrons in providing dowries for their daughters upon their marriage if the fathers had not sufficient means; to pay their ransom to the enemy if any of them or of their children were taken prisoner; to discharge out of their own purses their patrons' losses in private suits and the pecuniary fines which they were condemned to pay to the State, making these contributions to them not as loans but as thank-offerings; and to share with their patrons the costs incurred in their magistracies and dignities[11] and other public expenditures, in the same manner as if they were their relations.

For both patrons and clients alike it was impious and unlawful to accuse each other in law-suits or to bear witness or to give their votes against each other or to be found in the number of each other's enemies; and whoever was convicted of doing any of these things was guilty of treason by virtue of the law sanctioned by Romulus, and might lawfully be put to death by any man who so wished as a victim devoted to the Jupiter of the

---

[6] From ca. 472 to 404.

[7] This statement is puzzling, since the period actually extended from the surrender of Athens in 404 to the battle of Leuctra in 371. The text may be corrupt.

[8] Dionysius may have had in mind Pytheas' report of a πεπηγυῖα Θάλασσα (a sea filled with floating ice?) in the far north. From Eratosthenes we learn also that that other early navigator, the Carthaginian Hanno, who sailed far south along the west coast of Africa, was finally forced by many difficulties (of what sort we are not told) to turn back.

[9] Nero and Piso were consuls in 7 BCE This was the year 745 of the City according to Dionysius, who assigns its founding to the year 751.

[10] This would normally mean six full generations plus part of another. If Dionysius was counting from the battle of Pydna (168), he must have reckoned a generation here at less than twenty-eight years (his usual estimate); but he may have felt that the Macedonian power was broken at Cynoscephalae (197).

---

[11] The word γερηφορία should mean literally the "bearing, or enjoyment, of privileges," hence a "position of honour" or a "dignity." Presumably the reference is to priesthoods.

infernal regions.[12] For it was customary among the Romans, whenever they wished to put people to death without incurring any penalty, to devote their persons to some god or other, and particularly to the gods of the lower world; and this was the course what Romulus then adopted.

Accordingly, the connections between the clients and patrons continued for many generations, differing in no wise from the ties of blood-relationship and being handed down to their children's children. And it was a matter of great praise to men of illustrious families to have as many clients as possible and not only to preserve the succession of hereditary patronages but also by their own merit to acquire others. And it is incredible how great the contest of goodwill was between the patrons and clients, as each side strove not to be outdone by the other in kindness, the clients feeling that they should render all possible services to their patrons and the patrons wishing by all means not to occasion any trouble to their clients and accepting no gifts of money. So superior was their manner to all pleasure; for they measured their happiness by virtue, not by fortune.

It was not only in the city itself that the plebeians were under the protection of the patricians, but every colony of Rome and every city that had joined in alliance and friendship with her and also every city conquered in war had such protectors and patrons among the Romans as they wished. And the senate has often referred the controversies of these cities and nations to their Roman patrons and regarded their decisions binding.

And indeed, so secure was the Romans' harmony, which owed its birth to the regulations of Romulus, that they never in the course of six hundred and thirty years[13] proceeded to bloodshed and mutual slaughter, though many great controversies arose between the populace and their magistrates concerning public policy, as is apt to happen in all cities, whether large or small; but by persuading and informing one another, by yielding in some things and gaining other things from their opponents, who yielded in turn, they settled their disputes in a manner befitting fellow citizens. But from the time that C. Gracchus, while holding the tribunician power, destroyed the harmony of the government they have been perpetually slaying and banishing one another from the city and refraining from no irreparable acts in order to gain the upper hand.

---

[12] i.e. Dis or Pluto.
[13] Dionysius ignores the bloodshed in connection with the slaying of Tiberius Gracchus in 133 and the execution of many Gracchans that followed. The overthrow of C. Gracchus occurred at the very beginning of the year 121, which was the year 631 of the City according to Dionysius' reckoning.

Numa's Religious Settlement

Source: Livy 1.20–21. Translated by William Masfen Roberts. In *The History of Rome*. London: J.M. Dent, 1912.

Numa Pompilius, according to legend the second king of Rome, was credited with laying down the foundations of the Roman state religion. He is supposed to have been a Sabine and to have eschewed luxury.

Next he turned his attention to the appointment of priests. He himself, however, conducted a great many religious services, especially those which belong to the Flamen of Jupiter.[14] But he thought that in a warlike state there would be more kings of the type of Romulus than of Numa who would take the field in person. To guard, therefore, against the sacrificial rites which the king performed being interrupted, he appointed a Flamen as perpetual priest to Jupiter, and ordered that he should wear a distinctive dress and sit in the royal curule chair. He appointed two additional Flamens, one for Mars, the other for Quirinus, and also chose virgins as priestesses to Vesta. This order of priestesses came into existence originally in Alba and was connected with the race of the founder.[15] He assigned them a public stipend that they might give their whole time to the temple, and made their persons sacred and inviolable by a vow of chastity and other religious sanctions.

Similarly he chose twelve "Salii" for Mars Gradivus, and assigned to them the distinctive dress of an embroidered tunic and over it a brazen cuirass. They were instructed to march in solemn procession through the City, carrying the twelve shields called the "Ancilia," and singing hymns accompanied by a solemn dance in triple time.

The next office to be filled was that of the Pontifex Maximus.[16] Numa appointed the son of M., one of the senators—Numa Marcius—and all the regulations bearing on religion, written out and sealed, were placed in his charge. Here was laid down with what victims, on what days, and at what temples the various sacrifices were to be offered, and from what sources the expenses connected with them were to be defrayed.

He placed all other sacred functions, both public and private, under the supervision of the Pontifex, in order that there might be an authority for the people to consult, and so all trouble and confusion arising through

---

[14] A flamen was a priest devoted to a particular god. The three described as being created here—the Flamen Dialis, Flamen Martialis, and Flamen Quirinalis—were the only important ones, though a dozen minor flaminates were created later.
[15] The Vestales, or Vestal virgins, were the virgin priestesses of Vesta who ministered in her temple and watched the eternal fire, its extinction being considered as the most fearful of all prodigies, and emblemate of the extinction of the state.
[16] Chief priest. The origin of *pontifex* is disputed; it may relate to *pons* 'bridge,' so to archaic sacrifices made on the Sacred Bridge.

foreign rites being adopted and their ancestral ones neglected might be avoided. Nor were his functions confined to directing the worship of the celestial gods; he was to instruct the people how to conduct funerals and appease the spirits of the departed, and what prodigies sent by lightning or in any other way were to be attended to and expiated. To elicit these signs of the divine will, he dedicated an altar to Jupiter Elicius[17] on the Aventine, and consulted the god through auguries, as to which prodigies were to receive attention.

The deliberations and arrangements which these matters involved diverted the people from all thoughts of war and provided them with ample occupation. The watchful care of the gods, manifesting itself in the providential guidance of human affairs, had kindled in all hearts such a feeling of piety that the sacredness of promises and the sanctity of oaths were a controlling force for the community scarcely less effective than the fear inspired by laws and penalties. And whilst his subjects were molding their characters upon the unique example of their king, the neighboring nations, who had hitherto believed that it was a fortified camp and not a city that was placed amongst them to vex the peace of all, were now induced to respect them so highly that they thought it sinful to injure a State so entirely devoted to the service of the gods.

There was a grove through the midst of which a perennial stream flowed, issuing from a dark cave. Here Numa frequently retired unattended as if to meet the goddess, and he consecrated the grove to the Camaenae, because it was there that their meetings with his wife Egeria took place. He also instituted a yearly sacrifice to the goddess Fides and ordered that the Flamens should ride to her temple in a hooded chariot, and should perform the service with their hands covered as far as the fingers, to signify that Faith must be sheltered and that her seat is holy even when it is in men's right hands. There were many other sacrifices appointed by him and places dedicated for their performance which the pontiffs call the Argei.

The greatest of all his works was the preservation of peace and the security of his realm throughout the whole of his reign. Thus by two successive kings the greatness of the State was advanced; by each in a different way, by the one through war, by the other through peace. Romulus reigned thirty-seven years, Numa forty-three. The State was strong and disciplined by the lessons of war and the arts of peace.

LIVY

The Capture of the Sabine Women

Source: Livy 1.9–1.33. Translated by William Masfen Roberts. In *The History of Rome*. London: J.M. Dent, 1912.

According to legend, Rome, founded as it was by adventurers and immigrants, had an acute shortage of women. The story of Romulus's plan—to take their neighbors' maidens—was repeated in the later Republic most of all because it was justified in retrospect by the maidens' defense of their new home.

The Roman State had now become so strong that it was a match for any of its neighbors in war, but its greatness threatened to last for only one generation, since through the absence of women there was no hope of offspring, and there was no right of intermarriage with their neighbors. Acting on the advice of the senate, Romulus sent envoys amongst the surrounding nations to ask for alliance and the right of intermarriage on behalf of his new community....

As to the origin of Rome, it was well known that whilst it had received divine assistance, courage and self-reliance were not wanting. There should, therefore, be no reluctance for men to mingle their blood with their fellow-men. Nowhere did the envoys meet with a favorable reception....

The Roman youth could ill brook such insults, and matters began to look like an appeal to force. To secure a favorable place and time for such an attempt, Romulus, disguising his resentment, made elaborate preparations for the celebration of games in honor of "Equestrian Neptune," which he called "the Consualia."...

There was a great gathering; people were eager to see the new City, all their nearest neighbors ... and the whole Sabine population came, with their wives and families. They were invited to accept hospitality at the different houses, and after examining the situation of the City, its walls and the large number of dwelling-houses it included, they were astonished at the rapidity with which the Roman State had grown.

When the hour for the games had come, and their eyes and minds were alike riveted on the spectacle before them, the preconcerted signal was given and the Roman youth dashed in all directions to carry off the maidens who were present. The larger part were carried off indiscriminately....

Alarm and consternation broke up the games, and the parents of the maidens fled, distracted with grief, uttering bitter reproaches on the violators of the laws of hospitality and appealing to the god to whose solemn games they had come, only to be the victims of impious perfidy.

---

[17] Jupiter in his aspect as god of thunder and lightning.

The abducted maidens were quite as despondent and indignant. Romulus, however, went round in person, and pointed out to them that it was all owing to the pride of their parents in denying right of intermarriage to their neighbors. They would live in honorable wedlock, and share all their property and civil rights, and—dearest of all to human nature-would be the mothers of freemen.

[War breaks out between the Sabines and the Romans.] Then it was that the Sabine women, whose wrongs had led to the war, throwing off all womanish fears in their distress, went boldly into the midst of the flying missiles with disheveled hair and rent garments. Running across the space between the two armies they tried to stop any further fighting and calm the excited passions by appealing to their fathers in the one army and their husbands in the other not to bring upon themselves a curse by staining their hands with the blood of a father-in-law or a son-in-law, nor upon their posterity the taint of parricide. "If," they cried, "you are weary of these ties of kindred, these marriage-bonds, then turn your anger upon us; it is we who are the cause of the war, it is we who have wounded and slain our husbands and fathers. Better for us to perish rather than live without one or the other of you, as widows or as orphans."

DIONYSIUS OF HALICARNASSUS

Servius Tullius's Reform of the Comitia Centuriata

Source: Dion. Hal. RA 4.20-21. Translated by Earnest Cary. In *The Roman Antiquities of Dionysius of Halicarnassus*. Loeb classical library. Cambridge, Mass: Harvard University Press, 1937.

> *The comitia centuriata, or centuriate assembly, was conceived as the army sitting as a legislature. Just as the army was arranged according to class, so too was the comitia centuriata. Its structure as known in the middle republic was associated with Servius Tullius, the penultimate king.*

Having by this means laid upon the rich the whole burden of both the dangers and expenses and observing that they hand discontented, he contrived by another method to relieve their uneasiness and mitigate their resentment by granting to them an advantage which would make them complete masters of the commonwealth, while he excluded the poor from any part in the government; and he effected this without the plebeians noticing it. This advantage that he gave to the rich related to the assemblies, where the matters of greatest moment were ratified by the people.

I have already said before that by the ancient laws the people had control over the three most important and vital matters: they elected the magistrates, both civil and military; they sanctioned and repealed laws; and they declared war and made peace. In discussing and deciding these matters they voted by curiae, and citizens of the smallest means had an equal vote with those of the greatest; but as the rich were few in number, as may well be supposed, and the poor much more numerous, the latter carried everything by a majority of votes.

Tullius, observing this, transferred this preponderance of votes from the poor to the rich. For whenever he thought proper to have magistrates elected, a law considered, or war to be declared, he assembled the people by centuries instead of by curiae. And the first centuries that he called to express their opinion[18] were those with the highest rating, consisting of the eighteen centuries of cavalry and the eighty centuries of infantry.

As these centuries amounted to three more than all the rest together, if they agreed they prevailed over the others and the matter was decided. But in case these were not all of the same mind, then he called the twenty-two centuries of the second class; and if the votes were still divided, he called the centuries of the third class, and, in the fourth place, those of the fourth class; and this he continued to do till ninety-seven centuries concurred in the same opinion.

And if after the calling of the fifth class this had not yet happened but the opinions of the hundred and ninety-two centuries were equally divided, he then called the last century, consisting of the mass of the citizens who were poor and for that reason exempt from all military service and taxes; and whichever side this century joined, that side carried the day. But this seldom happened and was next to impossible. Generally the 1n was determined by calling the first class, and it rarely went as far as the fourth; so that the fifth and the last were superfluous.

In establishing this political system, which gave so great an advantage to the rich, Tullius outwitted the people, as I said, without their noticing it and excluded the poor from any part in public affairs. For they all thought that they had an equal share in the government because every man was asked his opinion, each in his own century; but they were deceived in this, that the whole century, whether it consisted of a small or a very large number of citizens, had but one vote; and also in that the centuries which voted first, consisting of men of the highest rating, though they were more in number than all the rest, yet contained fewer citizens; but, above all, in that the poor, who were very numerous, had but one vote and were the last called.

When this had been brought about, the rich, though paying out large sums and exposed without intermission

---

[18] If taken literally, this expression is erroneous. The popular assemblies were not deliberative bodies; they could merely vote "aye" or "no" to a specific proposal. But probably Dionysius meant no more by his expression than "give their vote."

to the dangers of war, were less inclined to feel aggrieved now that they had obtained control of the most important matters and had taken the whole power out of the hands of those who were not performing the same services; and the poor, who had but the slightest share in the government, finding themselves exempt both from taxes and from military service, prudently and quietly submitted to this diminution of their power; and the commonwealth itself had the advantage of seeing the same persons who were to deliberate concerning its interests allotted the greatest share of the dangers and ready to do whatever required to be done.

This form of government was maintained by the Romans for many generations, but is altered in our times and changed to a more democratic form, some urgent needs having forced the change, which was effected, not by abolishing the centuries, but by no longer observing the strict ancient manner of calling them[19]—a fact which I myself have noted, having often been present at the elections of their magistrates. But this is not the proper occasion to discuss these matters.

LIVY

The Rape of Lucretia

Source: Livy 1.57–59. Translated from the original in Jean Bayet, ed., *Tite-Live: Histoire Romaine*, Tome I, livre I. Paris: Societé d'Édition "les belles-lettres," 1954, pp. 92-95.

In this excerpt, Livy repeats a legend that was extremely important to Romans during the Republic. The sons of the King of Rome, L. Tarquinius Superbus, are at Ardea, a city which the army is attempting to conquer, when they hear of the virtue of the Roman matron Lucretia. The virtues this story puts forth for Roman society through the example of Lucretia helps explain why this story would have mattered to later Romans.

One day when the young men were drinking at the house of Sex. Tarquinius, after a supper where they had dined with the son of Egerius, Tarquinius Conlatinus, they fell to talking about their wives, and each man fell to praising his wife to excess. Finally Tarquinius Conlatinus declared that there was no need to argue; they might all be sure that no one was more worthy than his Lucretia. "Young and vigorous as we are, why don't we go get out horses and go and see for ourselves what our wives are doing? And we will base our judgment on whatever we see them doing when their husbands arrive unannounced." Encouraged by the wine, "Yes, let's go!" they all cried, and they went on horseback to the city. Darkness was beginning to fall when they arrived and they went to the house of Conlatinus. There, they found Lucretia behaving quite differently from the daughters-in-law of the King, whom they had found with their friends before a grand feast, preparing to have a night of fun. Lucretia, even though it was night, was still working on her spinning, with her servants, in the middle of her house. They were all impressed by Lucretia's chaste honor. When her husband and the Tarquins arrived, she received them, and her husband, the winner, was obliged to invite the king's sons in. It was then that Sex. Tarquinius was seized by the desire to violate Lucretia's chastity, seduced both by her beauty and by her exemplary virtue. Finally, after a night of youthful games, they returned to the camp.

Several days passed. Sex. Tarquinius returned to the house of Conlatinus, with one of his companions. He was well received and given the hospitality of the house, and maddened with love, he waited until he was sure everyone else was asleep. Then he took up his sword and went to Lucretia's bedroom, and placing his sword against her left breast, he said, "Quiet, Lucretia; I am Sextus Tarquinius, and I have a sword in my hand. If you speak, you will die." Awakening from sleep, the poor woman realized that she was without help and very close to death. Sex. Tarquinius declared his love for her, begging and threatening her alternately, and attacked her soul in every way. Finally, before her steadfastness, which was not affected by the fear of death even after his intimidation, he added another menace. "When I have killed you, I will put next to you the body of a nude servant, and everyone will say that you were killed during a dishonorable act of adultery." With this menace, Sex. Tarquinius triumphed over her virtue, and when he had raped her he left, having taken away her honor.

Lucretia, overcome with sorrow and shame, sent messengers both to her husband at Ardea and her father at Rome, asking them each to come "at once, with a good friend, because a very terrible thing had happened." S. Lucretius, her father, came with P. Valerius, the son of Volesus, and Conlatinus came with L. Junius Brutus; they had just returned to Rome when they met Lucretia's messenger. They found Lucretia in her chamber, overpowered by grief. When she saw them she began to cry. "How are you?" her husband asked. "Very bad," she replied, "how can anything go well for a woman who has lost her honor? There are the marks of another man in your bed, Conlatinus. My body is greatly soiled, though my heart is still pure, as my death will prove. But give me your right hand in faith that you will not allow the

---

[19] No ancient writer gives us an explicit account of this reform of the comitia centuriata; but from scattered allusions it is known that each of the five classes later contained 80 companies (one of seniores and one of iuniores from each of the 35 tribes). To these 350 centuries must be added the centuries of knights (probably 18, as before, though 35 and even 70 have been suggested), and perhaps also those of the artisans and musicians (4 as before?) and the one century of proletarii. The knights no longer voted first, but one century out of the first class (or possibly out of all five classes) was chosen by lot to give its vote first; then followed the knights and the several classes in a fixed order. This reform may have been introduced at the time when the last two tribes were created, in 241 BCE. Livy's statement (I.43.12) is tantalizingly brief.

guilty to escape. It was Sex. Tarquinius who returned our hospitality with enmity last night. With his sword in his hand, he came to take his pleasure for my unhappiness, but it will also be his sorrow if you are real men."

They promised her that they would pursue him, and they tried to appease her sorrow, saying that it was the soul that did wrong, and not the body, and because she had had no bad intention, she did no wrong. "It is your responsibility to see that he gets what he deserves," she said, "I will absolve myself of blame, and I will not free myself from punishment. No woman shall use Lucretia as her example in dishonor." Then she took up a knife which she had hidden beneath her robe, and plunged it into her heart, collapsing from her wound; she died there amid the cries of her husband and father.

Brutus, leaving them in their grief, took the knife from Lucretia's wound, and holding it all covered with blood up in the aid, cried, "By this blood, which was so pure before the crime of the prince, I swear before you, O gods, to chase the King L. Tarquinius Superbus, with his criminal wife and all their offspring, by fire, iron, and all the methods I have at my disposal, and never to tolerate Kings in Rome evermore, whether of that family of any other."

DIONYSIUS OF HALICARNASSUS
Coriolanus Opposes the Plebs

Source: Dion. Hal. *RA* 7..20–25 Translated by Earnest Cary. In *The Roman Antiquities of Dionysius of Halicarnassus.* Loeb classical library. Cambridge, Mass: Harvard University Press, 1937.

The story of C. Marcius Coriolanus, the famous turncoat, was later also identified with the conflict of the orders. When the aristocrats replaced the kings, who had sometimes intervened on behalf of the poor, the result was a debt crisis and open conflict between the patricians and the plebeians. It is difficult to establish the historical truth of the Coriolanus legend. The story of Coriolanus's conflict with the plebeians and his trial is probably an addition to an older story.[20]

When word was brought to the people in Rome that the ships had arrived from Sicily laden with corn, a long debate arose among the patricians concerning the disposal of it.[21] For those among them who were the most reasonable and the greatest friends of the people, having in view the public necessary, advised them to distribute all the corn given by the tyrant among the plebeians, and to sell to them at a low price that which had been purchased with the public funds, pointing out that by these favors more than by any other means the animosity of the poor against the rich would be moderated. On the other hand, those who were more arrogant and more zealous for the oligarchy thought that they ought to use every effort and every means to oppress the plebeians; and they advised making the provisions as costly as possible to them in order that they might through necessity become more moderate and more observant in general of the principles of justice prescribed by the constitution.

One of this oligarchic party was that Marcius, surnamed Coriolanus, who did not, like the rest, deliver his opinion with secrecy and caution, but with so much openness and boldness that many even of the plebeians heard him.[22] It seems that, besides the general grievance against them which he shared with the others, he had lately received some private provocations that seemed to justify his hatred of the plebeians.

For when he had stood for the consulship at the last election, in which he had been supported by the patricians, the people had opposed him and would not permit that magistracy to be conferred on him, since his brilliant reputation and daring inclined them to caution, lest he might make some move to overthrow the tribuneship, and they were particularly apprehensive because the whole body of the patricians promoted his interest with a zeal they had never before shown for any other candidate.

Marcius, therefore, being exasperated at this humiliation, and at the same time desirous of restoring the government to its ancient form, not only worked openly himself, as I have already said, to overthrow the power of the people, but also urged his associates on to the same end. He had about him a large faction of young men of noble birth and of the greatest fortunes, as well as many clients who had attached themselves to him for the sake of the booty to be gained in the wars. Elated by these advantages, he assumed a haughty air, became conspicuous, and attained to the greatest distinction.

And yet, for all this, he did not come to a fortunate end, as shall now be related. The senate having been assembled to consider the matters I have mentioned, and the older senators, according to custom, having delivered their opinions first, only a few of them declaring openly against the populace, when it came to the turn of the younger senators to speak, Marcius asked leave of the consuls to say what he wished; and meeting with loud acclaim and strict attention, he delivered the following harangue against the populace:

---

[20] It was supposedly after Coriolanus had made many enemies championing the power of the aristocracy that he was banished from Rome; embittered, he allied himself with Rome's enemies, the Volscians.
[21] The action takes place in 497 BCE, when Rome relieved a grain shortage with several new shipments from Sicily and other markets in Italy.

---

[22] That is, he expressed his opinions openly to the senate, loud enough that his speeches could be heard outside the meeting house, the doors of which were normally kept open.

"That the populace seceded, after him, not because of necessity and want, but because they were elated by the mischievous hope of destroying your aristocracy and of becoming themselves masters of the commonwealth, I think has become clear to nearly all of you when you observe the advantages which they gained by the accommodation. For they were not content, after they had destroyed the good faith which gave validity to their contracts and had abolished the laws made to secure it, to carry their meddling no farther, but introducing a new magistracy designed to overthrow that of the consuls, they made it sacred and inviolable by law, and have now, unobserved by you, senators, been acquiring a tyrannical power through this newly-enacted law.

"For when their leaders, in their great power putting forward the specious pretence of coming to the aid of such plebeians as are wronged, sack and pillage whatever they please by virtue of that power, and when there is no man, either private citizen or magistrate, who will oppose their lawless deeds for fear of this law, which destroys even our liberty of speech as well as of action by imposing the penalty of death on all who utter a word befitting freemen, what other name ought to be given by sensible men to this domination but that which is the true one and which you would all own to be such, namely, a tyranny? And if we are under the tyranny, not of one man, but of a whole populace, what is the difference? For the effect of both is the same.

"It would have been best, therefore, never to have permitted even the seed of this power to be sown, but rather to have submitted to everything, as the excellent Appius, who foresaw these mischiefs from afar, advised. But if that could not be, we ought now at least with one accord to pluck it up by the roots and cast it out of the city while it is yet weak and easily combated.

"And we are not the first or the only persons to whom this experience has come, senators, but oft-times in the part many who have been reduced to unenviable straits and have failed to take the best counsel in matters of the greatest consequence, since they did not check the beginnings of the evil, have endeavored to prevent its growth. And the repentance of those who are late in beginning to be wise, though inferior to foresight, yet, when viewed in another light, is seen to be no less valuable, since it wipes out the error originally made in ignorance by preventing its consequences.

"But if any of you, while looking upon the actions of the populace as outrageous and believing that they ought to be prevented from making any further mistakes, are nevertheless afraid of seeming to be the first to violate the agreement and transgress the oaths, let them know that, since they will not be the aggressors but will be repelling aggression, and will not be violating the agreement but rather punishing the violators of it, they will not only be guiltless towards the gods, but will also be doing an act of justice while they consult their own interest.

"And let this be a strong argument that it is not you who are taking the first steps to break the agreement and violate treaty, but rather the plebeian element, by not observing the conditions upon which they obtained their return. For, after asking for the tribunician power, not in order to injure the senate, but to secure themselves from being injured by the senate, they no longer employ this power for the purposes they ought or on the terms on which they obtained it, but for the overthrow and destruction of the established government.

"For surely you recall the recent assembly of the people and the harangues there made by their demagogues, what arrogance and unruliness they showed, and how these infatuated men vaunt themselves now, since they have discovered that the whole control of the commonwealth lies in the vote, which they will control, being more numerous than we.

"What, therefore, remains for us to do, now that they have begun to violate the compact and the law, but to repel to attacks of the aggressors, to deprive them justly of what they now unjustly possess, and for the future to put a stop to their craving for ever more and more? And we should return thanks to the gods for not having permitted them, when they had gained an unfair advantage at first, to act after that with moderation, but for having inspired them with this shamelessness and officiousness which have forced you to endeavor both to recover the rights you have lost and to guard with due care those that remain.

"The present opportunity is favorable as no other, if you really intend to begin to act with wisdom, since the greater part of the plebeians are now reduced to dire straits by the famine and the rest cannot hold out for want of money if they find proves scarce and dear. The worst of them and those who were never pleased with the aristocracy will be forced to leave the city, and the more reasonable will be compelled to behave themselves in an orderly manner without giving you any further trouble.

"Keep the provisions, therefore, under guard, and abate nothing of the price of commodities, but pass a vote that they shall now be sold at as high a price as ever. For this you have just grounds and plausible excuses in the ungrateful clamor of the populace to the effect that the scarcity of corn was contrived by you, whereas it was occasioned by their own revolt and the desolation of the country which they caused when they pillaged it just as if it had been the territory of an enemy; and again in the disbursements from the treasury to the men sent to purchase corn, and in many other instances in which you have been wronged by them. By this means we shall also know at last what that grievous treatment is which they are going to inflict upon us if we refuse to gratify the people in everything, as their demagogues threatened in order to frighten us.

"But if you let this opportunity also slip from your grasp, you will often pray for such another. Moreover, if the people should become aware that you desired to overthrow their power but were deterred, they will bear down much harder upon you, looking upon your desire as a proof of enmity and upon your inability to carry it out as evidence of cowardice."

After this speech of Marcius the opinions of the senators were divided and a great tumult arose among them. For those who from the beginning had opposed the plebeians and submitted to the accommodation against their will, among whom were almost all the youth and the richest and most ambitious of the older senators, some of them resenting the losses sustained in the loans they had made under contract and others their defeat when they sought office, applauded Marcius as a man of spirit and a lover of his country, who advised what was best for the commonwealth.

On the other hand, the senators whose sympathies were with the populace and who set no undue value on riches and thought nothing was or necessary than peace, were offended at his speech and rejected his advice. These maintained that they ought to surpass the humbler citizens, not in violence, but in kindness, and that they ought to regard reasonableness as not unbecoming, but necessary, particularly when it was manifested out of goodwill towards their fellow-citizens; and they declared that the advice of Marcius was madness, not frankness of speech or liberty. But this group was small and weak, and hence was overborne by the more violent party.

The tribunes, seeing this—for they were present in the senate at the invitation of the consuls—cried out and were in great conflict of mind, calling Marcius the pest and bane of the state for uttering malicious words against the populace; and unless the patricians should prevent his design of introducing civil war into the state by punishing him with death or banishment, they said they would do so themselves.

When a still greater tumult arose at these words of the tribunes, particularly on the part of the younger senators, who bore their threats with impatience, Marcius, inspired by these manifestations, now attacked the tribunes with greater arrogance and boldness, saying to them: "Unless you cease disturbing the commonwealth and stirring up the poor by your harangues, I shall no longer oppose you with words, but with deeds."

The Tribunes and their Manipulation

Source: Dion. Hal. *RA* 8.87, 9.1. Translated by Earnest Cary. In *The Roman Antiquities of Dionysius of Halicarnassus*. Loeb classical library. Cambridge, Mass: Harvard University Press, 1937.

> *The development of the unique role of the tribunate of the plebs is a topic taken up by every ancient commentator who strays into the time of the early Republic, always to reinforce a particular view of why the Republic evolved as it did. The actual facts are not known.*

Those elected consuls for the ensuing year[23] were M. Fabius, son of K.,[24] the younger brother of the consul who conducted the election, and L. Valerius, the son of M.,[25] the man who had accused Cassius, who had been thrice consul, of aiming at tyranny and caused him to be put to death.[26]

These men, having taken office, asked for the levying of fresh troops to replace those who had perished in the war against the Antiates, in order that the gaps in the various centuries might be filled; and having obtained a decree of the senate, they appointed a day on which all who were of military age must appear. Thereupon there was a great tumult throughout the city and seditious speeches were made by the poorest citizens, who refused either to comply with the decrees of the senate or to obey the authority of the consuls, since they had violated the promises made to them concerning the allotment of land. And going in great numbers to the tribunes, they charged them with treachery, and with loud outcries demanded their assistance.

Most of the tribunes did not regard it as a suitable time, when a foreign war had arisen, to fan domestic hatreds into flame again; but one of them, named C. Maenius, declared that he would not betray the plebeians or permit the consuls to levy an army unless they should first appoint commissioners for fixing the boundaries of the public land, draw up the decree of the senate for its allotment, and lay it before the people. When the consuls opposed this and made the war they had on their hands an excuse he says not granting anything he desired, the tribune replied that he would pay no heed to them, but would hinder the levy with all his power.

And this he attempted to do; nevertheless, he could prevail to the end. For the consuls, going outside the city, ordered their generals' chairs to be placed in the

---

[23] For 483 BCE.
[24] M. Fabius K. f. Vibulanus, consul in 483 and 480 BCE.
[25] L. Valerius Potitus, consul 483.
[26] S. Cassius Vecellinus: see "Treaties of Alliance with Rome's Neighbors," below.

near by field;[27] and there they not only enrolled the troops, but also fined those who refused obedience to the laws, since it was not in their power to seize their persons. If the disobedient owned estates, they laid them waste and demolished their country-houses; and if they were farmers who tilled fields belonging to others, they stripped them of the yokes of oxen, the cattle, and the beasts of burden that were on hand for the work, and all kinds of implements with which the land is tilled and the crops gathered.

And the tribune who opposed the levy was no longer able to do anything. For those who are invested with the tribuneship possess no authority over anything outside the city, since their jurisdiction is limited by the city walls, and it is not lawful for them even to pass a night away from the city, save on a single occasion, when all the magistrates of the commonwealth ascended the Alban Mount and offer up a common sacrifice to Jupiter in behalf of the Latin nation.

This custom by which the tribunes possess no authority over anything outside the city continues to our times. And indeed the motivating cause, among many others, of the civil war among the Romans which occurred in my day[28] and was greater than any war before it, the cause which seemed more important and sufficient to divide the commonwealth, was this—that some of the tribunes, complaining that they had been forcibly driven out of the city by the general[29] who was then in control of affairs in Italy, in order to deprive them henceforth of any power, fled to the general[30] who commanded the armies in Gaul, as having no place to turn to.

And the latter, availing himself of this excuse and pretending to come with right and justice to the aid of the sacrosanct magistracy of the people which had been deprived of its authority contrary to the oaths of the forefathers, entered the city himself in arms and restored the men to their office....

The following year,[31] a dispute having arisen between the populace and the senate concerning the men who were to be elected consuls, the senators demanding that both men promoted to that magistracy should be of the aristocratic party and the populace demanding that they be chosen from among such as were agreeable to them, after an obstinate struggle they finally convinced each other that a consul should be chosen from each party. Thus K. Fabius, who had accused Cassius of aiming at a tyranny, was elected consul,[32] for the second time, on the part of the senate, and S. Furius on the part of the populace,[33] in the seventy-fifth Olympiad, Calliades being archon at Athens, at the time when Xerxes made his expedition against Greece.

They had no sooner taken office than ambassadors of the Latins came to the senate asking them to send to them one of the consuls with an army to put a check to the insolence of the Aequians, and at the same time word was brought that all Tyrrhenia was aroused and would soon go to war. For that nation had been convened in a general assembly and at the urgent solicitation of the Veientes for aid in their war against the Romans had passed a decree that any of the Tyrrhenians who so desired might take part in the campaign; and it was a sufficiently strong body of men that voluntarily aided the Veientes in the war. Upon learning of this the authorities in Rome resolved to raise armies and also that both consuls should take the field, one to make war on the Aequians and to aid the Latins, and the other to march with his forces against Tyrrhenia.

All this was opposed by S. Icilius,[34] one of the tribunes, who, assembling the populace every day, demanded of the senate the performance of its promises relating to the allotment of land and said that he would allow none of their decrees, whether they concerned military or civil affairs, to take effect unless they should first appoint the decemvir so fix the boundaries of the public land and divide it among the people as they had promised.

When the senate was at a loss and did not know what to do, Ap. Claudius[35] suggested that they should consider how the other tribunes might be brought to dissent from Icilius, pointing out that there is no other method of putting an end to the power of a tribune who opposes and obstructs the decrees of the senate, since his person is sacred and this authority of his legal, than for another of the men of equal rank and possessing the same power to oppose him and to order to be done what the other tries to obstruct.

And he advised all succeeding consuls to do this and to consider how they might always have some of the tribunes well disposed and friendly to them, saying that only method of destroying the power of the college was to sow dissension among its members.

---

[27] The Campus Martius.
[28] I.e., the civil war between Caesar and Pompey.
[29] Pompey.
[30] Caesar.
[31] 482 BCE.
[32] K. Fabius Vibulanus was consul in 484, 481, and 479 BCE.
[33] S. Furius Medullinus Fusus, consul 481.

---

[34] The MSS. give this name here and below as Sicilius. Livy calls him Licinius.
[35] Ap. Claudius Sabinus Inregillensis, consul 495, a defender of the prerogatives of the patricians.

The Twelve Tables

Source: From: Oliver J. Thatcher, ed., The Library of Original Sources (Milwaukee: University Research Extension Co., 1901), Vol. III: The Roman World, pp. 9-11. Scanned by: J. S. Arkenberg, Dept. of History, Cal. State Fullerton. Prof. Arkenberg has modernized the text.

Cicero, De Oratore, I.44: "Though all the world exclaim against me, I will say what I think: that single little book of the Twelve Tables, if anyone look to the fountains and sources of laws, seems to me, assuredly, to surpass the libraries of all the philosophers, both in weight of authority, and in plenitude of utility."

What we have of the Tables is fragments only—quotations preserved in other, later sources. The division into tables and the numbering shown below is modern and arbitrary.

Table I.

1. If anyone summons a man before the magistrate, he must go. If the man summoned does not go, let the one summoning him call the bystanders to witness and then take him by force.

2. If he shirks or runs away, let the summoner lay hands on him.

3. If illness or old age is the hindrance, let the summoner provide a team. He need not provide a covered carriage with a pallet unless he chooses.

4. Let the protector of a landholder be a landholder; for one of the proletariat, let anyone that cares, be protector.

6-9. When the litigants settle their case by compromise, let the magistrate announce it. If they do not compromise, let them state each his own side of the case, in the comitium of the forum before noon. Afterwards let them talk it out together, while both are present. After noon, in case either party has failed to appear, let the magistrate pronounce judgment in favor of the one who is present. If both are present the trial may last until sunset but no later.

Table II.

2. He whose witness has failed to appear may summon him by loud calls before his house every third day.

Table III.

1. One who has confessed a debt, or against whom judgment has been pronounced, shall have thirty days to pay it in. After that forcible seizure of his person is allowed. The creditor shall bring him before the magistrate. Unless he pays the amount of the judgment or some one in the presence of the magistrate interferes in his behalf as protector the creditor so shall take him home and fasten him in stocks or fetters. He shall fasten him with not less than fifteen pounds of weight or, if he choose, with more. If the prisoner choose, he may furnish his own food. If he does not, the creditor must give him a pound of meal daily; if he choose he may give him more.

2. On the third market day let them divide his body among them. If they cut more or less than each one's share it shall be no crime.

3. Against a foreigner the right in property shall be valid forever.

Table IV.

1. A dreadfully deformed child shall be quickly killed.

2. If a father sell his son three times, the son shall be free from his father.

3. As a man has provided in his will in regard to his money and the care of his property, so let it be binding. If he has no heir and dies intestate, let the nearest agnate have the inheritance. If there is no agnate, let the members of his gens have the inheritance.

4. If one is mad but has no guardian, the power over him and his money shall belong to his agnates and the members of his gens.

5. A child born after ten months since the father's death will not be admitted into a legal inheritance.

Table V.

1. Females should remain in guardianship even when they have attained their majority.

Table VI.

1. When one makes a bond and a conveyance of property, as he has made formal declaration so let it be binding.

3. A beam that is built into a house or a vineyard trellis one may not take from its place.

5. *Usucapio* of movable things requires one year's possession for its completion; but *usucapio* of an estate and buildings two years.[36]

6. Any woman who does not wish to be subjected in this manner to the hand of her husband should be absent three nights in succession every year, and so interrupt the usucapio of each year.[37]

---

[36] *Usucapio* is the acquisition of ownership by continuous possession and use (*usus*).
[37] Because marriage was seen as a form of "conveyance," women could become bound to a man via a common-law marriage that corresponds to *usucapio*, acqustion by continuous possession.

Table VII.

1. Let them keep the road in order. If they have not paved it, a man may drive his team where he likes.

9. Should a tree on a neighbor's farm be bend crooked by the wind and lean over your farm, you may take legal action for removal of that tree.

10. A man might gather up fruit that was falling down onto another man's farm.

Table VIII.

2. If one has maimed a limb and does not compromise with the injured person, let there be retaliation. If one has broken a bone of a freeman with his hand or with a cudgel, let him pay a penalty of three hundred coins If he has broken the bone of a slave, let him have one hundred and fifty coins. If one is guilty of insult, the penalty shall be twenty-five coins.

3. If one is slain while committing theft by night, he is rightly slain.

4. If a patron shall have devised any deceit against his client, let him be accursed.

5. If one shall permit himself to be summoned as a witness, or has been a weigher, if he does not give his testimony, let him be noted as dishonest and incapable of acting again as witness.

10. Any person who destroys by burning any building or heap of corn deposited alongside a house shall be bound, scourged, and put to death by burning at the stake provided that he has committed the said misdeed with malice aforethought; but if he shall have committed it by accident, that is, by negligence, it is ordained that he repair the damage or, if he be too poor to be competent for such punishment, he shall receive a lighter punishment.

12. If the theft has been done by night, if the owner kills the thief, the thief shall be held to be lawfully killed.

13. It is unlawful for a thief to be killed by day....unless he defends himself with a weapon; even though he has come with a weapon, unless he shall use the weapon and fight back, you shall not kill him. And even if he resists, first call out so that someone may hear and come up.

23. A person who had been found guilty of giving false witness shall be hurled down from the Tarpeian Rock.

26. No person shall hold meetings by night in the city.

Table IX.

4. The penalty shall be capital for a judge or arbiter legally appointed who has been found guilty of receiving a bribe for giving a decision.

5. Treason: he who shall have roused up a public enemy or handed over a citizen to a public enemy must suffer capital punishment.

6. Putting to death of any man, whosoever he might be unconvicted is forbidden.

Table X.

1. None is to bury or burn a corpse in the city.

3. The women shall not tear their faces nor wail on account of the funeral.

5. If one obtains a crown himself, or if his chattel does so because of his honor and valor, if it is placed on his head, or the head of his parents, it shall be no crime.

Table XI.

1. Marriages should not take place between plebeians and patricians.

Table XII.

2. If a slave shall have committed theft or done damage with his master's knowledge, the action for damages is in the slave's name.

5. Whatever the people had last ordained should be held as binding by law.

LIVY, DIONYSIUS OF HALICARNASSUS

The Roman Way of Declaring War

Source: Livy I.32. From: William Stearns Davis, ed., Readings in Ancient History: Illustrative Extracts from the Sources, 2 Vols. (Boston: Allyn and Bacon, 1912-13), Vol. II: Rome and the West, pp. 7-9. Dion. Hal. *RA* 6.95, 9.59. Translated by Earnest Cary. In *The Roman Antiquities of Dionysius of Halicarnassus*. Loeb classical library. Cambridge, Mass: Harvard University Press, 1937.

Livy I.32

It was highly needful to observe all the necessary formalities in beginning hostilities; otherwise the angry gods would turn their favor to the enemy. Ancus Marcius, the fourth king of Rome, was a man of peace and a soldier; and on the outbreak of a war with the Latins he is said to have instituted the customs which later ages of Romans observed in war.

Inasmuch as Numa had instituted the religious rites for days of peace, Ancus Marcius desired that the ceremonies relating to war might be transmitted by himself to future ages. Accordingly he borrowed from an ancient folk, the Aequicolae, the form which the [Roman] heralds still observe, when they make public demand for restitution. The [Roman] envoy when he comes to the frontier of the offending nation, covers his head with a woolen fillet, and says: Hear, O Jupiter, and hear ye lands ____ [i.e., of such and such a nation], let Justice hear! I am a public messenger of the Roman people. Justly and religiously I come, and let my words bear credit! Then he makes his demands, and follows with a solemn appeal to Jupiter. If I demand unjustly and impiously that these men and goods [in question] be given to me, the herald of the Roman people, then suffer me never to enjoy again my native country!

These words he repeats when he crosses the frontiers; he says them also to the first man he meets [on the way]; again when he passes the gate; again on entering the [foreigners'] market-place, some few words in the formula being changed. If the persons he demands are not surrendered after thirty days, he declares war, thus: Hear, O Jupiter and you too, Juno—Romulus also, and all the celestial, terrestrial, and infernal gods! Give us ear! I call you to witness that this nation ____ is unjust, and has acted contrary to right. And as for us, we will consult thereon with our elders in our homeland, as to how we may obtain our rights.

After that the envoy returns to Rome to report, and the king was wont at once to consult with the Senators in some such words as these, Concerning such quarrels as to which the *pater patratus*[38] of the Roman people has conferred with the pater patratus of the ____ people, and with that people themselves, touching what they ought to have surrendered or done and which things they have not surrendered nor done [as they ought]; speak forth, he said to the senator first questioned, what think you? Then the other said, I think that [our rights] should be demanded by a just and properly declared war, and for that I give my consent and vote. Next the others were asked in order, and when the majority of those present had reached an agreement, the war was resolved upon.

It was customary for the fetialis[39] to carry in his hand a javelin pointed with steel, or burnt at the end and dipped in blood. This he took to the confines of the enemy's country, and in the presence of at least three persons of adult years, he spoke thus: Forasmuch as the state of the ____ has offended against the Roman People, the Quirites; and forasmuch as the Roman People the Quirites have ordered that there should be war with ____ and the Senate of the Roman People has duly voted that war should be made upon the enemy ____ : I, acting for the Roman People, declare and make actual war upon the enemy!

So saying he flung the spear within the hostile confines. After this manner restitution was at that time demanded from the Latins [by Ancus Marcius] and war proclaimed; and the usage then established was adopted by posterity.

---

[38] The head of the Roman heralds.
[39] *Fetiales* were a college of Roman priests who acted as the guardians of the public faith. It was their province, when any dispute arose with a foreign state, to demand satisfaction, to determine the circumstances under which hostilities might be commenced, to perform the various religious rites attendant on the solemn declaration of war, and to preside at the formal ratification of peace.

Dionysius of Halicarnassus: *RA* 6.95, 9.59

After a Latin rebellion was defeated at Lake Regillus (499 BCE), in 493 S. Cassius Vecellinus established a defensive military treaty of alliance between Rome and the other Latin cities. This treaty helped protect all parties against the Aequi and Volsci.

At the same time,[40] a new treaty of peace and friendship was made with all the Latin cities, and confirmed by oaths, inasmuch as they had not attempted to create any disturbance during the sedition, had openly rejoiced at the return of the populace, and seemed to have been prompt in assisting the Romans against those who had revolted from them.

The provisions of the treaty were as follows: "Let there be peace between the Romans and all the Latin cities as long as the heavens and the earth shall remain where they are. Let them neither make war upon another themselves nor bring in foreign enemies nor grant a safe passage to those who shall make war upon either. Let them assist one another, when warred upon, with all their forces, and let each have an equal share of the spoils and booty taken in their common wars. Let suits relating to private contracts be determined within ten days, and in the nation where the contract was made. And let it not be permitted to add anything to, or take anything away from these treaties except by the consent both of the Romans and of all the Latins."

This was the treaty entered into by the Romans and the Latins and confirmed by their oaths sworn over the sacrificial victims. The senate also voted to offer sacrifices to the gods in thanksgiving for their reconciliation with the populace, and added one day to the Latin festival,[41] as it was called, which previously had been celebrated for two days. The first day had been set apart as holy by Tarquinius when he conquered the Tyrrhenians; the second the people added after they had freed the commonwealth by the expulsion of the kings; and to these the third was now added because of the return of the seceders. The superintendence and oversight of the sacrifices and games performed during this festival was committed to the tribunes' assistants, who held, as I said, the magistracy now called the aedileship; and they were honored by the senate with a purple robe, an ivory chair, and the other insignia that the kings had had....

✳   ✳   ✳

Meanwhile [42] both consuls took the field, Aemilius marching into the country of the Sabines and Fabius into that of the Aequians.[43] Aemilius, though he remained a long time in the enemy's country, encountered no army

---

[40] 493 BCE ; cf. Livy II.33.4.
[41] Feriae Latinae.
[42] 467 BCE/
[43] Ti. Aemilius and Q. Fabius Vibulanus, consuls 467.

ready to fight for it, but ravaged it with impunity; then, when the time for the elections was at hand, he led his forces home. To Fabius the Aequians, even before they were compelled to do so by the destruction of their army or the capture of their walls, sent heralds to sue for a reconciliation and friendship.

The consul, after exacting from them two months' provisions for his army, two tunics for every man and six months' pay, and whatever else was urgently required, concluded a truce with them till they should go to Rome and obtain the terms of peace from the senate. The senate, however, when informed of this, gave Fabius full power to make peace with the Aequians upon such terms as he himself should elect.

After that the two nations by the mediation of the consul made a treaty as follows: the Aequians were to be subject to the Romans while still possessing their cities and lands, and were not to send anything to the Romans except troops, when so ordered, these to be maintained at their own expense. Fabius, having made this treaty, returned home with his army and together with his fellow consul nominated magistrates for the following year.

CICERO, DIONYSIUS OF HALICARNASSUS

The Mythology of the Farmer-General

Source: Cicero, *de sen* 16. Translated by Evelyn S. Shuckburgh. In *Two Essays on Old Age & Friendship*. Golden treasury series. London: Macmillan, 1903. Dion. Hal. *RA* 10.17. Translated by Earnest Cary. In *The Roman Antiquities of Dionysius of Halicarnassus*. Loeb classical library. Cambridge, Mass: Harvard University Press, 1937.

Cicero: *On Old Age* 16

Cicero is holding forth on the ancient Roman ideal of the farmer-citizen and, by extension, the farmer-general.

I might continue my list of the delights of country life; but even what I have said I think is somewhat overlong. However, you must pardon me; for farming is a very favorite hobby of mine, and old age is naturally rather garrulous—for I would not be thought to acquit it of all faults.

Well, it was in a life of this sort that M'. Curius, after celebrating triumphs over the Samnites, the Sabines, and Pyrrhus, spent his last days.[44] When I look at his villa—for it is not far from my own—I never can enough admire the man's own frugality or the spirit of the age. As Curius was sitting at his hearth the Samnites, who brought him a large sum of gold, were repulsed by him; for it was not, he said, a fine thing in his eyes to possess gold, but to rule those who possessed it. Could such a high spirit fail to make old age pleasant?

But to return to farmers—not to wander from my own métier. In those days there were senators, i.e., old men, on their farms. For L. Quinctius Cincinnatus was actually at the plough when word was brought him that he had been named Dictator.[45] It was by his order as Dictator, by the way, that C. Servilius Ahala, the Master of the Horse, seized and put to death S. Maelius when attempting to obtain royal power.[46] Curius as well as other old men used to receive their summonses to attend the Senate in their farm-houses, from which circumstances the summoners were called viatores or "travelers." Was these men's old age an object of pity who found their pleasure in the cultivation of the land? In my opinion, scarcely any life can be more blessed, not alone from its utility (for agriculture is beneficial to the whole human race), but also as much from the mere pleasure of the thing, to which I have already alluded, and from the rich abundance and supply of all things necessary for the food of man and for the worship of the gods above. So, as these are objects of desire to certain people, let us make our peace with pleasure. For the good and hard—working farmer's wine—cellar and oil store, as well as his larder, are always well filled, and his whole farm house is richly furnished. It abounds in pigs, goats, lambs, fowls, milk, cheese, and honey. Then there is the garden, which the farmers themselves call their "second flitch." A zest and flavor is added to all these by hunting and fowling in spare hours. Need I mention the greenery of meadows, the rows of trees, the beauty of vineyard and olive—grove? I will put it briefly: nothing can either furnish necessaries more richly, or present a fairer spectacle, than well—cultivated land. And to the enjoyment of that, old age does not merely present no hindrance—it actually invites and allures to it. For where else can it better warm itself, either by basking in the sun or by sitting by the fire, or at the proper time cool itself more wholesomely by the help of shade or water? Let the young keep their arms then to themselves, their horses, spears, their foils and ball, their swimming—baths and running—path. To us old men let them, out of the many forms of sport, leave dice and counters; but even that as they choose, since old age can be quite happy without them.

---

[44] M'. Curius Dentatus, consul 290 and 275, famous for frugality and incorruptibility.

[45] In 458 BCE.

[46] During Cincinnatus's second term as dictator, in 439 BCE.

Cincinnatus was made suffect, or replacement, consul in 460. The story of his being at his plow when called is told naming both to the suffect consulship (here, by Dionysius) and, two years later, to the dictatorship (by Livy).

The war[47] with the brigands being thus ended, the tribunes rekindled the civil strife once more by demanding of the surviving consul the fulfillment of the promises made to them by Valerius, who perished in the fighting,[48] with regard to the introduction of the law.[49] But Claudius[50] for a time kept procrastinating, now by performing lustrations for the city, now by offering sacrifices of thanksgiving to the gods, and again by entertaining the multitude with games and shows.

When all his excuses had been exhausted, he finally declared that another consul must be chosen in place of the deceased; for he said that the acts performed by him all would be neither legal nor lasting, whereas those performed by two of them would be legitimate and valid. Having put them off with this pretence, he appointed a day for the election, when he would nominate his colleague. In the meantime the leading men of the senate, consulting together in private, agreed among themselves upon the person to whom they would entrust the magistracy.

And when the day appointed for the election had come and the herald had called the first class, the eighteen centuries of knights together with the eighty centuries of foot, consisting of the wealthiest citizens, entering the appointed place, chose as consul L. Quinctius Cincinnatus, whose son K. Quinctius the tribunes had brought to trial for his life and compelled to leave the city. And no other class being called to vote—for the centuries which had voted were three more in be than the remaining centuries—the populace departed, regarding it as a grievous misfortune that a man who hated them was to be possessed of the consular power. Meanwhile the senate sent men to invite the consul and to conduct him to the city to assume his magistracy.

It chanced that Quinctius was just then plowing a piece of land for sowing,[51] he himself following the gaunt oxen that were breaking up the fallow; he had no tunic on, wore a small loin-cloth and had a cap upon his head.

Upon seeing a crowd of people come into the field he stopped his plough and for a long time was at a loss to know who they were or what they wanted of him; then, when some one ran up to him and bade him make himself more presentable, he went into the cottage and after putting on his clothes came out to them.

Thereupon the men who were sent to escort him all greeted him, not by his name, but as consul; and clothing him with the purple-bordered robe and placing before him the axes and the other insignia of his magistracy, they asked him to follow them to the city. And he, pausing for a moment and shedding tears, said only this: "So my field will go unsown this year, and we shall be indicate danger of having not enough to live on." Then he kissed his wife, and charging her to take care of things at home, went to the city.

I am led to relate these particulars for no other reason than to let all the world see what kind of men the leaders of Rome were at that time, that they worked with their own hands, led frugal lives, did not chafe under honorable poverty, and, far from aiming at positions of royal power, actually refused them when offered. For it will be seen that the Romans of to-day do not bear the least resemblance to them, but follow the very opposite practices in everything—with the exception of a very few by whom the dignity of the commonwealth is still maintained and a resemblance to those men preserved. But enough on this subject.

LIVY

The Defeat of the Latins

Source: Livy 8.6.15, 8.11, 8.14. Translated by William Masfen Roberts. In *The History of Rome*. London: J.M. Dent, 1912.

Livy tells of the problems faced by the Romans in fighting the Latins, their ethnic kin, as well as the difficulties administering a settlement after the war. The Latins, alarmed by Roman expansionism, waged war on Rome a final time in 341 and were defeated in 340; the settlement described here took place in 338.

The council of war also decided that if ever any war had been conducted with the strict enforcement of orders, on this occasion certainly, military discipline should be brought back to the ancient standard. Their anxiety was increased by the fact that it was against the Latins that they had to fight, a people resembling them in language, manners, arms, and especially in their military organization. They had been colleagues and comrades, as soldiers, centurions, and tribunes, often stationed together in the same posts and side by side in the same maniples. That this might not prove a source of error

---

[47] I.e., the slave uprising of 460. Cf. Livy III.19.1□3.
[48] P. Valerius Publicola, consul 460, was killed during the slave uprising.
[49] One of the tribunes of 462, C. Terentilius Harsa, proposed that a commission be appointed to gather up the law, and to publish it to the whole people. This would have eliminated the stranglehold the patricians had on drafting and administering law, which was unpublished and secret prior to the Twelve Tables.
[50] C. Claudius, consul 460 (i.e., the surviving consul).
[51] Compare Livy's description (III.26.8 ff.) of Cincinnatus' humble activities at the time of his appointment to the dictatorship.

and confusion, orders were given that no one was to leave his post to fight with the enemy....

In some authors I find it stated that it was only after the battle was over that the Samnites who had been waiting to see the result came to support the Romans. Assistance was also coming to the Latins from Lanuvium whilst time was being wasted in deliberation, but whilst they were starting and a part of their column was already on the march, news came of the defeat of the Latins. They faced about and re-entered their city, and it is stated that Milionius, their praetor, remarked that for that very short march they would have to pay a heavy price to Rome.

Those of the Latins who survived the battle retreated by many different routes, and gradually assembled in the city of Vescia. Here the leaders met to discuss the situation, and Numisius assured them that both armies had really experienced the same fortune and an equal amount of bloodshed; the Romans enjoyed no more than the name of victory, in every other respect they were as good as defeated. The headquarters of both consuls were polluted with blood; the one had murdered his son, the other had devoted himself to death; their whole army was massacred, their hastati and principes killed; the companies both in front of and behind the standards had suffered enormous losses; the triarii in the end saved the situation.

The Latin troops, it was true, were equally cut up, but Latium and the Volsci could supply reinforcements more quickly than Rome. If, therefore, they approved, he would at once call out the fighting men from the Latin and Volscian peoples and march back with an army to Capua, and would take the Romans unawares; a battle was the last thing they were expecting. He dispatched misleading letters throughout Latium and the Volscian country, those who had not been engaged in the battle being the more ready to believe what he said, and a hastily levied body of militia, drawn from all quarters, was got together.

This army was met by the consul at Trifanum, a place between Sinuessa and Menturnae. Without waiting even to choose the sites for their camps, the two armies piled their baggage, fought and finished the war, for the Latins were so utterly worsted that when the consul with his victorious army was preparing to ravage their territory, they made a complete surrender and the Campanians followed their example. Latium and Capua were deprived of their territory.

The Latin territory, including that of Privernum, together with the Falernian, which had belonged to the Campanians as far as the Volturnus, was distributed amongst the Roman plebs. They received two jugera a head in the Latin territory, their allotment being made up by three-quarters of a jugerum in the Privernate district; in the Falernian district they received three entire jugera, the additional quarter being allowed owing to the distance. The Laurentes, amongst the Latins and the aristocracy of the Campanians, were not thus penalized because they had not revolted. An order was made for the treaty with the Laurentes to be renewed, and it has since been renewed annually on the tenth day after the Latin Festival. The Roman franchise was conferred on the aristocracy of Campania, and a brazen tablet recording the fact was fastened up in Rome in the temple of Castor, and the people of Campania were ordered to pay them each—they numbered 1600 in all— the sum of 450 denarii annually....

The leaders of the senate applauded the way in which the consul had introduced the motion, but as the circumstances differed in different cases they thought that each case ought to be decided upon its merits, and with the view of facilitating discussion they requested the consul to put the name of each place separately. Lanuvium received the full citizenship and the restitution of her sacred things, with the proviso that the temple and grove of Juno Sospita should belong in common to the Roman people and the citizens living at Lanuvium. Aricium, Nomentum, and Pedum obtained the same political rights as Lanuvium. Tusculum retained the citizenship which it had had before, and the responsibility for the part it took in the war was removed from the State as a whole and fastened on a few individuals.

The Veliternians, who had been Roman citizens from old times, were in consequence of their numerous revolts severely dealt with; their walls were thrown down, their senate deported and ordered to live on the other side of the Tiber; if any of them were caught on this side of the river, he was to be fined 1000 ases, and the man who caught him was not to release him from confinement till the money was paid. Colonists were sent on to the land they had possessed, and their numbers made Velitrae look as populous as formerly. Antium also was assigned to a fresh body of colonists, but the Antiates were permitted to enroll themselves as colonists if they chose; their warships were taken away, and they were forbidden to possess any more; they were admitted to citizenship.

Tibur and Praeneste had their domains confiscated, not owing to the part which they, in common with the rest of Latium, had taken in the war, but because, jealous of the Roman power, they had joined arms with the barbarous nation of the Gauls.[52] The rest of the Latin cities were deprived of the rights of intermarriage, free trade, and common councils with each other. Capua, as a reward for the refusal of its aristocracy to join the Latins, were allowed to enjoy the private rights of Roman citizens, as were also Fundi and Formiae, because they had always allowed a free passage through

_____

[52] After the Gauls' sack of Rome in 390.

their territory. It was decided that Cumae and Suessula should enjoy the same rights as Capua. Some of the ships of Antium were taken into the Roman docks, others were burnt and their beaks (rostra) were fastened on the front of a raised gallery which was constructed at the end of the Forum, and which from this circumstance was called the Rostra.

POLYBIUS

The Constitution of the Roman Republic

Source: Polybius 6.11.11-6.18.3: John Porter, translator.

> *Polybius here sets forth a general analysis of the Roman constitution, which he had had ample opportunity to observe first-hand, at the time of the Second Punic War (i.e., the late third century BCE).*

I have already mentioned the three divisions of government in control of state affairs. Regarding their respective roles, everything was so equally and fittingly set out and administered, in all respects, that no one, not even any of the Romans themselves, could say for certain whether their system of government was aristocratic in its general nature, or democratic, or monarchical. And this uncertainty is only reasonable, for if we were to focus on the powers of the consuls it would appear to be altogether monarchical and kingly in nature. If, however, we were to focus on the powers of the Senate, it would appear to be a government under the control of an aristocracy. And yet if one were to look at the powers enjoyed by the People, it would seem plain that it was democratic in nature. As for the parts of government controlled by each element, they were at that time and (with a few exceptions) still are as follows:

The consuls, when in Rome prior to leading out their legions, are in charge of all public affairs. For all of the other public officials, with the exception of the tribunes, are below the consuls and subject to their authority, and it is the consuls who introduce ambassadors to the Senate. In addition to the powers just mentioned, the consuls introduce to the Senate urgent matters for its consideration and bring about the detailed implementation of its decrees. Moreover, it is the consuls' duty to consider all matters of public concern which are to be decided by the People: they summon the assemblies, introduce measures requiring a vote, and have authority over the execution of the decisions of the majority. Further, they enjoy nearly autocratic powers as regards preparations for war and the general conduct of military affairs in the field. It is within their power to give whatever commands to the allies that they think right, to appoint military tribunes, to levy soldiers, and to choose those fit for military service. When in the field

they also may punish any of those under their command whom they wish. And they have the power to dispense whatever public funds they might propose, a quaestor being appointed to accompany them and carry out their orders in such matters. As a result, one might reasonably say, if one were to look at this section of the government, that the Roman constitution was a pure monarchy or kingship....

The Senate, first of all, has control of the treasury, for it has complete authority over all revenues and expenditures. For the quaestors are unable to disburse funds for any particular purpose without a decree from the Senate, the only exception being in the case of the consuls. The Senate is in charge of by far the most important and the greatest expenditure of public funds—that which the censors make every *lustrum*[53] for the repair and construction of public works: it is through the Senate that the funds are allocated to the censors. Similarly, crimes committed in Italy requiring a public investigation—for example, treason, conspiracy, poisoning, assassination—all fall under the jurisdiction of the Senate. In addition, if some private person or one of the communities in Italy requires legal settlement of a dispute or indeed the assessment of a penalty or aid or protection, all of these things lie in the Senate's care. And indeed, if it should be necessary to send an embassy to any people outside of Italy—either to effect a truce, or to call for aid, or to impose duties on them, or to accept their submission, or to declare war on them—the Senate makes provision for such things. In the same way, when embassies arrive in Rome, the Senate handles the question of how to deal with them and what reply is to be given them. Not one of the above matters is presented to the People for consideration. As a result, if one were in Rome when the consuls were not present, the constitution would appear altogether aristocratic in nature. This, indeed, is the firm conviction of many of the Greeks and likewise of many eastern kings, on account of the Senate's authority in nearly all dealings that these foreign peoples have with Rome.

After this who would not reasonably enquire as to just what sort of role is left in the Roman state for the People, and just what that role is, seeing that the authority of the Senate extends over the various jurisdictions that I have detailed—and over the greatest of all, that being revenues and expenditures—while the consuls in turn have absolute authority concerning preparations for war and operations in the field? But in fact there is a role left for the People as well, and a most weighty one. For the People alone amid the organs of state have jurisdiction over the conferring of rewards and punishments, these representing the sole bonds by which kingdoms and states and, in short, all human society are held together.... The People often pass

---

[53] The censors took the lustrum every five years.

judgment, then, even where a financial penalty is concerned, whenever the punishment for a crime involves a substantial penalty, and especially when the accused have held high office. And the People alone pass judgment in capital cases.... It is the People who grant offices to the deserving, the most noble prize for virtue in a state. They also have authority over the ratifying of laws and—the greatest of their powers—they deliberate and pass judgment concerning war and peace. Also, as for military alliances, truces, and other treaties, they approve the particulars, rendering them valid or rejecting them. The result is that, with a view to these powers, one might reasonably say that the People have the greatest role in the state, and that the constitution is democratic in nature.

I have now indicated how the various functions of the state are divided among the different parts of the government. Now I will indicate how each can counteract the others, should it so wish, or work in harmony with them. Whenever the consul sets out with his forces, invested with the aforementioned powers, he appears to have absolute authority as regards the mission at hand, yet he requires the cooperation of both the People and the Senate, and without them he lacks sufficient power to bring his operation to a successful conclusion. For it is clear that supplies must always be sent to accompany his armies, but neither food nor clothing nor pay for the soldiers can be allocated without a decree of the Senate, with the result that the commander's plans are rendered ineffectual if the Senate chooses to be negligent or obstructionist. Furthermore, it lies with the Senate whether the commander's plans and designs ultimately come to fulfillment or not, since the Senate has the authority to send another commander out to supersede the old at the end of a year's time or to extend the command of the consul in the field.[54] It also has the power to celebrate and thus increase the fame of the consul's achievements, or to belittle them and render them obscure. For the celebrations that they call triumphs, in which the spectacle of the general's achievements is brought strikingly before the eyes of the citizens, cannot be organized as is fitting—and at times cannot be held at all—unless the Senate should concur and should provide the requisite expenditures. As for the People, it is altogether necessary for the consuls to court their favor, even if they should happen to be quite far from Rome. For it is the People who reject or ratify truces and other treaties, as I have noted above. Of greatest weight is the fact that, upon laying aside their office, it is before the People that they must submit an account of their actions. The result is that it is in no way safe for the commanders to slight the Senate or the good will of the People.

The Senate, in turn, which enjoys so much authority, first of all must pay attention to the masses and court the favor of the People in matters of public concern. The most important and greatest enquiries into crimes against the state, and the penalties thereby adjudicated—those that involve the death sentence—cannot be carried out by it unless the People first ratify what it has proposed. The same is true of those things that concern the Senate itself: for if ever anyone introduces a law that would strip the Senate of some part of the powers accorded it by tradition, or would abolish their right of precedence in seating and other honors accorded senators, or, indeed, would effect a reduction in their livelihoods—the People have authority over all such matters, whether to pass them or not. Most important of all, if a single one of the tribunes interposes his veto, the Senate is unable to put into effect any of its resolutions; indeed, it cannot even convene or come together at all. And the tribunes are bound always to effect the will of the People and to be guided by their wishes. As a result of all of these factors, the Senate fears the masses and is ever mindful of the People.

Similarly, in turn, the People are subordinate to the Senate and must have regard for its wishes, both in public matters and private. Many projects are contracted out by the censors for the repair and construction of public works throughout all of Italy—so many that one could scarcely number them all—and also the rights to collect the revenues from many rivers, harbors, gardens, mines, lands—everything that falls under Roman control. All of the aforementioned are administered through the People, and nearly everyone, so to speak, has an interest in the contracts and the works derived therefrom. For some in fact purchase the grants of these contracts from the censors, others act as partners in such ventures, others provide sureties for the purchasers, and others still pledge their property to the public treasury for this purpose. But the Senate has authority over all of these procedures: it is able to grant extensions and, in the case of an unforeseen catastrophe, can lessen the contractor's liability, or can release him from his contract altogether should he prove unable to complete it. And there are in fact many ways in which the Senate either greatly harms or greatly benefits those who have charge of public works, for all of the aforementioned are referred to it. Most important, it is from the Senate that judges are appointed in most public and private suits that concern charges of any weight. As a result, everyone, being bound to the good will of the Senate and fearing the uncertainty of litigation, takes care with regard to obstructing or opposing its wishes. Similarly, as regards the initiatives of the consuls, the People are loathe to oppose them since all citizens, both privately and collectively, fall under their authority in the field.

---

[54] A consul can remain in command by being made a proconsul, that is, an ex-consul acting in the capacity of a consul.

Such then are the powers of each of the parts of government both to oppose one another and to work in conjunction. In unison they are a match for any and all emergencies, the result being that it is impossible to find a constitution that is better constructed. For whenever some common external danger comes upon them and compels them to band together in counsel and in action, the power of their state becomes so great that nothing that is required is neglected, inasmuch as all compete without fail to devise some means of meeting the emergency, nor do they dally in reaching a decision until too late, but each, both communally and individually, work together to complete the task that lies before them. The result is that their unique form of constitution comes to be unconquerable and successfully achieves every goal upon which it resolves.

POLYBIUS

The Roman Maniple vs. the Macedonian Phalanx

Source: Polybius, *The Histories* XVIII.28–32. From:, The Histories of Polybius, 2 Vols., trans. Evelyn S. Shuckburgh (London: Macmillan, 1889), pp. 226-230. Scanned by: J. S. Arkenberg, Dept. of History, Cal. State Fullerton. Prof. Arkenberg has modernized the text.

Credit for the military success of the Macedonians in the fourth century BCE goes partly to their innovations to the Greek style of hoplite warfare. Polybius naturally wanted to compare the greatest conquerors of the east to the greatest conquerors of the west, the Romans, who—also in the fourth century—abandoned the hoplite phalanx in favor of the more flexible maniple.

In my sixth book I made a promise, still unfulfilled, of taking a fitting opportunity of drawing a comparison between the arms of the Romans and Macedonians, and their respective system of tactics, and pointing out how they differ for better or worse from each other. I will now endeavor by a reference to actual facts to fulfill that promise. For since in former times the Macedonian tactics proved themselves by experience capable of conquering those of Asia and Greece; while the Roman tactics sufficed to conquer the nations of Africa and all those of Western Europe; and since in our own day there have been numerous opportunities of comparing the men as well as their tactics, it will be, I think, a useful and worthy task to investigate their differences, and discover why it is that the Romans conquer and carry off the palm from their enemies in the operations of war: that we may not put it all down to Fortune, and congratulate them on their good luck, as the thoughtless of mankind do; but, from a knowledge of the true causes, may give their leaders the tribute of praise and admiration which they deserve.

Now as to the battles which the Romans fought with Hannibal and the defeats which they sustained in them, I need say no more. It was not owing to their arms or their tactics, but to the skill and genius of Hannibal that they met with those defeats: and that I made quite clear in my account of the battles themselves. And my contention is supported by two facts. First, by the conclusion of the war: for as soon as the Romans got a general of ability comparable with that of Hannibal, victory was not long in following their banners. Secondly, Hannibal himself, being dissatisfied with the original arms of his men, and having immediately after his first victory furnished his troops with the arms of the Romans, continued to employ them thenceforth to the end. Pyrrhus, again, availed himself not only of the arms, but also of the troops of Italy, placing a maniple of Italians and a company of his own phalanx alternately, in his battles against the Romans. Yet even this did not enable him to win; the battles were somehow or another always indecisive.

It was necessary to speak first on these points, to anticipate any instances which might seem to make against my theory. I will now return to my comparison.

Many considerations may easily convince us that, if only the phalanx has its proper formation and strength, nothing can resist it face to face or withstand its charge. For as a man in close order of battle occupies a space of three feet; and as the length of the sarissae are sixteen cubits according to the original design, which has been reduced in practice to fourteen; and as of these fourteen four must be deducted, to allow for the weight in front; it follows clearly that each hoplite will have ten cubits of his sarissa projecting beyond his body, when he lowers it with both hands, as he advances against the enemy: hence, too, though the men of the second, third, and fourth rank will have their sarissae projecting farther beyond the front rank than the men of the fifth, yet even these last will have two cubits of their sarissae beyond the front rank; if only the phalanx is properly formed and the men close up properly both flank and rear, like the description in Homer:

"So buckler pressed on buckler; helm on helm; And man on man; and waving horse-hair plumes In polished head-piece mingled, as they swayed In order: in such serried rank they stood."[55]

And if my description is true and exact, it is clear that in front of each man of the front rank there will be five sarissae projecting to distances varying by a descending scale of two cubits.

With this point in our minds, it will not be difficult to imagine what the appearance and strength of the whole phalanx is likely to be, when, with lowered sarissae, it advances to the charge sixteen deep. Of these sixteen ranks, all above the fifth are unable to reach with their

---

[55] Iliad, 13.131.

sarissae far enough to take actual part in the fighting. They, therefore, do not lower them, but hold them with the points inclined upwards over the shoulders of the ranks in front of them, to shield the heads of the whole phalanx; for the sarissae are so closely serried, that they repel missiles which have carried over the front ranks and might fall upon the heads of those in the rear. These rear ranks, however, during an advance, press forward those in front by the weight of their bodies; and thus make the charge very forcible, and at the same time render it impossible for the front ranks to face about.

Such is the arrangement, general and detailed of the phalanx. It remains now to compare with it the peculiarities and distinctive features of the Roman arms and tactics. Now, a Roman soldier in full armor also requires a space of three square feet. But as their method of fighting admits of individual motion for each man—because he defends his body with a shield, which he moves about to any point from which a blow is coming, and because he uses his sword both for cutting and stabbing—it is evident that each man must have a clear space, and an interval of at least three feet both on flank and rear if he is to do his duty with any effect. The result of this will be that each Roman soldier will face two of the front rank of a phalanx, so that he has to encounter and fight against ten spears, which one man cannot find time even to cut away, when once the two lines are engaged, nor force his way through easily—seeing that the Roman front ranks are not supported by the rear ranks, either by way of adding weight to their charge, or vigor to the use of their swords. Therefore, it may readily be understood that, as I said before, it is impossible to confront a charge of the phalanx, so long as it retains its proper formation and strength.

Why is it then that the Romans conquer? And what is it that brings disaster on those who employ the phalanx? Why, just because war is full of uncertainties both as to time and place; whereas there is but one time and one kind of ground in which a phalanx can fully work. If, then, there were anything to compel the enemy to accommodate himself to the time and place of the phalanx, when about to fight a general engagement, it would be but natural to expect that those who employed the phalanx would always carry off the victory. But if the enemy finds it possible, and even easy, to avoid its attack, what becomes of its formidable character? Again, no one denies that for its employment it is indispensable to have a country flat, bare, and without such impediments as ditches, cavities, depressions, steep banks, or beds of rivers: for all such obstacles are sufficient to hinder and dislocate this particular formation. And that it is, I may say, impossible, or at any rate exceedingly rare to find a piece of country of twenty stades, or sometimes of even greater extent, without any such obstacles, every one will also admit. However, let us suppose that such a district has been found. If the enemy decline to come down into it, but traverse the country sacking the towns and territories of the allies, what use will the phalanx be? For if it remains on the ground suited to itself, it will not only fail to benefit its friends, but will be incapable even of preserving itself; for the carriage of provisions will be easily stopped by the enemy, seeing that they are in undisputed possession of the country: while if it quits its proper ground, from the wish to strike a blow, it will be an easy prey to the enemy. Nay, if a general does descend into the plain, and yet does not risk his whole army upon one charge of the phalanx or upon one chance, but maneuvers for a time to avoid coming to close quarters in the engagement, it is easy to learn what will be the result from what the Romans are now actually doing.

For no speculation is any longer required to test the accuracy of what I am now saying: that can be done by referring to accomplished facts. The Romans do not, then, attempt to extend their front to equal that of a phalanx, and then charge directly upon it with their whole force: but some of their divisions are kept in reserve, while others join battle with the enemy at close quarters. Now, whether the phalanx in its charge drives its opponents from their ground, or is itself driven back, in either case its peculiar order is dislocated; for whether in following the retiring, or flying from the advancing enemy, they quit the rest of their forces: and when this takes place, the enemy's reserves can occupy the space thus left, and the ground which the phalanx had just before been holding, and so no longer charge them face to face, but fall upon them on their flank and rear. If, then, it is easy to take precautions against the opportunities and peculiar advantages of the phalanx, but impossible to do so in the case of its disadvantages, must it not follow that in practice the difference between these two systems is enormous? Of course, those generals who employ the phalanx must march over ground of every description, must pitch camps, occupy points of advantage, besiege, and be besieged, and meet with unexpected appearances of the enemy: for all these are part and parcel of war, and have an important and sometimes decisive influence on the ultimate victory. And in all these cases the Macedonian phalanx is difficult, and sometimes impossible, to handle, because the men cannot act either in squads or separately.

The Roman order on the other hand is flexible: for every Roman, once armed and on the field, is equally well-equipped for every place, time, or appearance of the enemy. He is, moreover, quite ready and needs to make no change, whether he is required to fight in the main body, or in a detachment, or in a single maniple, or even by himself. Therefore, as the individual members of the Roman force are so much more serviceable, their plans are also much more often attended by success than those of others.

I thought it necessary to discuss this subject at some length, because at the actual time of the occurrence many Greeks supposed when the Macedonians were beaten that it was incredible; and many will afterwards be at a loss to account for the inferiority of the phalanx to the Roman system of arming.

LIVY

The Samnites' 'Linen Legion' Remains Undaunted

Source: Livy 10.38.

This discussion of the Samnites' furious resistance to Roman dominance occurs during Livy's discussion of the Samnite uprising that followed Pyrrhus's departure from Italy in 272.

The year following was marked by the consulship of L. Papirius Cursor,[56] who had not only inherited his father's glory but enhanced it by his management of a great war and a victory over the Samnites, second only to the one which his father had won.[57] It happened that this nation had taken the same care and pains to adorn their soldiery with all the wealth of splendor as they had done on the occasion of the elder Papirius' victory. They had also called in the aid of the gods by submitting the soldiers to a kind of initiation into an ancient form of oath.

A levy was conducted throughout Samnium under a novel regulation; any man within the military age who had not assembled on the captain-general's proclamation, or any one who had departed without permission, was devoted to Jupiter and his life forfeited. The whole of the army was summoned to Aquilonia, and 40,000 men, the full strength of Samnium, were concentrated there. A space, about 200 feet square, almost in the centre of their camp, was boarded off and covered all over with linen cloth. In this enclosure a sacrificial service was conducted, the words being read from an old linen book by an aged priest, Ovius Paccius, who announced that he was taking that form of service from the old ritual of the Samnite religion. It was the form which their ancestors used when they formed their secret design of wresting Capua from the Etruscans.

When the sacrifice was completed the captain-general sent a messenger to summon all those who were of noble birth or who were distinguished for their military achievements. They were admitted into the enclosure one by one. As each was admitted he was led up to the altar, more like a victim than like one who was taking part in the service, and he was bound on oath not to divulge what he saw and heard in that place. Then they compelled him to take an oath couched in the most terrible language, imprecating a curse on himself, his family, and his race if he did not go into battle where the commanders should lead him or if he either himself fled from battle or did not at once slay any one whom he saw fleeing. At first there were some who refused to take this oath; they were massacred beside the altar, and their dead bodies lying amongst the scattered remains of the victims were a plain hint to the rest not to refuse.

After the foremost men among the Samnites had been bound by this dread formula, ten were especially named by the captain-general and told each to choose a comrade-in-arms, and these again to choose others until they had made up the number of 16,000. These were called the "linen legion," from the material with which the place where they had been sworn was covered. They were provided with resplendent amour and plumed helmets to distinguish them from the others. The rest of the army consisted of something under 20,000 men, but they were not inferior to the linen legion either in their personal appearance or soldierly qualities or in the excellence of their equipment. This was the number of those in camp at Aquilonia, forming the total strength of Samnium.

CORNELIUS NEPOS

Hannibal

Source: Cornelius Nepos, "Hannibal," *De Viribus Illustris*. Translated by J. Thomas.

Cornelius Nepos is a Northern Italian biographer writing in the first century BCE. His essay on Hannibal is the earliest surviving biography of the general in Latin.

Hannibal the Carthaginian, son of Hamilcar. If it be true, as no one doubts, that the Roman people have surpassed all other nations in valor, it must be admitted that Hannibal excelled all other commanders in skill as much as the Roman people are superior to all nations in bravery. For as often as he engaged with that people in Italy, he invariably came off victor; and if his strength had not been impaired by the jealousy of his fellow-citizens at home, he would have been able, to all appearance, to conquer the Romans. But the disparagement of the multitude overcame the courage of one man. Yet after all, he so cherished the hatred of the Romans which had, as it were, been left him as an inheritance by his father, that he would have given up his life rather than renounce it. Indeed, even after he had been driven from his native land and was dependent on

---

[56] L. Papirius Cursor the Younger, consul 272.
[57] L. Papirius Cursor the Elder, consul 326, 320, 319, 315, 313; dictator 324, 309. He is credited with Rome's victory in the Second Samnite War (326–304 BCE).

the aid of foreigners, he never ceased to war with the Romans in spirit.

Aside from Philip, whom from afar Hannibal had made an enemy of the Romans, he fired up Antiochus, the most powerful of all kings in those times, with such a desire for war, that from far away on the Red Sea he made preparations to invade Italy.

To his court came envoys from Rome to sound his intentions and try by secret intrigues to arouse his suspicions of Hannibal, alleging that they had bribed him and that he had changed his sentiments. These attempts were not made in vain, and when Hannibal learned it and noticed that he was excluded from the king's more intimate councils, he went to Antiochus, as soon as the opportunity offered, and after calling to mind many proofs of his loyalty and his hatred of the Romans, he added, "My father Hamilcar, when I was a small boy not more than nine years old, just as he was setting out from Carthage to Spain as commander-in-chief, offered up victims to Jupiter, Greatest and Best of gods. While this ceremony was being performed, he asked me if I would like to go with him on the campaign. I eagerly accepted and began to beg him not to hesitate to take me with him. Thereupon he said, I will do it, provided you will give me the pledge that I ask. With that he led me to the altar on which he had begun his sacrifice, and having dismissed all the others, he bade me lay hold of the altar and swear that I would never be a friend to the Romans. For my part, up to my present time of life, I have kept the oath which I swore to my father so faithfully, that no one ought to doubt that in the future I shall be of the same mind. Therefore, if you have any kindly intentions with regard to the Roman people, you will be wise to hide them from me; but when you prepare war, you will go counter to your own interests if you do not make me the leader in that enterprise."

Accordingly, at the age which I have named, Hannibal went with his father to Spain, and after Hamilcar died and Hasdrubal succeeded to the chief command, he was given charge of all the cavalry. When Hasdrubal died in his turn, the army chose Hannibal as its commander, and on their action being reported at Carthage, it was officially confirmed. So it was that when he was less than twenty-five years old, Hannibal became commander-in-chief; and within the next three years he subdued all the peoples of Spain by force of arms, stormed Saguntum, a town allied with Rome, and mustered three great armies. Of these armies he sent one to Africa, left the second with his brother Hasdrubal in Spain, and led the third with him into Italy. He crossed the range of the Pyrenees. Wherever he marched, he warred with all the natives, and he was everywhere victorious.

When he came to the Alps separating Italy from Gaul, which no one before him had ever crossed with an army except Hercules (the Greek) because of which that place is called the Greek Pass, he cut to pieces the Alpine tribes that tried to keep him from crossing, opened up the region, built roads, and made it possible for an elephant with its equipment to go over places along which before that a single unarmed man could barely crawl. By this route he led his forces across the Alps and came into Italy.

He had already fought at the Rhone with P. Cornelius Scipio, the consul, and routed him; with the same man he engaged at Clastidium on the Po River, wounded him, and drove him from the field. A third time that same Scipio, with his colleague Ti. Longus, opposed him at the Trebia. With those two he joined battle and routed them both. Then he passed through the country of the Ligurians over the Apennines, on his way to Etruria. In the course of that march he contracted such a severe eye trouble that he never afterwards had equally good use of his right eye. While he was still suffering from that complaint and was carried in a litter, he ambushed the consul C. Flaminius with his army at Trasumenus and slew him; and not long afterwards C. Centenius, the praetor, who was holding a pass with a body of picked men, met the same fate.

Next, he arrived in Apulia. There he was opposed by two consuls, C. Terentius and L. Aemilius, both of whose armies he put to flight in a single battle; the consul Paulus was slain, besides several ex-consuls, including Cn. Servilius Geminus, who had been consul the year before.

After having fought that battle, Hannibal advanced upon Rome without resistance. He halted in the hills near the city. After he had remained in camp there for several days and was returning to Capua, the Roman dictator Q. Fabius Maximus opposed himself to him in the Falernian region. But Hannibal, although caught in a defile, extricated himself by night without the loss of any of his men, and thus tricked Fabius, that most skillful of generals. For under cover of night the Carthaginian bound torches to the horns of cattle and set fire to them, then sent a great number of animals in that condition to wander about in all directions. The sudden appearance of such a sight caused so great a panic in the Roman army that no one ventured to go outside the entrenchments. Not so many days after this exploit, when M. Minucius Rufus, master of horse, had been given the same powers as the dictator, he craftily lured him into fighting, and utterly defeated the Roman. Although not present in person, he enticed Ti. Sempronius Gracchus, who had been twice consul into an ambuscade in Lucania and destroyed him. In a similar manner, at Venusia, he slew M. Claudius Marcellus, who was holding his fifth consulship.

It would be a long story to enumerate all his battles. Therefore it will suffice to add this one fact, to show how great a man he was: so long as he was in Italy, no one was a match for him in the field, and after the battle of

Cannæ no one encamped face to face with him on open ground.

Then, undefeated, he was recalled to defend his native land; there he carried on war against P. Scipio, the son of that Scipio whom he had put to flight first at the Rhone, then at the Po, and a third time at the Trebia. With him, since the resources of his country were now exhausted, he wished to arrange a truce for a time, in order to carry on the war later with renewed strength. He had an interview with Scipio, but they could not agree upon terms. A few days after the conference he fought with Scipio at Zama. Defeated incredible to relate he succeeded in a day and two nights in reaching Hadrumetum, distant from Zama about three hundred miles. In the course of that retreat the Numidians who had left the field with him laid a trap for him, but he not only eluded them, but even crushed the plotters. At Hadrumetum he rallied the survivors of the retreat and by means of new levies mustered a large number of soldiers within a few days.

While he was busily engaged in these preparations, the Carthaginians made peace with the Romans. Hannibal, however, continued after that to command the army and carried on war in Africa until the consulship of P. Sulpicius and C. Aurelius. For in the time of those magistrates Carthaginian envoys came to Rome, to return thanks to the Roman senate and people for having made peace with them; and as a mark of gratitude they presented them with a golden crown, at the same time asking that their hostages might live at Fregellae and that their prisoners should be returned. To them, in accordance with a decree of the senate, the following answer was made: that their gift was received with thanks; that the hostages should live where they had requested; that they would not return the prisoners, because Hannibal, who had caused the war and was bitterly hostile to the Roman nation, still held command in their army, as well as his brother Mago. Upon receiving that reply the Carthaginians recalled Hannibal and Mago to Carthage. On his return Hannibal was made a king, after he had been general for twenty-one years. For, as is true of the consuls at Rome, so at Carthage two kings were elected annually for a term of one year.

In that office Hannibal gave proof of the same energy that he had shown in war. For by means of new taxes he provided, not only that there should be money to pay to the Romans according to the treaty, but also that there should be a surplus to be deposited in the treasury. Then in the following year, when M. Claudius and L. Furius were consuls, envoys came to Carthage from Rome. Hannibal thought that they had been sent to demand his surrender; therefore, before they were given audience by the senate, he secretly embarked on a ship and took refuge with King Antiochus in Syria. When this became known, the Carthaginians sent two ships to arrest Hannibal, if they could overtake him; then they

confiscated his property, demolished his house from its foundations, and declared him an outlaw.

But Hannibal, in the third year after he had fled from his country, in the consulship of L. Cornelius and Q. Minucius, with five ships landed in Africa in the territories of Cyrene, to see whether the Carthaginians could by any chance be induced to make war by the hope of aid from King Antiochus, whom Hannibal had already persuaded to march upon Italy with his armies. To Italy also he dispatched his brother Mago. When the Carthaginians learned this, they inflicted on Mago in his absence the same penalty that Hannibal had suffered. The brothers, regarding the situation as desperate, raised anchor and set sail. Hannibal reached Antiochus; as to the death of Mago there are two accounts; some have written that he was shipwrecked; others, that he was killed by his own slaves. As for Antiochus, if he had been as willing to follow Hannibal's advice in the conduct of the war as he had been in declaring it, he would not have fought for the rule of the world at Thermopylae, but nearer to the Tiber. But although Hannibal saw that many of the king's plans were unwise, yet he never deserted him. On one occasion he commanded a few ships, which he had been ordered to take from Syria to Asia, and with them he fought against a fleet of the Rhodians in the Pamphylian Sea. Although in that engagement his forces were defeated by the superior numbers of their opponents, he was victorious on the wing where he fought in person.

After Antiochus had been defeated, Hannibal, fearing that he would be surrendered to the Romans—as undoubtedly would have happened, if he had let himself be taken—came to the Gortynians in Crete, there to deliberate where to seek asylum. But being the shrewdest of all men, he realized that he would be in great danger, unless he devised some means of escaping the avarice of the Cretans; for he was carrying with him a large sum of money, and he knew that news of this had leaked out. He therefore devised the following plan: he filled a number of large jars with lead and covered their tops with gold and silver. These, in the presence of the leading citizens, he deposited in the temple of Diana, pretending that he was entrusting his property to their protection. Having thus misled them, he filled some bronze statues which he was carrying with him with all his money and threw them carelessly down in the courtyard of his house. The Gortynians guarded the temple with great care, not so much against others as against Hannibal, to prevent him from taking anything without their knowledge and carrying it off with him.

Thus he saved his goods, and having tricked all the Cretans, the Carthaginian joined Prusias in Pontus. At his court he was of the same mind towards Italy and gave his entire attention to arming the king and training his forces to meet the Romans. And seeing that Prusias' personal resources did not give him great strength, he won him the friendship of the other kings of that region and allied him with warlike nations. Prusias had quarreled with Eumenes, king of Pergamum, a strong friend of the Romans, and they were fighting with each other by land and sea. But Eumenes was everywhere the stronger because of his alliance with the Romans, and for that reason Hannibal was the more eager for his overthrow, thinking that if he got rid of him, all his difficulties would be ended.

To cause his death, he formed the following plan. Within a few days they were intending to fight a decisive naval battle. Hannibal was outnumbered in ships; therefore it was necessary to resort to a ruse, since he was unequal to his opponent in arms. He gave orders to collect the greatest possible number of venomous snakes and put them alive in earthenware jars. When he had got together a great number of these, on the very day when the sea-fight was going to take place he called the marines together and bade them concentrate their attack on the ship of Eumenes and be satisfied with merely defending themselves against the rest; this they could easily do, thanks to the great number of snakes. Furthermore, he promised to let them know in what ship Eumenes was sailing, and to give them a generous reward if they succeeded in either capturing or killing the king.

After he had encouraged the soldiers in this way, the fleets on both sides were brought out for battle. When they were drawn up in line, before the signal for action was given, in order that Hannibal might make it clear to his men where Eumenes was, he sent a messenger in a skiff with a herald's staff. When the emissary came to the ships of the enemy, he exhibited a letter and said that he was looking for the king. He was at once taken to Eumenes since no one doubted that it was some communication about peace. The letter-carrier, having pointed out the commander's ship to his men, returned to the place from which he came. But Eumenes, on opening the missive, found nothing in it except what was designed to mock at him. Although he wondered at the reason for such conduct and could not find one, he nevertheless did not hesitate to join battle at once.

When the clash came, the Bithynians did as Hannibal had ordered and fell upon the ship of Eumenes in a body. Since the king could not resist their force, he sought safety in flight, which he secured only by retreating within the entrenchments which had been thrown up on the neighboring shore. When the other Pergamene ships began to press their opponents too hard, on a sudden the earthenware jars of which I have spoken began to be hurled at them. At first these projectiles excited the laughter of the combatants, and they could not understand what it meant. But as soon as they saw their ships filled with snakes, terrified by the strange weapons and not knowing how to avoid them, they turned their ships about and retreated to their naval

camp. Thus Hannibal overcame the arms of Pergamum by strategy; and that was not the only instance of the kind, but on many other occasions in land battles he defeated his antagonists by a similar bit of cleverness.

While this was taking place in Asia, it chanced that in Rome envoys of Prusias were dining with T. Quinctius Flamininus, the ex-consul, and that mention being made of Hannibal, one of the envoys said that he was in the kingdom of Prusias. On the following day Flamininus informed the senate. The Fathers, believing that while Hannibal lived they would never be free from plots. sent envoys to Bithynia, among them Flamininus, to request the king not to keep their bitterest foe at his court, but to surrender him to the Romans. Prusias did not dare to refuse; he did, however, stipulate that they would not ask him to do anything which was in violation of the laws of hospitality. They themselves, if they could, might take him; they would easily find his place of abode. As a matter of fact, Hannibal kept himself in one place, in a stronghold which the king had given him, and he had so arranged it that he had exits in every part of the building, evidently being in fear of experiencing what actually happened.

When the envoys of the Romans had come to the place and surrounded his house with a great body of troops, a slave looking out from one of the doors reported that an unusual number of armed men were in sight. Hannibal ordered him to go about to all the doors of the building and hasten to inform him whether he was beset in the same way on every side. The slave having quickly reported the facts and told him that all the exits were guarded, Hannibal knew that it was no accident; that it was he whom they were after and he must no longer think of preserving his life. But not wishing to lose it at another's will, and remembering his past deeds of valor, he took the poison which he always carried about his person.

Thus that bravest of men, after having performed many and varied labors, entered into rest in his seventieth year. Under what consuls he died is disputed. For Atticus has recorded in his Annals that he died in the consulate of M. Claudius Marcellus and Q. Fabius Labeo; Polybius, under L. Aemilius Paulus and Cn. Baebius Tamphilus; and Sulpicius Blitho, in the time of P. Cornelius Cethegus and M. Baebius Tamphilus. And that great man, although busied with such great wars, devoted some time to letters; for there are several books of his, written in Greek, among them one, addressed to the Rhodians, on the deeds of Cn. Manlius Volso in Asia. Hannibal's deeds of arms have been recorded by many writers, among them two men who were with him in camp and lived with him so long as fortune allowed, Silenus and Sosylus of Lacedaemon. And it was this Sosylus whom Hannibal employed as his teacher of Greek.

The Battle of Cannæ

Source: Polybius, III.107–118. In *The Histories of Polybius*, 2 Vols., trans. Evelyn S. Shuckburgh (London: Macmillan, 1889), I. 264–275. Scanned by: J. S. Arkenberg, Dept. of History, Cal. State Fullerton. Prof. Arkenberg has modernized the text.

The Battle of Cannæ in 216 BCE, in which Hannibal smashed the Roman army, was one of Rome's greatest defeats.

Thus through all that winter and spring the two armies remained encamped facing each other. But when the season for the new harvest was come, Hannibal began to move from the camp at Geronium; and making up his mind that it would be to his advantage to force the enemy by any possible means to give him battle, he occupied the citadel of a town called Cannæ, into which the corn and other supplies from the district round Canusium were collected by the Romans, and conveyed thence to the camp as occasion required. The town itself, indeed, had been reduced to ruins the year before: but the capture of its citadel and the material of war contained in it, caused great commotion in the Roman army; for it was not only the loss of the place and the stores in it that distressed them, but the fact also that it commanded the surrounding district. They therefore sent frequent messages to Rome asking for instructions: for if they approached the enemy they would not be able to avoid an engagement, in view of the fact that the country was being plundered, and the allies all in a state of excitement. The Senate passed a resolution that they should give the enemy battle: they, however, bade Cn. Servilius wait, and dispatched the Consuls to the seat of war.

It was to Aemilius[58] that all eyes turned, and on him the most confident hopes were fixed; for his life had been a noble one, and he was thought to have managed the recent Illyrian war with advantage to the state. The Senate determined to bring eight legions into the field, which had never been done at Rome before, each legion consisting of five thousand men besides allies. For the Romans, as I have state before, habitually enroll four legions per year, each consisting of about four thousand foot and two hundred horse; and when any unusual necessity arises, they raise the number of foot to five thousand and of the horse to three hundred. Of allies, the number in each legion is the same as that of the citizens, but of the horse three times as great. Of the four legions thus composed, they assign two to each of the Consuls for whatever service is going on. Most of their wars are decided by one Consul and two legions, with their quota of allies;[59] and they rarely employ all four at one time and on one service. But on this occasion, so great was the alarm and terror of what would happen, they resolved to bring not only four but eight legions into the field.[60]

With earnest words of exhortations, therefore, to Aemilius, putting before him the gravity in every point of view of the result of the battle, they dispatched him with instructions to seek a favorable opportunity to fight a decisive battle with a courage worthy of Rome. Having arrived at the camp and united their forces, they made known the will of the Senate to the soldiers, and Aemilius exhorted them to do their duty in terms which evidently came from his heart. ...

Up to that time both Consuls had never been engaged together, or employed thoroughly trained soldiers: the combatants on the contrary had been raw levies, entirely inexperienced in danger; and what was most important of all, they had been entirely ignorant of their opponents, that they had been brought into the field, and engaged in a pitched battle with an enemy that they had never once set eyes upon. Those who had been defeated on the Trebia were drawn up on the field at daybreak, on the very next morning after their arrival from Sicily; while those who had fought in Etruria,[61] not only had never seen the enemy before, but did not do so even during the very battle itself, owing to the unfortunate state of the atmosphere. ...

Next morning the two Consuls broke up their camp, and advanced to where they heard that the enemy were entrenched. On the second day they arrived within sight of them, and pitched their camp at about fifty stadia distance. But when Aemilius observed that the ground was flat and bare for some distance round, he said that they must not engage there with an enemy superior to them in cavalry; but that they must rather try to draw him off, and lead him to ground on which the battle would be more in the hands of the infantry. But C. Terentius[62] being, from inexperience, of a contrary opinion, there was a dispute and misunderstanding between the two leaders, which of all things is the most dangerous. It is the custom, when the two Consuls are present, that they should take the chief command on alternate days; and the next day happening to be the turn of Terentius, he ordered an advance with a view of approaching the enemy, in spite of the protests and active opposition of his colleague.

Hannibal set his light-armed troops and cavalry in motion to meet him, and charging the Romans while they were still marching, took them by surprise and caused a great confusion in their ranks. The Romans repulsed the first charge by putting some of their heavy-armed in front; and then sending forward their light-armed and cavalry, began to get the best of the fight all

---

[58] L. Aemilius Paullus, Consul for 216 BCE.
[59] Thus two citizen legions and two allied legions combined.

[60] Thus eight citizen legions and eight allied legions combined—about 90,000 men.
[61] At the defeat at Lake Trasimene.
[62] C. Terentius Varro, Consul for 216 BCE.

along the line: the Carthaginians having no reserves of any importance, while certain companies of the legionaries were mixed with the Roman light-armed, and helped to sustain the battle. Nightfall for the present put an end to a struggle which had not at all answered to the hopes of the Carthaginians.

But next day Aemilius, not thinking it right to engage, and yet being unable any longer to lead off his army, encamped with two-thirds of it on the banks of the Apennines—that chain of mountains which forms the watershed of all Italian rivers, which flow either west to the Tuscan sea, or east to the Adriatic. This chain is, I say, pierced by the Aufidus, which rises on the side of Italy nearest the Tuscan Sea, and is discharged into the Adriatic. For the other third of his army he caused a camp to be made across the river, to the east of the ford, about ten stades from his own lines, and a little more from those of the enemy; that these men, being on the other side of the river, might protect his own foraging parties, and threaten those of the enemy.

Then Hannibal, seeing that his circumstances called for a battle with the enemy, being anxious lest his troops should be depressed by their previous reverse, and believing that it was an occasion which required some encouraging words, summoned a general meeting of his soldiers. When they were assembled, he bid them all look round upon the country, and asked them "What better fortune they could have asked from the gods, if they had had the choice, than to fight in such ground as they saw there, with the vast superiority of cavalry on their side?" ...

Next day he gave orders that all should employ themselves in making preparations and getting themselves into a fit state of body. On the day after that he drew out his men along the bank of the river, and showed that he was eager to give the enemy battle. But Aemilius, dissatisfied with his position, and seeing that the Carthaginians would soon be obliged to shift their quarters for the sake of supplies, kept quiet in his camps, strengthening both with extra guards. After waiting a considerable time, when no one came out to attack him, Hannibal put the rest of the army into camp again, but sent out his Numidian horse to attack the enemy's water parties from the lesser camp. These horsemen riding right up to the lines and preventing the watering, C. Terentius became more than ever inflamed with the desire of fighting, and the soldiers were eager for a battle, and chafed at the delay. For there is nothing more intolerable to mankind than suspense; when a thing is once decided, men can but endure whatever out of their catalogue of evils it is their misfortune to undergo.

But when the news arrived at Rome that the two armies were face to face, and that skirmishes between advanced parties of both sides were daily taking place, the city was in a state of high excitement and uneasiness; the people dreading the result, owing to the disasters which had now befallen them on more than one occasion; and foreseeing and anticipating in their imaginations what would happen if they were utterly defeated. All the oracles preserved at Rome were in everybody's mouth; and every temple and house was full of prodigies and miracles: in consequence of which the city was one scene of vows, sacrifices, supplicatory processions, and prayers. For the Romans in time of danger take extraordinary pains to appease gods and men, and look upon no ceremony of that kind in such times as unbecoming or beneath their dignity.

When he took over the command on the following day, as soon as the sun was above the horizon, C. Terentius got the army in motion from both the camps. Those from the larger camp he drew up in order of battle, as soon as he had got them across the river, and bringing up those of the smaller camp he placed them all in the same line, selecting the south as the aspect of the whole. The Roman horse he stationed on the right wing along the river, and their foot next to them in the same line, placing the maniples, however, closer together than usual, and making the depth of each maniple several times greater than its front. The cavalry of the allies he stationed on the left wing, and the light-armed troops he placed slightly in advance of the whole army, which amounted with its allies to eighty thousand infantry and a little more than six thousand horse. At the same time Hannibal brought his Balearic slingers and spearmen across the river, and stationed them in advance of his main body; which he led out of their camp, and, getting them across the river at two spots, drew them up opposite the enemy. On his left wing, close to the river, he stationed the Iberian and Celtic horse opposite the Roman cavalry; and next to them half the Libyan heavy-armed foot; and next to them the Iberian and Celtic foot; next, the other half of the Libyans, and, on the right wing, the Numidian horse. Having now got them all into line he advanced with the central companies of the Iberians and Celts; and so arranged the other companies next these in regular gradations, that the whole line became crescent-shaped, diminishing in depth towards its extremities: his object being to have his Libyans as a reserve in the battle, and to commence the action with his Iberians and Celts.

The armor of the Libyans was Roman, for Hannibal had armed them with a selection of the spoils taken in previous battles. The shield of the Iberians and Celts was about the same size, but their swords were quite different. For that of the Roman can thrust with as deadly effects as it can cut, while the Gallic sword can only cut, and that requires some room. And the companies coming alternately—the naked Celts, and the Iberians with their short linen tunics bordered with purple stripes, the whole appearance of the line was strange and terrifying. The whole strength of the Carthaginian cavalry was ten thousand, but that of their foot was not more than forty thousand, including the Celts. Aemilius commanded on the Roman right, C. Terentius on the left, M. Atilius and Cn. Servilius, the consuls of the previous year, on the center. The left of the Carthaginians was commanded by Hasdrubal, the right by Hanno, the center by Hannibal in person, attended by his brother Mago. And as the Roman line faced the south, as I said before, and the Carthaginian the north, the rays of the rising sun did not inconvenience either of them.

The battle was begun by an engagement between the advanced guard of the two armies; and at first the affair between these light-armed troops was indecisive. But as soon as the Iberian and Celtic cavalry got at the Romans, the battle began in earnest, and in the true barbaric fashion: for there was none of the usual formal advance and retreat; but when they once got to close quarters, they grappled man to man, and, dismounting from their horses, fought on foot. But when the Carthaginians had got the upper hand in this encounter and killed most of their opponents on the ground—because the Romans all maintained the fight with spirit and determination—and began chasing the remainder along the river, slaying as they went along and giving no quarter; then the legionaries took the place of the light-armed and closed with the enemy. For a short time the Iberian and Celtic lines stood their ground and fought gallantly; but, presently overpowered by the weight of the heavy-armed lines, they gave way and retired to the rear, thus breaking up the crescent. The Roman maniples followed with spirit, and easily cut their way through the enemy's line; since the Celts had been drawn up in a thin line, while the Romans had closed up from the wings towards the center and the point of danger. For the two wings did not come into action at the same time as the center: but the center was first engaged, because the Gauls, having been stationed on the arc of the crescent, had come into contact with the enemy long before the wings, the convex of the crescent being towards the enemy.

The Romans, however, going in pursuit of these troops, and hastily closing in towards the center and the part of the enemy which was giving ground, advanced so far that the Libyan heavy-armed troops on either wing got on their flanks. Those on the right, facing to the left, charged from the right upon the Roman flank; while those who were on the left wing faced to the right, and, dressing by the left, charged their right flank, the exigency of the moment suggesting to them what they ought to do. Thus it came about, as Hannibal had planned, that the Romans were caught between two hostile lines of Libyans—thanks to their impetuous pursuit of the Celts. Still they fought, though no longer in line, yet singly, or in maniples, which faced to meet those who charged them on the flanks.

Though he had been from the first on the right wing, and had taken part in the cavalry engagement, L.

Aemilius still survived. Determined to act up to his own exhortatory speech, and seeing that the decision of the battle rested mainly on the legionaries, riding up to the center of the line he led the charge himself, and personally grappled with the enemy, at the same time cheering on and exhorting his soldiers to the charge. Hannibal, on the other side, did the same, for he too had taken his place on the center from the commencement. The Numidian horse on the Carthaginian right were meanwhile charging through the cavalry on the Roman left; and though, from the peculiar nature of their mode of fighting, they neither inflicted nor received much harm, they yet rendered the enemy's horse useless by keeping them occupied, and charging them first on one side and then another. But when Hasdrubal, after all but annihilating the cavalry by the river, came from the left to the support of the Numidians, the Roman allied cavalry, seeing his charge approaching, broke and fled. At that point Hasdrubal appears to have acted with great skill and discretion. Seeing the Numidians to be strong in numbers, and more effective and formidable to troops that had once been forced from their ground, he left the pursuit to them; while he himself hastened to the part of the field where the infantry were engaged, and brought his men up to support the Libyans. Then, by charging the Roman legions on the rear, and harassing them by hurling squadron after squadron upon them at many points at once, he raised the spirits of the Libyans, and dismayed and depressed that of the Romans.

It was at this point that L. Aemilius fell, in the thick of the fight, covered with wounds: a man who did his duty to his country at that last hour of his life, as he had throughout its previous years, if any man ever did. As long as the Romans could keep an unbroken front, to turn first in one direction and then in another to meet the assaults of the enemy, they held out; but the outer files of the circle continually falling, and the circle becoming more and more contracted, they at last were all killed on the field; and among them M. Atilius and Cn. Servilius, the Consuls of the previous year, who had shown themselves brave men and worthy of Rome in the battle. While this struggle and carnage were going on, the Numidian horse were pursuing the fugitives, most of whom they cut down or hurled from their horses; but some few escaped into Venusia, among whom was C. Terentius, the Consul, who thus sought a flight, as disgraceful to himself, as his conduct in office had been disastrous to his country.

Such was the end of the battle of Cannæ, in which both sides fought with the most conspicuous gallantry, the conquered no less than the conquerors. This is proved by the fact that, out of six thousand horse, only seventy escaped with C. Terentius to Venusia, and about three hundred of the allied cavalry to various towns in the neighborhood. Of the infantry ten thousand were taken prisoners in fair fight, but were not actually engaged in the battle: of those who were actually engaged only about three thousand perhaps escaped to the towns of the surrounding district; all the rest died nobly, to the number of seventy thousand, the Carthaginians being on this occasion, as on previous ones, mainly indebted for their victory to their superiority in cavalry: a lesson to posterity that in actual war it is better to have half the number of infantry, and the superiority in cavalry, than to engage your enemy with an equality in both. On the side of Hannibal there fell four thousand Celts, fifteen hundred Iberians and Libyans, and about two hundred horse.

The ten thousand Romans who were captured had not, as I said, been engaged in the actual battle; and the reason was this. L. Aemilius left ten thousand infantry in his camp that, in case Hannibal should disregard the safety of his own camp, and take his whole army onto the field, they might seize the opportunity, while the battle was going on, of forcing their way in and capturing the enemy's baggage; or if, on the other hand, Hannibal should, in view of this contingency, leave a guard in his camp, the number of the enemy in the field might thereby be diminished. These men were captured in the field in the following circumstances. Hannibal, as a matter of fact, did leave a sufficient guard in his camp; and as soon as the battle began, the Romans, according to their instructions, assaulted and tried to take those thus left by Hannibal. At first they held their own: but just as they were beginning to waver, Hannibal, who was by this time gaining a victory all along the line, came to their relief, and routing the Romans, shut them up in their own camp; killed two thousand of them; and took all the rest prisoners. In like manner the Numidian horse brought in all those who had taken refuge in the various strongholds about the district, amounting to two thousand of the routed cavalry.

The result of this battle, such as I have described it, had the consequences which both sides expected. For the Carthaginians by their victory were thenceforth masters of nearly the whole of the Italian coast which is called Magna Græcia. Thus the Tarentines immediately submitted; and the Arpani and some of the Campanian states invited Hannibal to come to them; and the rest were with one consent turning their eyes to the Carthaginians: who, accordingly, began now to have high hopes of being able to carry even Rome itself by assault. On their side the Romans, even after this disaster, despaired of retaining their supremacy over the Italians, and were in the greatest alarm, believing their own lives and the existence of their city to be in danger, and every moment expecting that Hannibal would be upon them. For, as though Fortune herself were in league with the disasters that had already befallen them to fill up the measure of their ruin, it happened that only a few days afterwards, while the city was still in this panic, the Praetor who had been sent to the Gaul fell unexpectedly

into an ambush and perished, and his army was utterly annihilated by the Celts.

In spite of all, however, the Senate left no means untried to save the State. It exhorted the people to fresh exertions, strengthened the city with guards, and deliberated on the crisis in a brave and manly spirit. And subsequent events made this manifest. For though the Romans were on that occasion indisputably beaten in the field, and had lost their reputation for military prowess; by the peculiar excellence of their political constitution, and the prudence of their counsels, they not only recovered their supremacy over Italy, by eventually conquering the Carthaginians, but before very long became masters of the whole world.

LIVY, PRUDENTIUS

The Magna Mater

Source: Livy, 29.10, 14; Prudentius: "The Taurobolion of Magna Mater," in *Peristephanon.* In Thatcher, Oliver J. *The Library of Original Sources; Ideas That Have Influenced Civilization, in the Original Documents, Translated.* Metuchen, N.J.: Mini-Print Corp, 1971.

> *The Romans absorbed some alien religions and persecuted others; the case of the Magna Mater was special.*

Livy: 29.10, 14

About this time[63] the citizens were much exercised by a religious question which had lately come up. Owing to the unusual number of showers of stones which had fallen during the year, an inspection had been made of the Sibylline Books, and some oracular verses had been discovered which announced that whenever a foreign foe should carry war into Italy he could be driven out and conquered if the Mater Magna were brought from Pessinos [in Phrygia] to Rome. The discovery of this prediction produced all the greater impression on the senators because the deputation who had taken the gift to Delphi reported on their return that when they sacrificed to the Pythian Apollo the indications presented by the victims were entirely favorable, and further, that the response of the oracle was to the effect that a far grander victory was awaiting Rome than the one from whose spoils they had brought the gift to Delphi. In order, therefore, to secure all the sooner the victory which the Fates, the omens, and the oracles alike foreshadowed, they began to think out the best way of transporting the goddess to Rome....

203 BCE In this state of excitement men's minds were filled with superstition and the ready credence given to announcement of portents increased their number. Two suns were said to have been seen; there were intervals of daylight during the night; a meteor was seen to shoot

[63] 204 BCE.

from east to west; a gate at Tarracina and at Anagnia a gate and several portions of the wall were struck by lightning; in the temple of Juno Sospita at Lanuvium a crash followed by a dreadful roar was heard. To expiate these portents special intercessions were offered for a whole day, and in consequence of a shower of stones a nine days' solemnity of prayer and sacrifice was observed. The reception of Mater Magna was also anxiously discussed. M. Valerius, the member of the deputation who had come in advance, had reported that she would be in Italy almost immediately and a fresh messenger had brought word that she was already at Tarracina. Scipio was ordered to go to Ostia, accompanied by all the matrons, to meet the goddess. He was to receive her as she left the vessel, and when brought to land he was to place her in the hands of the matrons who were to bear her to her destination.

As soon as the ship appeared off the mouth of the Tiber he put out to sea in accordance with his instructions, received the goddess from the hands of her priestesses, and brought her to land. Here she was received by the foremost matrons of the City, amongst whom the name of Claudia Quinta stands out pre-eminently. According to the traditional account her reputation had previously been doubtful, but this sacred function surrounded her with a halo of chastity in the eyes of posterity. The matrons, each taking their turn in bearing the sacred image, carried the goddess into the temple of Victory on the Palatine. All the citizens flocked out to meet them, censers in which incense was burning were placed before the doors in the streets through which she was borne, and from all lips arose the prayer that she would of her own free will and favor be pleased to enter Rome. The day on which this event took place was 12th April, and was observed as a festival; the people came in crowds to make their offerings to the deity; a lectisternium[64] was held, and Games were constituted which were known afterwards as the Megalesian.

Prudentius: The Taurobolion of Magna Mater

The high priestess who is to be consecrated is brought down under ground in a pit dug deep, marvelously adorned with a fillet, binding her festive temples with chaplets, her hair combed back under a golden crown, and wearing a silken toga caught up with Gabine girding. Over this they make a wooden floor with wide spaces, woven of planks with an open mesh; they then divide or bore the area and repeatedly pierce the wood with a pointed tool that it may appear full of small holes. Here a huge bull, fierce and shaggy in appearance, is led, bound with flowery garlands about its flanks, and with its horns sheathed—its forehead sparkles with gold, and the flash of metal plates colors its hair. Here, as

is ordained, they pierce its breast with a sacred spear; the gaping wound emits a wave of hot blood, and the smoking river flows into the woven structure beneath it and surges wide. Then by the many paths of the thousand openings in the lattice the falling shower rains down a foul dew, which the priestess buried within catches, putting her head under all the drops. She throws back her face, she puts her cheeks in the way of the blood, she puts under it her ears and lips, she interposes her nostrils, she washes her very eyes with the fluid, nor does she even spare her throat but moistens her tongue, until she actually drinks the dark gore. Afterwards, the corpse, stiffening now that the blood has gone forth, is hauled off the lattice, and the priestess, horrible in appearance, comes forth, and shows her wet head, her hair heavy with blood, and her garments sodden with it. This woman, all hail and worship at a distance, because the ox's blood has washed her, and she is born again for eternity.

POLYBIUS

The Siege of Syracuse

Source: Polybius VIII.3–7. Translated by Ian Scott-Kilvert. Penguin, 1979.

The great kingdom of Syracuse declared for Carthage during the Second Punic War and was subjected to a siege (214–212). The Syracusans held out not so much through the brilliance not of their generals but through that of their engineer, Archimedes.

The subsequent sack of Syracuse and Marcellus's triumph, in which the opulence of the Greek city was paraded before the populace, was later seen as the beginning of the erosion of Roman austerity.

After Epicydes and Hippocrates had seized power in Syracuse, they managed to transfer the friendship and allegiance which their compatriots had previously cherished for Rome to the side of Carthage. Meanwhile, the Romans, who had already been informed of the fate which had befallen Hieronymous, the tyrant of Syracuse, appointed Ap. Claudius Pulcher as pro-praetor to command the land forces, and M. Claudius Marcellus to take charge of the fleet. These officers then took up a position not far from the city and decided to assault it with their land forces at the quarter known as the Hexapyli; the fleet was to attack at the so-called portico of Scytice in Achradina, where the city wall extends to the quay-side. The Romans' wicker screens, missiles and other siege apparatus had been made ready beforehand, and they felt confident that with the number of men at their disposal they could within five days bring their preparations to a point which would give them the advantage over the enemy. But here they failed to

---

[64] A seven-day citywide feast.

reckon with the talents of Archimedes or to foresee that in some cases the genius of one man is far more effective than superiority in numbers. This lesson they now learned by experience.

The strength of the defenses of Syracuse is due to the fact that the city wall extends in a circle along high ground with steeply overhanging crags, which are by no means easy to climb, except at certain definite points, even if the approach is uncontested. Accordingly Archimedes had constructed the defenses of the city in such a way—both on the landward side and to repel any attack from the sea—that there was no need for the defenders to busy themselves with improvisations; instead they would have everything ready to hand, and could respond to any attack by the enemy with a counter-move. For his part Ap. Claudius Pulcher, who was equipped with penthouses and scaling-ladders, brought these into operation to attack the part of the wall which adjoins the Hexapyli gate to the east.

Meanwhile Marcellus was attacking the quarter of Achradina from the sea with sixty quinqueremes, each vessel being filled with archers, slingers and javelin-throwers, whose task was to drive the defenders from the battlements. Besides these vessels he had eight quinqueremes grouped in pairs. Each pair had had half of their oars removed, the starboard bank for the one and the port for the other, and on these sides the vessels were lashed together. They were then rowed by the remaining oars of their outer sides, and brought up to the walls the siege engines known as sambucae. These are constructed as follows. A ladder is made, four feet in width and high enough to reach the top of the wall from the place where its feet are to rest. Each side is fenced in with a high protective breastwork, and the machine is also shielded by a wicker covering high overhead. It is then laid flat over the two sides of the ships where are lashed together, the top protruding a considerable distance beyond the bows. To the tops of the ships' masts are fixed pulleys with ropes, and when the sambuca is about to be used, the ropes are attached to the top of the ladder, and men standing in the stern haul up the machine by means of the pulleys, while others stand in the bows to support it with long poles and make sure that it is safely raised. After this the oarsmen on the two outer sides of the ships row the vessels close inshore, and the crews then attempt to prop the sambuca against the wall. At the top of the ladder there is a wooden platform which is protected on three sides by wicker screens; four men are stationed on this to engage the defenders, who in the meanwhile are struggling to prevent the sambuca from being lodged against the battlements. As soon as the attackers have got it into position, and are thus standing on a higher level that the wall, they pull down the wicker screens on each side of the platform and rush out on to the battlements or towers. Their comrades climb up the

sambuca after them, the ladder being held firm by ropes which are attached to both ships. This device is aptly named, because when it is raised the combination of the ship and the ladder looks remarkably like the musical instrument in question.

This was the siege equipment with which the Romans planned to assault the city's towers. But Archimedes had constructed artillery which could cover a whole variety of ranges, so that while the attacking ships were still at a distance he scored so many hits with his catapults and stone-throwers that he was able to cause them severe damage and harass their approach. Then, as the distance decreased and these weapons began to carry over the enemy's heads, he resorted to smaller and smaller machines, and so demoralized the Romans that their advance was brought to a standstill. In the end Marcellus was reduced in despair to bringing up his ships secretly under cover of darkness. But when they had almost reached the shore, and were therefore too close to be struck by the catapults, Archimedes had devised yet another weapon to repel the marines, who were fighting from the decks. He had had the walls pierced with large numbers of loopholes at the height of a man, which were about a palm's breadth wide at the outer surface of the walls. Behind each of these and inside the walls were stationed archers with rows of so-called 'scorpions', a small catapult which discharged iron darts, and by shooting through these embrasures they put many of the marines out of action. Through these tactics he not only foiled all the enemy's attacks, both those made at long range and any attempt at hand-to-hand fighting, but also caused them heavy losses.

Then, whenever the enemy tried to work their sambucae, he had other engines ready all along the walls. At normal times these were kept out of sight, but as soon as they were needed they were hoisted above the walls, with their beams projecting far over the battlements, some of them carrying stones weighing as much as ten talents, and others large lumps of lead. As soon as the sambucae approached, these beams were swung round on a universal joint and by means of a release mechanism or trigger dropped the weight on the sambuca; the effect was not only to smash the ladder but to endanger the safety of the ships and of their crews.

Other machines invented by Archimedes were directed against the assault parties as they advanced under the shelter of screens which protected them against the missiles shot through the walls. Against these attackers the machines could discharge stones heavy enough to drive back the marines from the bows of the ships; at the same time a grappling-iron attached to a chain would be let down, and with this the man controlling the beam would clutch at the ship. As soon as the prow was securely gripped, the lever of the machine inside the wall would be pressed down. When the operator had lifted up the ship's prow in this way and made her stand on her stern, he made fast the lower parts of the machine, so that they would not move, and finally by means of a rope and pulley suddenly slackened the grappling-iron and the chain. The result was that some of the vessels heeled over and fell on the sides, and others capsized, while the majority when their bows were let fall from a height plunged under water and filled, and thus threw all into confusion. Marcellus' operations were thus completely frustrated by these inventions of Archimedes, and when he saw that the garrison not only repulsed his attacks with heavy losses but also laughed at his efforts, he took his defeat hard. At the same time he could not refrain from making a joke against himself when he said: 'Archimedes uses my ships to ladle sea-water into his wine-cups, but my sambuca band have been whipped out of the wine-party as intruders!' So ended the efforts to capture Syracuse from the sea.

At the same time Ap. Claudius Pulcher found himself faced with similar difficulties when he attacked by land, and finally he abandoned the attempt. While his troops were still at a distance from the walls they suffered many casualties from the mangonels and catapults. This artillery was extraordinarily effective both in the volume of its fire, as was to be expected when Hiero had provided the supplies, and Archimedes designed the various engines. Then, even when the soldiers did get close to the wall, they were so harassed by the volleys of arrows and darts which continually poured through the embrasures, as I described above, that their advance was effectually halted. Alternatively, if they attacked under cover of their penthouses, they were crushed by the stones and beams that were dropped on their heads. The defenders also killed many men by means of the iron grappling-hooks let down from cranes, which I mentioned earlier: these were used to lift up men, amour and all, and then allow them to drop. In the end Pulcher withdrew to his camp and summoned a council of the military tribunes, at which it was unanimously decided to use any other methods rather than persist in the attempt to capture Syracuse by storm. And this resolution was never reversed, for during the eight months' siege of the city which followed, although they left no stratagem or daring attempt untried, they never again ventured to mount a general assault. So true it is that the genius of one man can become an immense, almost a miraculous asset, if it is properly applied to certain problems. In this instance, at any rate, the Romans, having brought up such numerous forces both by sea and by land, had every hope of capturing the city immediately, if only one old man out of all the Syracusans could have been removed; but so long as he was present they did not dare even to attempt an attack by any method which made it possible for Archimedes to oppose them. Instead they concluded that in view of the large population of the town, the best way to reduce it

was by starvation; they therefore cut off supplies from the sea by means of the fleet, and by land by means of the army, and rested their hopes on this solution. But as they were anxious to achieve some useful results outside, and not waste all the time during which they would be blockading Syracuse, the two commanders separated and divided their forces. Pulcher took command of two-thirds and invested the city, while Marcellus with the remaining third made raids on those parts of Sicily which were supporting the Carthaginians.

POLYBIUS

The Destruction of Corinth

Source: Polybius, *The Histories*, 38.1, 39.7-17. From: The Histories of Polybius, 2 Vols., trans. Evelyn S. Shuckburgh (London: Macmillan, 1889), II.515-525, 530-540. Scanned by: J. S. Arkenberg, Dept. of History, Cal. State Fullerton. Prof. Arkenberg has modernized the text.

The destruction of Corinth, one of the greatest cities of Greece, ended the Achaean War—a desperate bid by the Greeks of Peloponnese to fend off Roman domination. A severe departure for Roman foreign policy, and taking place in the same year (146 BCE) as the destruction of Carthage that ended in the Third Punic War, the sack of Corinth seemed an ominous turning point for the Romans.

On his arrival in the Peloponnese, the consul L. Mummius Achaicus was joined by allies who greatly enlarged his army. The Achaeans made a sudden attack upon them and gained a slight success, which was a few days afterwards revenged by a signal defeat. Diaeus, leader of the Achaeans, fled to Megalopolis, where he killed his wife and himself. The rest of the beaten Achaean army took refuge in Corinth, which Mummius took and destroyed on the third day. Then the commissioners were sent from Rome to settle the whole of Greece.

My thirty-eighth book embraces the consummation of the misfortunes of Greece. For though Greece as a whole, as well as separate parts of it, has on several occasions sustained grave disasters, yet to none of her previous defeats could the word "misfortune" be more properly applied, than to those which have befallen her in our time. For it is not only that the sufferings of Greece excite compassion: stronger still is the conviction, which a knowledge of the truth of the several occurrences must bring, that in all she undertook she was supremely unfortunate. At any rate, though the disaster of Carthage is looked upon as of the severest kind, yet one cannot but regard that of Greece as not less, and in some respects even more so. For the Carthaginians at any rate left something for posterity to say on their behalf; but the mistakes of the Greeks were so glaring that they made it impossible for those who wished to support them to do so. Besides, the destruction of the

Carthaginians was immediate and total, so that they had no feeling afterwards of their disasters: but the Greeks, with their misfortunes ever before their eyes, handed down to their children's children the loss of all that once was theirs. And in proportion as we regard those who live in pain as more pitiable than those who lose their lives at the moment of their misfortunes, in that proportion must the disasters of the Greeks be regarded as more pitiable than those of the Carthaginians—unless a man thinks nothing of dignity and honor, and gives his opinion from a regard only to material advantage. To prove the truth of what I say, one has only to remember and compare the misfortunes in Greece reputed to be the heaviest with what I have just now mentioned....

The incidents of the capture of Corinth were melancholy. The soldiers cared nothing for the works of art and the consecrated statues. I saw with my own eyes pictures thrown on the ground and soldiers playing dice on them; among them was a picture of Dionysus by Aristeides—in reference to which they say that the proverbial saying arose, "Nothing to the Dionysus,"—and the Hercules tortured by the shirt of Deianeira...

Owing to the popular reverence for the memory of Philopoemen, they did not take down the statues of him in the various cities. So true is it, as it seems to me, that every genuine act of virtue produces in the mind of those who benefit by it an affection which it is difficult to efface.... One might fairly, therefore, use the common saying: "He has been foiled not at the door, but in the road."... There were many statues of Philopoemen, and many erections in his honor, voted by the several cities; and a Roman at the time of the disaster which befell Greece at Corinth, wished to abolish them all and to formally indict him, laying an information against him, as though he were still alive, as an enemy and ill-wisher to Rome. But after a discussion, in which Polybius spoke against this sycophant, neither Mummius nor the commissioners would consent to abolish the honors of an illustrious man.... Polybius, in an elaborate speech, conceived in the spirit of what has just been said, maintained the cause of Philopoemen. His arguments were that "This man had indeed been frequently at variance with the Romans on the matter of their injunctions, but he only maintained his opposition so far as to inform and persuade them on the points in dispute; and even that he did not do without serious cause. He gave a genuine proof of his loyal policy and gratitude, by a test as it were of fire, in the periods of the wars with Philip and Antiochus. For, possessing at those times the greatest influence of any one in Greece, from his personal power as well as that of the Achaeans, he preserved his friendship for Rome with the most absolute fidelity, having joined in the vote of the Achaeans in virtue of which, four months before the Romans crossed from Italy, they levied a war from their own territory upon Antiochus and the Aetolians, when nearly all the other Greeks had become estranged from the Roman friendship." Having listened to this speech and approved of the speaker's view, the ten commissioners granted that the complimentary erections to Philopoemen in the several cities should be allowed to remain. Acting on this pretext, Polybius begged of the Consul the statues of Achaeus, Aratus, and Philopoemen, though they had already been transported to Acarnania from the Peloponnese: in gratitude for which action people set up a marble statue of Polybius himself ...

After the settlement made by the ten commissioners in Achaia, they directed the Quaestor, who was to superintend the selling of Diaeus's property, to allow Polybius to select anything he chose from the goods and present it to him as a free gift, and to sell the rest to the highest bidders. But, so far from accepting any such present, Polybius urged his friends not to covet anything whatever of the goods sold by the Quaestor anywhere:— for he was going a round of the cities and selling the property of all those who had been partisans of Diaeus, as well of such as had been condemned except those who left children or parents. Some of these friends did not take his advice; but those who did follow it earned a most excellent reputation among their fellow-citizens.

After completing these arrangements in six months, the ten commissioners sailed for Italy, at the beginning of spring, having left a noble monument of Roman policy for the contemplation of all Greece. They also charged Polybius, as they were departing, to visit all the cities and to decide all questions that might arise, until such plain time as they were grown accustomed to their constitution and laws. Which he did: and after a while caused the inhabitants to be contented with the constitution given them by the commissioners, and left no difficulty connected with the laws on any point, private or public, unsettled.

The Roman Proconsul, after the commissioners had left Achaia, having restored the holy places in the Isthmus and ornamented the temples in Olympia and Delphi, proceeded to make a tour of the cities, receiving marks of honor and proper gratitude in each. And indeed he deserved honor both public and private, for he conducted himself with self-restraint and disinterestedness, and administered his office with mildness, although he had great opportunities of enriching himself, and immense authority in Greece. And, in fact, in the points in which he was thought to have at all overlooked justice, he appears not to have done it for his own sake, but for that of his friends. And the most conspicuous instance of this was in the case of the Chalcidian horsemen whom he put to death.....

Cato Opposes Extravagance

Source: Livy XXXIV. 1-3. Translated by Cyrus Edmonds. In Kevin Guinagh and Alfred P. Dorjahn (eds.). *Latin Literature in Translation*. New York: Longmans, Green and Co, 1942.

> *In 215 BCE, Hannibal was ravaging Italy. The Oppian Law was passed to restrain women from extravagance in dress. When Carthage was defeated, the law was repealed despite the vigorous efforts of M. Porcius Cato, or Cato the Elder, consul 195 and one of the most formidable men in Roman history.*

Amid the serious concerns of important wars, either scarcely brought to a close or impending, an incident intervened, trivial indeed to be mentioned, but which, through the zeal of the parties concerned, issued in a violent contest. M. Fundanius and L. Valerius, plebeian tribunes, proposed to the people the repealing of the Oppian law. This law, which had been introduced by C. Oppius, plebeian tribune, in the consulate of Q. Fabius and Ti. Sempronius, during the heat of the Punic war, enacted that "no woman should possess more than half an ounce of gold, or wear a garment of various colors, or ride in a carriage drawn by horses, in a city, or any town, or any place nearer thereto than one mile; except on occasion of some public religious solemnity."

M. and P. Junius Brutus, plebeian tribunes, supported the Oppian law, and declared, that they would never suffer it be repealed; while many of the nobility stood forth to argue for and against the motion proposed. The Capitol was filled with crowds, who favored or opposed the law; nor could the matrons be kept at home, either by advice or shame, nor even by the commands of their husbands; but beset every street and pass in the city, beseeching the men as they went down to the forum, that in the present flourishing state of the commonwealth, when the private fortune of all was daily increasing, they would suffer the women to have their former ornaments of dress restored. This throng of women increased daily, for they arrived even from the country towns and villages; and they had at length the boldness to come up to the consuls, praetors, and magistrates, to urge their request. One of the consuls, however, they found especially inexorable—M. Porcius Cato, who, in support of the law proposed to be repealed, spoke to this effect:

"If, Romans, every individual among us had made it a rule to maintain the prerogative and authority of a husband with respect to his own wife, we should have less trouble with the whole sex. But now, our privileges, overpowered at home by female contumacy, are, even here in the forum, spurned and trodden under foot; and because we are unable to withstand each separately, we now dread their collective body. I was accustomed to think it a fabulous and fictitious tale, that, in a certain island, the whole race of males was utterly extirpated by a conspiracy of the women. But the utmost danger may be apprehended equally from either sex, if you suffer cabals, assemblies, and secret consultations to be held: scarcely, indeed, can I determine, m my own mind, whether the act Itself, or the precedent that it affords, is of more pernicious tendency. The latter of these more particularly concerns us consuls, and the other magistrates' the former, yourselves, my fellow-citizens. For, whether the measure proposed to your consideration be profitable to the state or not, is to be determined by you, who are about to go to the vote. As to the outrageous behavior of these women, whether it be merely an act of their own, or owing to your instigations, M. Fundanius and L. Valerius, it unquestionably implies culpable conduct in magistrates. I know not whether it reflects greater disgrace on you, tribunes, or on the consuls: on you certainly, if you have, on the present occasion, brought these women hither for the purpose of raising tribunician seditions; on us, if we suffer laws to be imposed on us by a secession of women, as was done formerly by that of the common people. It was not without painful emotions of shame, that I, just now, made my way into the forum through the midst of a band of women. Had I not been restrained by respect for the modesty and dignity of some individuals among them, rather than of the whole number, and been unwilling that they should be seen rebuked by a consul, I should have said to them, 'What sort of practice is this, of running out into public, besetting the streets, and addressing other women's husbands? Could not each have made the same request to her husband at home? Are your blandishments more seducing in public than in private; and with other women's husbands, than with your own? Although if the modesty of matrons confined them within the limits of their own rights, it did not' become you, even at home, to concern yourselves about what laws might be passed or repealed here.' Our ancestors thought it not proper that women should perform any, even private business, without a director; but that they should be ever under the control of parents, brothers, or husbands. We, it seems, suffer them, now, to interfere in the management of state affairs, and to introduce themselves into the forum, into general assemblies, and into assemblies of election. For, what are they doing, at this moment, in your streets and lanes? What, but arguing, some in support of the motion of the plebeian tribunes~ others, for the repeal of the law? Will you give the reins to their intractable nature, and their uncontrolled passions, and then expect that themselves should set bounds to their licentiousness, when you have failed to do so? This is the smallest of the injunctions laid on them by usage or the laws, as which women bear with impatience: they long for liberty; or rather, to speak the truth, for unbounded freedom in every particular. For what will they not attempt, if they now come off victorious?

"Recollect all the institutions respecting the sex, by which our forefathers restrained their undue freedom, and by which they subjected them to their husbands; and yet, even with the help of all these restrictions, you can scarcely keep them within bounds. If, then, you suffer them to throw these off one by one, to tear them all asunder, and, at last, to be set on an equal footing with yourselves, can you imagine that they will be any longer tolerable by you? The moment they have arrived at an equality with you, they will have become your superiors. .But, forsooth, they only object to any new law being made against them' they mean to deprecate, not justice, but severity. Nay, their wish is, that a law which you have admitted, established by your suffrages, and confirmed by the practice and experience of so many years to be beneficial, should now be repealed; that is, that, by abolishing one law, you should weaken all the rest. No law perfectly suits the convenience of every member of the community: the only consideration is, whether, upon the whole, it be profitable to the greater part. If, because a law proves obnoxious to a private individual, that circumstance should destroy and sweep it away, to what purpose is it for the community to enact general laws, which those, with reference to whom they were passed, could presently repeal? I should like, however, to hear what this important affair is which has induced the matrons thus to run out into public in this excited manner, scarcely restraining from pushing into the forum and the assembly of the people. Is it to solicit that their parents, their husbands, children, and brothers may be ransomed from captivity under Hannibal? By no means: and far be ever from the commonwealth so unfortunate a situation. Yet, even when such was the case, you refused this to their prayers. But it is not duty, nor solicitude for their friends; it is religion that has collected them together. They are about to receive the Idaean Mother, coming out of Phrygia from Pessinus! What motive, that even common decency will allow to be mentioned, is pretended for this female insurrection? Why, say they, that we may shine in gold and purple; that, both on festal and common days, we may ride through the city in our chariots, triumphing over vanquished and abrogated law, after having captured and wrested from you your suffrages; and that there may be no bounds to our expenses and our luxury.

"Often have you heard me complain of the profuse expenses of the women—often of those of the men; and that not only of men in private stations, but of the magistrates: and that the state was endangered by two opposite vices, luxury and avarice; those pests, which have been the ruin of all great empires. These I dread the more, as the circumstances of the commonwealth grow daily more prosperous and happy; as the empire increases; as we have now passed over into Greece and Asia, places abounding with every kind of temptation that can inflame the passions, and as we have begun to handle even royal treasures: so much the more do I fear that these matters will bring us into captivity, rather than we them. Believe me, those statues from Syracuse were brought into this city with hostile effect. I already hear too many commending and admiring the decorations of Athens and Corinth, and ridiculing the earthen images of our Roman gods that stand on the fronts of their temples. For my part I prefer these gods,—propitious as they are, and I hope will continue to be, if we allow them to remain in their own mansions. In the memory of our fathers, Pyrrhus, by his ambassador Cineas, made trial of the dispositions, not only of our men, but of our women also, by offers of presents: at that time the Oppian law, for restraining female luxury, had not been made; and yet not one woman accepted a present. What, think you, was the reason? That for which our ancestors made no provision by law on this subject: there was no luxury existing which needed to be restrained. As diseases must necessarily be known before their remedies, so passions come into being before the laws which prescribe limits to them. What called forth the Licinian law, restricting estates to five hundred acres, but the unbounded desire for enlarging estates? What the Cincian law, concerning gifts and presents, but that the plebeians had become vassals and tributaries to the senate? It is not therefore in any degree surprising, that no want of the Oppian law, or of any other, to limit the expenses of the women, was felt at that time, when they refused to receive gold and purple that was thrown in their way, and offered to their acceptance. If Cineas were now to go round the city with his presents he would find numbers of women standing in the public streets to receive them. There are some passions, the causes or motives of which I can no way account for. For that that should not be lawful for you which is permitted to another, may perhaps naturally excite some degree of shame or indignation; yet, when the dress of all is alike, why should anyone of you fear, lest she should not be an object of observation? Of all kinds of shame, the worst, surely, is the being ashamed of frugality or of poverty; but the law relieves you with regard to both; since that which you have not it is unlawful for you to possess. This equalization, says the rich matron, is the very thing that I cannot endure. Why do not I make a figure, distinguished with gold and purple? Why is the poverty of others concealed under this cover of a law, so that it should be thought that, if the law permitted, they would have such things as they are not now able to procure?

"Romans, do you wish to excite among your wives an emulation of this sort, that the rich should wish to have what no other can have; and that the poor, lest they should be despised as such, should extend their expenses beyond their means? Be assured, that when a woman once begins to be ashamed of what she ought not to be ashamed of, she will not be ashamed of what she ought. She who can, will purchase out of her own purse; she who cannot, will ask her husband. Unhappy is the husband, both he who complies with the request, and he who does not; for what he will not give himself, he will see given by another. Now, they openly solicit favors from other women's husbands; and, what is more, solicit a law and votes. From some they obtain them; although, with regard to yourself, your property, or your children, they would be inexorable. So soon as the law shall cease to limit the expenses of your wife, you yourself will never be able to do so. Do not suppose that the matter will hereafter be in the same state in which it was before the law was made on the subject. It is safer that a wicked man should even never be accused, than that he should be acquitted; and luxury, if it had never been meddled with, would be more tolerable than it will be, now, like a wild beast, irritated by having been chained, and then let loose. My opinion is, that the Oppian law ought, on no account, to be repealed. Whatever determination you may come to, I pray all the gods to prosper it."

PLAUTUS

From *The Menaechmi*

Source: Plautus, *The Menaechmi*, Act IV. Translated by Richard W. Hyde and Edward C. Weist. In Kevin Guinagh and Alfred P. Dorjahn (eds.). *Latin Literature in Translation*. New York: Longmans, Green and Co, 1942.

Plautus, one of the few playwrights of the New Comedy school whose work has survived, lived 254–184 BCE, but we do not know the circumstances of this play's original performance. It is one of the inspirations for Shakespeare's Comedy of Errors.

Synopsis: Moschus, a merchant of Syracuse, had identical twin sons. When the boys were seven years old, Moschus took one of them, Menaechmus, with him on a business trip to Tarentum. There the boy became separated from his father and lost in the crowd. He was found later and adopted by a wealthy merchant of Epidamnus. In this city he grew to manhood and married a rich wife.

Meanwhile, so great was the parents' grief for the lost boy that the remaining twin, Sosicles, was renamed Menaechmus. When the latter reached young manhood he set out with his slave Messenio in search of his twin. At the opening of the action, Menaechmus Sosicles has arrived at Epidamnus after six years of wandering.

Just prior to their appearance on the street where Menaechmus of Epidamnus lives, the latter has as usual been quarreling with his wife. To spite her he has stolen a rich mantle of hers to give to the courtesan, Erotium,

who later unwittingly gives the mantle to the other twin, asking that it be repaired.

[Prelude]

[Enter MENAECHMUS SOSICLES, R.]

MEN. II: That was a foolish thing I did a while ago when I handed over my purse and money to Messenio. He has got himself into a chop-house somewhere, I suppose.

[Enter WIFE, from her house.]

WIFE: I'll watch and see how soon my husband will get home. Ah ha, there he is. I'm saved! He is bringing back the cloak.

MEN. II *[to- himself]*: I wonder where Messenio can be rambling now.

WIFE: I'll go up to the fellow and welcome him as he deserves. *[to MEN. II]* You scoundrel, aren't you ashamed to come into my sight with that garment?

MEN. II *[surprised]*: What's this? What is troubling you, madam?

WIFE : You shameless wretch, do you dare say a single word to me? Do you dare to speak?

MEN. II: Pray, what have I done, that I shouldn't dare to speak to you?

WIFE: You ask me? Oh, the shameless impudence of the man!

MEN. II *[mockingly]*: I suppose you know, madam, why it was that the Greeks used to call Hecuba a bitch?

WIFE: No, I do *not*.

MEN. II: Because Hecuba used to act just the way you do now. She used to heap abuse on everybody that she saw. That's how she got to be called a bitch, and she deserved it, too.

WIFE: It's impossible to put up with such outrages. I'd rather be husbandless all my life than stand for such outrages!

MEN. II: Is it any of *my* business whether you can put up with the state of marriage or whether you are going to leave your husband? Or is it the custom here to babble to perfect strangers?

WIFE: Babble, you say? I swear I'll remain married not an instant longer—to put up with your ways!

MEN. II: For all of me, by heaven, you can be a widow as long as Jove sits on his throne.

WIFE: For that, by goodness, I'll call my father and tell him about your outrages. *[calls within the house to slave, who comes at once]* Here, Decio, go find my father, and ask him to come with you to me. *[Slave runs off L.]* Tell him it's absolutely necessary. *[to MEN. II]* I'll tell him of all your outrages!

MEN. II: Are you mad? What outrages? *[mocking her]*

WIFE: You steal cloaks and money from your wife and take them to your mistress. Is that straight enough?

MEN. II *[applauding]:* Bravo, woman! You certainly are a bad one, and a bold one, too! Do you dare *say* that I stole this when I got it from another woman, who wanted me to have it repaired?

WIFE: A few minutes ago you didn't deny stealing it; and are you going to hold it now before my very eyes? Aren't you ashamed?

MEN. II: I beg of you, woman, tell me, if you can, what potion I can drink that will make me able to put up with your bad humor. I don't know whom you take me for. As for you, I don't know you any more than I know the man in the moon.

WIFE: You may make fun of me, but you won't be able to make fun of my father. He's coming now. *[pointing off L., where FATHER appears hobbling towards them]* Back there. Do you know *him?*

MEN II *[facetiously]:* Yes, I knew him when I knew Methuselah. I met him the same day I met you.

WIFE : You deny that you know me? that you know my father?

MEN. II : Yes, and your grandfather too, if you want to lug *him* in. *[stalks to extreme R.]*

WIFE: By heaven, that's the way you always are about everything.

[Enter FATHER.]

SONG—FATHER

I'm getting along just as fast as my age will permit and this business requires,

But if some of you say that that's easy for me— very briefly I'll show that you're liars:

My body's a burden, my nimbleness gone, and of strength I've a notable lack,

I am quite overgrown with my years—oh, confounded old age is a curse on the back!

Why, if I were to tell all the terrible evils that age, when it comes, brings along,

I'm certain as certain can be that past suitable limits I'd lengthen this song.

However my mind is a little disturbed at this thing, for it seems a bit queer

That my daughter should suddenly send to my house with directions for me to come here.

And how the affair is related to me, she has not let me know up to now;

But I'm a good guesser, and feel pretty sure that her husband and she's had a row.

That's what usually happens when men are enslaved by their wives and must come when they call;

And then it's the wives who are mostly to blame, while the husbands aren't guilty at all.

And yet there are bounds, which we all must observe, to the things that a wife can endure,

And a woman won't call in her father unless the offense of her husband is sure. .

But I think very soon the suspense will be over, and then I'll know what is the matter-

But look, there's my daughter in front of the door, and her husband; he's not looking at her. It's just as I suspected.

I'll speak to her.

WIFE: I'll go meet him. *[meeting him C.]* I hope you are well, father.

FATHER: I hope you are well. Do I find you well? Are you well, that you summoned me? Why are you sad? Why does he *[pointing with staff]* stand apart from you, in anger? You have been quarreling about something. Tell me which of you is at fault, and be brief about it; no rigmarole.

WIFE: I am guilty of nothing on my part; I'll ease you on this point first, father. But I can't live here, and I can't stand it another minute. Take me away.

FATHER: Why, what's the matter?

WIFE: I'm made fun of, father.

FATHER: By whom?

WIFE: By *him,* to whom you gave me: my husband.

FATHER *[to audience]:* Look at that now! A squabble! *[to WIFE]* How many times have I told you to see to it that neither of you come to me with your complaints?

WIFE *[tearfully]:* But father, how could I help it? I think you could understand—unless you don't want to.

FATHER: How many times have I told you to humor your husband? Pay. no attention to what he does, or where he goes, or what he is about. .

WIFE: Why, he has been making love to a courtesan who lives right next door.

FATHER: That's sensible enough. And I'll warrant he'll make love to her all the more, with you spying on him this way.

WIFE: And he drinks there, too.

FATHER: Well, will he drink any the less on your account, here or anywhere else that he chooses? Devil take it, why will you be so foolish? You might as well expect to forbid him to accept dinner invitations or to entertain guests at his own house. Do you want husbands to be slaves ? You might as well expect to give him a stint of work, and have him sit among the slave-girls and card wool.

WIFE [resentfully]: Apparently I had you come here to defend my husband's case, father, not mine! You're *my* attorney, but you plead *his* case.

FATHER: If he has been delinquent in any way, I'll be even more severe with him than I was with you. But since he keeps you well supplied with gold trinkets and clothes and gives you servants and provisions as he should, it is better for you, girl, to take a sane view of things.

WIFE: But he steals my gold and my cloaks from the cupboard. He robs me and takes my trinkets to courtesans on the sly.

FATHER: He does wrong if he does; you do wrong if he doesn't: that's accusing an innocent man.

WIFE: But he has the cloak right now, father, and the bracelet that he took to the woman. He is bringing them back now because I have found out about it.

FATHER: I'll find out from him just what has happened. I'll go speak to him. [goes over to MEN. II and taps him with staff] Menaechmus, for my enlightenment tell me what you are quarreling about. Why are you sad? Why does she stand apart from you, in anger?

MEN. II: Whoever you are, whatever your name is, old man, I call as my witnesses great Jupiter and the gods—

FATHER: Why? Wherefore?' And for what?

MEN. II: That I have neither wronged this woman, who accuses me of stealing this cloak from her house—

WIFE: Perjury, eh?

MEN. II: If I have ever set my foot inside the house in which she lives, may I be the most accursedly accursed!

FATHER: Are you in your right mind, to make such a wish? Do you deny that you have ever set foot in the house you live in, you utter madman?

MEN. II: Old man, do you say I live in that house?

FATHER: Do you deny it?

MEN. II: I' faith, I do deny it.

FATHER: No; you deny not "in faith" but in joke - unless, of course, you have moved out overnight. [motions WIFE to C.]—Come here, please, daughter. What do you say? You haven't moved from the house, have you?

WIFE: Why should we, or where should we move *to*, I ask you?

FATHER: By heaven, I don't know.

WIFE: It's clear that he is making fun of you. Don't you get that?

FATHER: Menaechmus, you have joked long enough; now attend to business.

MEN. II: I ask you, what business have I with you? Or who are you? Are you sane? And this woman, who has been plaguing me this way and that—is she sane? [tears his hair in exasperation]

WIFE [to FATHER, frightened]: Do you see the color of his eyes? See how a green color is coming over his temples and forehead! How his eyes shine!

MEN. II [to audience]: Alack, they say I'm crazy, whereas it is they who are really that way themselves. What could be better for me, since they say I am mad, than to pretend to be insane, to scare them off? [begins to jump about madly]

WIFE: How he stretches and gapes! What shall I do, father?

FATHER: Come over here, my child, as far as you can from him. [retreating L.]

MEN. II [pretending madness]: Ho, Bacchus! Ho, Bromius! Where in this forest do you bid me to the hunt? I hear. but cannot leave this place, so closely am I guarded by that rabid bitch upon my left. And behind there is that bald goat, who often in his time has ruined innocent citizens by his false testimony.

FATHER: Curse you!

MEN. II: Lo, Apollo from his oracle bids me to burn out the eyes of that woman with flaming torches. [charges at WIFE, then immediately retreats]

WIFE: I am lost, father! He threatens to burn out my eyes.

FATHER [to WIFE, aside]: Hist, daughter!

WIFE: What? What shall we do?

FATHER: Suppose I summon the slaves? I'll go bring some people to take this .man away and chain him up indoors before he makes any more disturbance.

MEN. II [aside] I'm stuck; if I don't hit upon a scheme, they'll take me into the house with them. [aloud] Apollo, you forbid me to spare her face with my fists unless she leaves my sight and goes utterly to the devil? [advances threateningly] I'll do your bidding Apollo!

FATHER: Run home as fast as you can, before he thumps you.

WIFE : I am running: Watch him, father; don't let him get away! Oh! am I not a miserable woman to have to listen to such things! [Exit into her house.]

MEN. II [aside]. I got rid of her rather well. [aloud, threatening FATHER] No, Apollo, as for this most filthy wretch, this bearded tremulous Tilthonus, who is called the son of Cygnus, you bid me break his limbs and bones and joints with that staff which he holds?

FATHER [*retreats, shaking his staff*]: You'll get a beating if you touch me or come any closer.

MEN. II I'll do your. bidding! I'll take a double-edged axe and chop the flesh of this old man .to mince meat, down to the very bones!

FATHER [*aside*]: Well then, I must beware and take care of myself Really, I am afraid, from the way he threatens, that he may do me harm. [MEN. *retreats* C.]

MEN. II: You give me many commands, Apollo! Now you bid me take my. fierce untamed yoked horses and mount my chariot, to crush this old stinking toothless lion. Now I've mounted! [*business*] Now I hold the reins! Now the goad is in my hand! Forward, my steeds, make loud the clatter of your hooves! And in swift flight make undiminished the fleetness of your feet! [*gallops about the stage*]

FATHER: Do you threaten me with yoked horses?

MEN. II: Lo, Apollo, again you bid me make a charge at him, this fellow who stands here, and slay him. [*rushes forward, then suddenly stops*] But who is this, who drags me from my chariot by the hair? He alters your commands, even the commands of Apollo! [*pretends to fall senseless to the ground*]

FATHER [*advances cautiously*]' Alas, by heaven, it is a severe disease! 0 gods, by your faith, what sudden changes do ye work! Take this madman—how strong he was a little while before. This disease has smitten him all of a sudden. I'll go get a doctor as quick as I can. [*Exit, L.*]

MEN. II [*getting up*]: Lord! These idiots who compel me, a sane man, to act like a madman! Have they got out of my sight now, I wonder? Why don't I go straight back to the ship while the going is good? [*as he starts to go, R., to audience*] I beg of all of you, if the old man comes back don't tell him what street I've taken. [*Exit, R.*]

APPIAN

On Tiberius Gracchus

Source: Appian, Civil Wars, I: I-3, in Oliver J. Thatcher, ed., The Library of Original Sources (Milwaukee: University Research Extension Co., 1907), Vol. III: The Roman World, pp. 77-89. Scanned by: J. S. Arkenberg, Dept. of History, Cal. State Fullerton.

The conflict between rich and poor in the late Republic was expressed by means of the struggle over public lands. Public lands—including vast acreages taken over from Italian allies of Hannibal at the end of the third century—had been encroached upon by rich estates; one effect of this was the reduction in number of the smallholding farmer, once the backbone of the Roman army.

(One side effect of this shortfall in farmer-soldiers was an increasing reliance on Italian allied troops levied by tribute; as Rome fought more and bloodier wars this dependence exacerbated tensions with the allies, leading to the Social War.)

Tiberius Gracchus and his brother Gaius pushed relentlessly for land reform, in part to improve Rome's armies, but the elite painted them as ambitious demagogues. Both were killed, marking the beginning of the end of the Republic.

[For 134-133 BCE]: As the Romans conquered the Italian tribes, one after another, in war, they seized part of the lands and founded towns there, or placed colonies of their own in those already established, and used them as garrisons. They allotted the cultivated part of the land obtained through war, to settlers, or rented or sold it. Since they had not time to assign the part which lay waste by the war, and this was usually the greater portion, they issued a proclamation that for the time being any who cared to work it could do so for a share of the annual produce, a tenth part of the grain and a fifth of the fruit. A part of the animals, both of the oxen and sheep was exacted from those keeping herds. They did this to increase the Italian peoples, considered the hardest working of races, in order to have plenty of supporters at home. But the very opposite result followed; for the wealthy, getting hold of most of the unassigned lands, and being encouraged through the length of time elapsed to think that they would never be ousted, and adding, part by purchase and part by violence, the little farms of their poor neighbors to their possessions, came to work great districts instead of one estate, using to this end slaves as laborers and herders, because free laborers might be drafted from agriculture into the army. The mere possession of slaves brought them great profit through the number of their children, which increased because they were absolved from service in the wars. Thus the powerful citizens became immensely wealthy and the slave class all over the country multiplied, while the Italian race decreased in numbers and vigor, held down as they were by poverty, taxes, and military service. If they had any rest from these burdens, they wasted their time in idleness, because the land was in the hands of the wealthy, who used slaves instead of free laborers.

Because of these facts the people began to fear that they should no longer have enough Italian allies, and that the state itself would be imperiled by such great numbers of slaves. Not seeing any cure for the trouble, as it was not practicable nor entirely fair to dispossess men of their possessions so long occupied, including their own trees, buildings and improvements, a decree was at one time got through by the efforts of the tribunes that no one should hold more than five hundred jugera,[65] or graze more than a hundred cattle or five hundred sheep upon it. To make sure the law was observed, it was provided, also, that there should be a stated number of freemen employed on the lands, whose duty it should be to watch and report what took place. Those holding lands under the law were compelled to make oath to obey it, and penalties were provided against breaking it. It was thought that the surplus land would soon be subdivided amongst the poor in small lots, but there was not the slightest respect shown for the law or the oaths. The few that seemed to give some heed to them fraudulently made over their lands to their relatives, but most paid no attention to the law whatsoever.

At last Ti. Sempronius Gracchus, an eminent man, ambitious for honor, a forceful orator, and for these causes well known to everybody, made an eloquent speech, while tribune, on the subject of the Italian race, deploring that a people so warlike, and related in descent to the Romans, were gradually sinking into pauperism and decreasing in numbers, with no hope of betterment. He denounced the swarm of slaves as useless in war and faithless to their masters, and instanced the recent disaster brought upon the owners in Sicily by their slaves, where the requirements of agriculture had greatly increased their number. He called to mind, also, the war waged by the Romans against the slaves, a war neither trivial nor short, but long drawn but long drawn out and filled with misfortunes and perils. After this address he once more brought forward the law providing that no one should hold more than five hundred jugera of the public land, but he made this addition to the previous law, that the sons of the present occupants might each hold half as large an allotment and that the surplus land should be divided among the poor by triumvirs, that were to be changed yearly.

This greatly vexed the wealthy, because, on account of the triumvirs, they could no longer pass by the law as they had done before; nor could they purchase the lands allotted to others, because Gracchus had provided

against this by prohibiting sales. They gathered into groups, complaining and charging the poor with seizing the results of their cultivation, their vineyards, and their houses. Some said they had paid their neighbors the price of the land; were they to lose their money as well as the land? Others declared that the graves of their fathers were in the ground that had been assigned to them in the partition of their family estate. Others stated that their wives' dowries had been spent on the land or that it had been given to their own daughters as such. Loaners of money could show advances made on this security. All sorts of complaints and denunciations were heard at the same time. On the other hand rose the wails of the poor, crying that they had been reduced from plenty to the lowest pauperism and from that to enforced lack of offspring, because they could not support children. They enumerated the services they had rendered in war, by which this very land had been obtained, and were indignant at being despoiled of their part of the public property. They upbraided the wealthy for using slaves, who were always faithless and sulky, and for that cause useless in war, in the place of freemen, citizens and men at arms. While these classes were complaining and reproaching each other, a vast multitude, consisting of colonists or dwellers in the free cities, or others in some way interested in the lands and with similar fears, thronged into town and sided with their respective parties. Angry at each other, they gathered in riotous crowds, made bold by numbers, and, waiting for the new law, tried in every way, some to obstruct its passage and others to carry it. Party spirit in addition to individual interest stimulated both sides in the preparation against each other which they were making for the voting day.

What Gracchus sought in framing the law was the increase, not of wealth, but of serviceable population. He was highly enthused with the usefulness of the proposal and, believing that nothing more beneficial or desirable could happen to Italy, he attached no weight to the difficulties involved. When the time came for voting he brought forward at some length many other arguments, asking whether it was not right to allot among the common people what belonged to them in common, whether a citizen did not always deserve more concern than a slave, whether a man that fought in the army was not more serviceable than one that did not, and whether one that had an interest in the country was not the surer to be faithful to the public weal. He did not tarry long on this contrast between freemen and slaves, which he thought debasing, but plunged at once into an outline of their hopes and fears for the state, saying that the Romans had obtained most of their lands by conquest and that they had the opportunities of acquiring the rest of the inhabitable world, but now the question most doubtful of all was whether, with plenty of warlike men, they should conquer the rest, or whether, through their

---

[65] About three hundred acres.

internal dissensions and weaknesses, their foes should deprive them of what they already had. After enlarging upon the honor and wealth on one side and the peril and need of apprehension on the other, he warned the rich to reflect, and said that for the accomplishment of such hopes they should be willing to give this very land as a gift, if need be, to men that would bring up offspring, and not, by wrangling over trivial matters, lose sight of the more important ones—especially since they were getting full pay for the labor they had expended in the clear title to five hundred jugera of land, in a high state of cultivation, to each of them without cost, and half as much again for each son to those that had them. After saying much else in the same strain and getting the poor aroused, as well as those that were influenced by reason rather than the hope of profit, he commanded the clerk to read the measure proposed.

Another tribune, M. Octavius, who had been prevailed on by those holding land to interpose his veto (for among the Romans the veto of the tribune always had absolute authority), ordered the clerk to be silent. Upon this Gracchus rebuked him sternly and adjourned the meeting to the next day. This time he placed quite a force around, as if to coerce Octavius against his will, and with threats bade the clerk read the measure proposed to the assemblage. He began reading, but upon Octavius again interposing his veto, stopped. Then the tribunes commenced quarreling with each other, and something of an uproar broke forth from among the people. The influential citizens begged the tribunes to lay their disagreements before the senate for arbitration. Gracchus acted upon this advice, thinking the measure to be agreeable to all patriotic people, and hurried to the senate. As he found only a few supporters there, and was reproached by the wealthy, he rushed back to the forum and announced that he would take a vote in the assembly on the following day upon the law, and also upon the tenor of office of Octavius, to find out whether a tribune of the plebs, acting contrary to the welfare of the plebs, could continue to retain his magistracy.

So he did, and when Octavius, not at all intimidated, again put in his veto, Gracchus had the pebbles distributed to vote on him first. As the first tribe voted to impeach Octavius, Gracchus, turning to him, pleaded with him to withdraw his veto. As he would not do so, the votes of the other tribes were taken. At that time there were thirty-five tribes. The seventeen voting first wrathfully approved the measure. If the eighteenth should do likewise it would constitute a majority. Once more in full view of the people Gracchus passionately begged Octavius, in his great jeopardy, not to obstruct this most devout work, so beneficial to all Italy, and not to dash down the hopes so deeply grounded among the people, whose wishes he ought, as a tribune, the rather to share in, and not to run the risk of losing his office by public impeachment. Upon saying this he called the gods to witness that he did not of his own accord do any injury to his colleague, but, as Octavius was still firm, he continued taking the vote, and Octavius was thereupon reduced to the rank of private citizen and stole away unnoticed.

Q. Mummius was elected tribune in his stead and the agrarian law was passed. The three men first appointed to allot the land were Gracchus himself, the framer of the measure, his brother of the same name, and his father-in-law, Ap. Claudius, for the people were still afraid that the law might not be executed unless Gracchus, with all his family, should be placed at the helm. Gracchus became enormously popular on account of the law and was attended home by the mass of the people, as if he were the founder, not merely of one city or people, but of all the states of Italy. After this the victors returned to the fields whence they had journeyed to conduct the affair, while the defeated ones stayed in the city and went over the subject with one another, feeling incensed and declaring that when Gracchus became a private citizen he would be made sorry that he had dishonored the sacred and inviolable office of tribune and had opened the way to such a flood of strife in Italy.

At the coming of summer the announcement of the election of tribunes was made, and as the day for voting drew near, it was clear that the wealthy were vigorously aiding the election of those most opposed to Gracchus. Fearing that misfortune would come upon him if he should not be re-elected for the next year, Gracchus sent to his friends in the fields to attend the assembly, but as their time was taken up with the harvest he was forced, when the day fixed for the voting was at hand, to depend upon the plebeians of the city. So he went about canvassing each one to elect him tribune for the next year, on account of the jeopardy he had put himself in on their account. When the voting commenced, the first two tribes went for Gracchus. The wealthy held that it was not constitutional for a man to hold the office twice in succession. The tribune, Rubrius, who had been selected by lot to preside over the comitia, was in doubt upon the question, and Mummius, who had been elected instead of Octavius, besought him to hand the assembly over to his charge. So he did, but the other tribunes objected that the chairmanship should be decided by lot, maintaining that when Rubrius, who had been selected in that way, relinquished it, the casting of lots ought to be done all over again. Since there was a deal of wrangling on this point, Gracchus, who was being bested, postponed the election until the next day. In deep despondency he robed himself in black, though still in office, and led his son about the forum, introducing him to each man and putting him in their care, as if he himself were about to die at the hands of his foes.

The poor were afflicted with great grief, and justly so, both on account of themselves, for they thought that they would no longer dwell in a free state under equitable laws, but were to be reduced to slavery by the rich, and on account of Gracchus personally, who had brought upon himself such peril for their sakes. Therefore, they all escorted him with lamentations to his home at nighttime, and bade him take heart for the next day. Gracchus gathered courage, and calling together his friends before daylight, imparted to them a sign to be made for a resort to violence. Then he placed himself in the temple on the Capitoline hill, where the election was to be held, and put himself in the middle of the comitia. As he was checked by the other tribunes and by the wealthy, who would not permit the votes to be taken on this question, he gave the sign. A sudden uproar arose from those who saw it and the resort to arms followed. Part of the faction of Gracchus took their stand about him like a body-guard. Others that had girded themselves, laid hold of the fasces and staves in the hands of lictors and shattered them into pieces. The rich were thrown out of the comitia with so much tumult and so many wounds that the tribunes rushed from their seats in consternation, and the priests closed the doors of the temple. Many ran hither and thither and cast wild reports abroad. Some said that Gracchus had impeached all the other tribunes and this was given credence because none of them were in sight. Others said that he had declared himself tribune for the next year without a vote.

Under these conditions the senate came together at the Temple of Fides [Faith]. It is astounding to me that they never thought of electing a dictator in this crisis, though they had often been defended by the rule of an absolute magistrate amid such periods of danger. Though this expedient had been found very serviceable in ancient times, few thought of it either then or afterwards. After coming to the decision they arrived at, they marched to the Capitol, the high priest, Cornelius Scipio Nasica, at their head, crying out in a sonorous voice, "Let those who would save the state follow me." He gathered the border of his toga around his head, either to attract a larger crowd to follow him by his peculiar appearance, or to make for himself, as it were, a helmet as a signal for violence to the spectators, or to hide from the gods what he was about to do. When he came to the temple and stepped forward against the adherents of Gracchus, they yielded to the prestige of so eminent a citizen, for they saw the senate behind him. The senators wrenched clubs from the very hands of the followers of Gracchus, or with pieces of torn-up benches or other things that had been brought for the use of the comitia, began mauling them and in hot pursuit, drove them over the precipice. In the riot many followers of Gracchus were killed and Gracchus himself, being seized near the temple, was slain at the door near the statues of the kings. All the corpses were thrown into the Tiber at night.

Thus died on the Capitol and while still tribune, Ti. Gracchus, the son of the Gracchus who was twice consul and of Cornelia, the daughter of the Scipio that conquered Carthage. He lost his life because he followed up an excellent plan in too lawless a way. This awful occurrence, the first of the kind that took place in the public assembly, was never long without a new parallel thereafter. On the matter of the killing of Gracchus, the city was divided between grief and joy. Some sorrowed for themselves and him and bewailed the existing state of affairs, believing that the republic no longer existed, but had been usurped by coercion and violence. Others congratulated themselves that everything had turned out just as they wanted it to. This event happened at the time that Aristonicus was struggling with the Romans for the mastery of Asia.[66]

PLUTARCH

On Tiberius Gracchus

Source: Plutarch, *Ti. Gracchus*. Translated by John Dryden.

Plutarch's biography emphasizes Tiberius's effectiveness as a leader and speaker, which yielded him the loyalty of the populace.

When he returned to Rome, he found the whole transaction censured and reproached, as a proceeding that was base and scandalous to the Romans. But the relations and friends of the soldiers, forming a large body among the people, came flocking to Tiberius, whom they acknowledged as the preserver of so many citizens, imputing to the general all the miscarriages which had happened. Those who cried out against what had been done, urged for imitation the example of their ancestors, who stripped and handed over to the Samnites not only the generals who had consented to the terms of release, but also all the quaestors, for example, and tribunes, who had in any way implicated themselves in the agreement, laying the guilt of perjury and breach of conditions on their heads. But, in this all the populace, showing an extraordinary kindness and affection for Tiberius, indeed voted that the consul should be stripped and put in irons, and so delivered to the Numantines; but, for the sake of Tiberius, spared all the other officers. It may be probable, also, that Scipio, who at that time was the greatest and most powerful man among the Romans, contributed to save him, though indeed he was also censured for not protecting Mancinus too, and that he did not exert himself to maintain the observance of the articles of peace which had been agreed upon by his kinsman and friend Tiberius. But it may be presumed that the difference

---

[66] The Fourth Macedonian War (150–148 BCE).

between them was for the most part due to ambitious feelings, and to the friends and reasoners who urged on Tiberius, and, as it was, it never amounted to anything that might not have been remedied, or that was really bad. Nor can I think that Tiberius would ever have met with his misfortunes, if Scipio had been concerned in dealing with his measures; but he was away fighting at Numantia when Tiberius, upon the following occasion, first came forward as a legislator.

Of the land which the Romans gained by conquest from their neighbors, part they sold publicly, and turned the remainder into common; this common land they assigned to such of the citizens as were poor and indigent, for which they were to pay only a small acknowledgment into the public treasury. But when the wealthy men began to offer larger rents, and drive the poorer people out, it was enacted by law that no person whatever should enjoy more than five hundred acres of ground. This act for some time checked the avarice of the richer, and was of great assistance to the poorer people, who retained under it their respective proportions of ground, as they had been formerly rented by them. Afterwards the rich men of the neighborhood contrived to get these lands again into their possession, under other people's names, and at last would not stick to claim most of them publicly in their own. The poor, who were thus deprived of their farms, were no longer either ready, as they had formerly been, to serve in war or careful in the education of their children; insomuch that in a short time there were comparatively few freemen remaining in all Italy, which swarmed with workhouses full of foreign-born slaves. These the rich men employed in cultivating their ground of which they dispossessed the citizens. C. Laelius, the intimate friend of Scipio, undertook to reform this abuse; but meeting with opposition from men of authority, and fearing a disturbance, he soon desisted, and received the name of the Wise or the Prudent, both which meanings belong to the Latin word Sapiens.

But Tiberius, being elected tribune of the people, entered upon that design without delay, at the instigation, as is most commonly stated, of Diophanes, the rhetorician, and Blossius, the philosopher. Diophanes was a refugee from Mitylene, the other was an Italian, of the city of Cuma, and was educated there under Antipater of Tarsus, who afterwards did him the honor to dedicate some of his philosophical lectures to him.

Some have also charged Cornelia, the mother of Tiberius, with contributing towards it, because she frequently upbraided her sons, that the Romans as yet rather called her the daughter of Scipio, than the mother of the Gracchi. Others again say that S. Postumius was the chief occasion. He was a man of the same age with Tiberius, and his rival for reputation as a public speaker; and when Tiberius, at his return from the campaign,

found him to have got far beyond him in fame and influence, and to be much looked up to, he thought to outdo him, by attempting a popular enterprise of this difficulty and of such great consequence. But his brother Gaius has left it us in writing, that when Tiberius went through Tuscany to Numantia, and found the country almost depopulated, there being hardly any free husbandmen or shepherds, but for the most part only barbarian, imported slaves, he then first conceived the course of policy which in the sequel proved so fatal to his family. Though it is also most certain that the people themselves chiefly excited his zeal and determination in the prosecution of it, by setting up writings upon the porches, walls, and monuments, calling upon him to reinstate the poor citizens in their former possessions.

However, he did not draw up his law without the advice and assistance of those citizens that were then most eminent for their virtue and authority; amongst whom were Crassus, the high-priest, Mucius Scaevola, the lawyer, who at that time was consul, and Claudius Appius, his father-in-law. Never did any law appear more moderate and gentle, especially being enacted against such great oppression and avarice. For they who ought to have been severely punished for transgressing the former laws, and should at least have lost all their titles to such lands which they had unjustly usurped, were notwithstanding to receive a price for quitting their unlawful claims, and giving up their lands to those fit owners who stood in need of help. But though this reformation was managed with so much tenderness that, all the former transactions being passed over, the people were only thankful to prevent abuses of the like nature for the future, yet, on the other hand, the moneyed men, and those of great estates, were exasperated, through their covetous feelings against the law itself, and against the lawgiver, through anger and party-spirit. They therefore endeavored to seduce the people, declaring that Tiberius was designing a general redivision of lands, to overthrow the government, and cut all things into confusion.

But they had no success. For Tiberius, maintaining an honorable and just cause, and possessed of eloquence sufficient to have made a less creditable action appear plausible, was no safe or easy antagonist, when, with the people crowding around the hustings, he took his place, and spoke in behalf of the poor. "The savage beasts," said he, "in Italy, have their particular dens, they have their places of repose and refuge; but the men who bear arms, and expose their lives for the safety of their country, enjoy in the meantime nothing more in it but the air and light and, having no houses or settlements of their own, are constrained to wander from place to place with their wives and children." He told them that the commanders were guilty of a ridiculous error, when, at the head of their armies, they exhorted the common soldiers to fight for their sepulchers and altars; when not any amongst so many Romans is possessed of either altar or monument, neither have they any houses of their own, or hearths of their ancestors to defend. They fought indeed and were slain, but it was to maintain the luxury and the wealth of other men. They were styled the masters of the world, but in the meantime had not one foot of ground which they could call their own.

A harangue of this nature, spoken to an enthusiastic and sympathizing audience, by a person of commanding spirit and genuine feelings, no adversaries at that time were competent to oppose.

APPIAN

On Gaius Gracchus

Source: Appian, Civil Wars, I: I-3, in Oliver J. Thatcher, ed., The Library of Original Sources (Milwaukee: University Research Extension Co., 1907), Vol. III: The Roman World, pp. 77-89. Scanned by: J. S. Arkenberg, Dept. of History, Cal. State Fullerton.

Gaius Gracchus had his brother's fervor but was said to be more flamboyant than the reserved Tiberius.

[For 132-124 BCE] After Ti. Gracchus was killed, Ap. Claudius, his father-in-law, died and Fulvius Flaccus and Papirius Carbo were selected, together with the younger [Gaius] Gracchus, to divide the land. As those in possession failed to hand in lists of what they held, it was announced that informers should give evidence against them. A large number of perplexing lawsuits sprang up. Where a new field had been purchased next to an old one, or where the land had been divided with allies, the whole section had to be gone over in the surveying of this one field, in order to discover how it had been sold or partitioned. Some owners had not kept their bills of sale or deeds of allotment, and even those that were unearthed were often ambiguous. On the remeasuring of the land, some had to give up orchards and farm buildings for bare fields. Others were moved from tilled to untilled lands or to swamps or ponds. In short, the surveying had been carelessly done when the land was first taken away from the enemy. Since the first proclamation sanctioned anyone's cultivating the unassigned land that wished to, men had been impelled to till the parts lying next to their own land until the boundary line between the two had been lost sight of. The lapse of time had also made many changes. Thus, what injustice had been done by the rich, though great, was not easily discovered. So nothing less than a general commotion followed, everybody being ousted from his own place and set down in somebody else's.

The Italian allies that remonstrated at this disturbance and especially against the lawsuits suddenly brought against them, selected Cornelius Scipio [Aemilianus], the destroyer of Carthage, to protect them from these annoyances. As he had used their powerful aid in war, he did not like to refuse their request. So, coming into the senate, he explained the difficulty in enforcing Gracchus' law, although, for the sake of the plebs, he did not openly attack it. He held that these cases ought not to be judged by the triumvirs, as they did not have the confidence of the disputants, but should be handed over to others. As his point of view seemed just, they let themselves be persuaded, and the consul, Tuditanus, was chosen to sit in these cases. But when he began on the matter he saw its difficulties, and then led the army against the Illyrians as an excuse to get out of acting as judge, and since no one could bring the cases before the triumvirs they fell into abeyance. Hence ill feeling and resentment sprung up against Scipio among the people, because they saw him for whose sake they had often taken sides against the aristocracy and brought upon themselves hostility, twice electing him consul contrary to law, now siding with the Italian allies against them. When Scipio's foes saw this, they charged that he was intent on annulling the law of Gracchus entirely, and to that end was about to incite armed violence and bloodshed.

When the populace heard these accusations they were much disturbed until Scipio, who had placed near his couch at home one evening a tablet, on which he intended during the night to write the speech he was to deliver before the people, was found dead on his couch without a wound. Whether this was caused by Cornelia, the mother of the Gracchi, assisted by her daughter, Sempronia, who was the wife of Scipio, but unloved and unaffectionate because she was deformed and childless, to prevent the law of Gracchus being abolished, or whether, as some believed, he committed suicide because he saw clearly that he could not do what he had said he would, is not certain. Some say that slaves, after being exposed to torture, confessed that unknown persons, who were brought through the rear of the house by night, strangled him, and that those who knew about it refrained from telling because the people were still incensed at him and were glad he died. So Scipio perished, and though he had been of enormous service to the Roman state, he was not given the honor of a public funeral. Thus does the irritation of the moment efface the appreciation of past service. This event, important enough in itself, happened as an incident of the undertaking of Gracchus.

Even after this those holding the lands long put off upon various excuses the division of their holdings. Some thought the Italian allies, who objected to it most strenuously, should be admitted to Roman citizenship, in order that, out of thankfulness for so great a favor, they should not longer protest about the land. The Italians were ready to accept this compromise, since they had rather have Roman citizenship than the ownership of these fields. Fulvius Flaccus, at that time both consul and triumvir, did his best to carry it through, but the senate was wroth at the proposition to make their subjects of equal rank with themselves. So the effort was dropped and the people, who had been so long hopeful of obtaining land, began to be discouraged.

[For 124-122 BCE] While they were in this frame of mind, C. Gracchus, who had made himself popular as a triumvir, stood for the tribuneship. He was the younger brother of Ti. Gracchus, the originator of the law. He had kept silent concerning the killing of his brother for some time, but as some of the senate treated him disdainfully, he offered himself as a candidate for the tribuneship, and as soon as he was elected to this high office began to intrigue against the senate. He proposed that a monthly distribution of grain should be made to each citizen at the expense of the state. This had not been the custom prior to this. Thus he put himself at the head of the populace at a bound by one stroke of politics, in which he had the assistance of Fulvius Flaccus. Right after this he was elected tribune for the next year also, for in cases where there were not enough candidates the law permitted the people to fill out the list from those in office.

In this way C. Gracchus became tribune a second time. After, so to say, buying the plebs, he began to court the equites, who hold the rank midway between the senate and the plebs, by another similar stroke of politics. He handed over the courts of justice, which had become distrusted on account of bribery, from the senators to the equites, upbraiding the senators particularly for the recent instances of Aurelius Cotta, Salinator, and, thirdly, M'. Aquilius (the one that conquered Asia), all shameless bribe-takers, who had been set free by the judges, even though envoys sent to denounce them were still present, going about making disgraceful charges against them. The senate was very much ashamed of such things and agreed to the law and the people passed it. Thus the courts of justice were handed over from the senate to the knights. It is reported that soon after the enactment of this law Gracchus made the remark that he had destroyed the supremacy of the senate once for all, and this remark of his has been corroborated by experience throughout the course of history. The privilege of judging all Romans and Italians, even the senators themselves, in all affairs of property, civil rights and exile, raised the equites like governors over them, and placed the senators on the same plane as subjects. As the equites also voted to support the power of the tribunes in the comitia and received whatever they asked from them in return, they became more and more dangerous opponents to the senators. Thus it soon resulted that the supremacy in the state was reversed, the real mastery going into the hands of the equites and only the honor to the senate. The equites went so far in using their power over the senators as to openly mock them beyond all reason. They, too, imbibed the habit of bribe-taking and,

after once tasting such immense acquisitions, they drained the draft even more shamefully and recklessly than the senators had done. They hired informers against the rich and put an end to prosecutions for bribe-taking entirely, partly by united action and partly by actual violence, so that the pursuit of such investigations was done away with entirely. Thus the judiciary law started another factional contest that lasted for a long time and was fully as harmful as the previous ones.

Gracchus constructed long highways over Italy and thus made an army of contractors and workmen dependent on his favor and rendered them subject to his every wish. He proposed the establishment of a number of colonies. He prompted the Latin allies to clamor for all the privileges of Roman citizenship, for the senate could not becomingly deny them to the kinsmen of the Romans. He attempted to give the right to vote to those allies that were not permitted to take part in Roman elections, so as to have their assistance in the passing of measures that he had in mind. The senate was greatly perturbed at this and commanded the consuls to set forth the following proclamation, "No one that does not have the right to vote shall remain in the city or come within forty stadia of it during the time that the voting is taking place upon these laws." The senate also got Livius Drusus—another tribune, to intercede his veto against the measures brought forward by Gracchus without telling the plebs his reasons for so doing; for a tribune did not have to give his reasons for a veto. In order to curry favor with the plebs they gave Drusus permission to found twelve colonies, and the people were so much taken with this that they began to jeer at the measures that Gracchus proposed.

[For 122-121 BCE] As he had lost the good will of the populace, Gracchus set sail for Africa along with Fulvius Flaccus, who, after his consulship, had been elected tribune through the same causes for which Gracchus had. A colony had been assigned to Africa, because of the reported richness of its soil, and these men had been selected as its founders for the very sake of getting rid of them for awhile, in order that the senate might be untrammeled by demagogy for a time. They laid out a town for the colony in the same place where Carthage had formerly lain, paying no heed to the fact that Scipio, when he razed it, had consigned it with imprecations to eternal sheep-grazing. They allotted six thousand colonists to this town, as against the smaller number assigned by law in order thus to further conciliate the people. Then, returning to Rome, they solicited the six thousand from all Italy. The managers that had remained in Africa laying out the town sent back word that wolves had dragged out and carried far and wide the boundary marks placed by Gracchus and Fulvius, and the sooth-sayers held this to be a bad omen for the colony. So the senate called together the comitia proposing to repeal the law authorizing the colony. When Gracchus and Fulvius saw that they were about to fail in this affair they became desperate and charged that the senate had lied about the wolves. The rashest of the plebs, with daggers in hand, gathered about them and accompanied them to the assembly where the comitia was to be held in regard to the colony.

The people were already assembled and Fulvius had commenced to address them about the matter when Gracchus reached the Capitol surrounded by a body-guard of his friends. Agitated by his knowledge of the unwonted schemes in hand, he turned away from the meeting place of the comitia, passing into the porch, and walked about, waiting to learn what would take place. Just then a pleb by the name of Antyllus, who was making a sacrifice in the porch, saw him thus troubled in mind, and, grasping him by the hand, because he had either heard or guessed something or was prompted through some impulse to speak to him, begged him to spare his fatherland. Still more agitated and starting as if caught in the act of a crime, Gracchus gave a sharp glance at the man. One of his partisans, without any sign or order being given, gathered from the piercing look itself given by Gracchus to Antyllus, that the moment to strike was at hand, and thought he should render Gracchus a kindness by giving the first blow; so he drew forth his dagger and stabbed Antyllus. An uproar was raised, the dead man being seen in the midst of the throng, and every one outside fled away from the temple, fearful of a similar fate. Gracchus went into the comitia in order to exonerate himself of the act, but no one would even listen to him. Everyone turned away from him as from one tainted with bloodshed. Gracchus and Flaccus were confounded, and having missed the opportunity to carry out their plans, they hurried home along with their adherents. The rest of the great mass of people stayed in the forum during the night, as if some fearful crisis were at hand. One of the consuls, who was staying in the city, Opimius, ordered an armed guard to be placed at the Capitol at daybreak and dispatched heralds to convene the senate. He stationed himself in the Temple of Castor and Pollux in the middle of the city, and awaited the outcome there.

When these preparations had been made, the senate called Gracchus and Flaccus from their homes to the senate-house to make their defense, but with arms in their hands, they fled to the Aventine hill, hoping that if they could get possession of it first the senate would come to some understanding with them. They ran through the city promising liberty to slaves, but none paid heed to them. Nevertheless, with such troops as they had, they seized and barricaded the Temple of Diana and dispatched Quintus, the son of Flaccus, to the senate, trying to make terms and dwell in peace. The senate sent back word for them to put down their arms, and to come to the senate-house and tell what they

desired, or else send no more emissaries. As they sent Quintus a second time, the consul Opimius seized him, as no longer an envoy after being thus warned, and sent a force in arms against the followers of Gracchus. Gracchus fled to a grove across the river by the wooden bridge, accompanied by one slave, to whom he bared his throat when on the point of being taken. Flaccus sought shelter in the shop of an acquaintance. As those pursuing him did not know what shop he was in they threatened to set fire to the whole line. The man that had given the suppliant refuge was loath to point out his hiding place, but told some one else to do so. Flaccus was caught and slain. The heads of Gracchus and Flaccus were brought to Opimius and he gave an equal weight in gold to the ones presenting them. The mob pillaged their homes. Opimius seized their confederates and threw them into prison, ordering them to be strangled to death. After this a lustration on account of the bloodshed was made by the city and the senate ordered the erection of a temple to Harmony in the forum.

SALLUST

Speech of Marius Against the Nobility

Source: Sallust, *Jugurthine War* LXIII-LXV. Translated by John S. Watson. In Kevin Guinagh and Alfred P. Dorjahn (eds.). *Latin Literature in Translation*. New York: Longmans, Green and Co, 1942.

After serving for a year under Q. Caecilius Metellus, the consul of 109, in the war against the anti-Roman Numidian usurper Jugurtha (a war that lasted from 112 to 105), the populist Marius went to Rome where he was elected to the consulship (in 108, for 107) and given the command of the army in Numidia. During his absence Metellus made considerable headway in his campaign against Jugurtha who, in spite of his reverses, succeeded in winning Bocchus, the King of Mauritania, over to his side. Before returning to his new duties, Marius denounced the aristocrats.

On arriving at his new post, Marius pushed the campaign against the Numidian with vigor and gained many successes. Bocchus betrayed his ally, Jugurtha, into the hands of Sulla, Marius's quaestor.

Marius who, as I said before, had been made consul with great eagerness on the part of the populace, began, though he had always been hostile to the patricians, to inveigh against them, after the people gave him the province of Numidia, with great frequency and violence; he attacked them sometimes individually and sometimes in a body; he said that he had snatched from them the consulship as spoils from vanquished enemies; and uttered other remarks laudatory to himself and offensive to them. Meanwhile he made the provisions for the war his chief object; .he asked for reinforcements for the legions; he sent for auxiliaries from foreign states, kings, and allies; he also enlisted all the bravest men from Latium, most of whom were known to him by actual service, some few only by report and, induced by earnest solicitation, even discharged veterans to accompany him. Nor did the senate, though adverse to him, dare to refuse him anything; the additions to the legions they had voted even with eagerness, because military service was thought to be unpopular with the multitude, and Marius seemed likely to lose either the means of warfare or the favor of the people. But such expectations were entertained in vain, so ardent was the desire of going with Marius that had seized on almost all. Everyone cherished the fancy that he should return home laden with spoil, crowned with victory, or attended with some similar good fortune. Marius himself; too, had excited them in no small degree by a speech; for, when all that he required was granted and he was anxious to commence a levy, he called an assembly of the people as well to encourage them to enlist as to inveigh, according to his practice, against the nobility. He spoke, on the occasion, as follows:

"I am aware, my fellow-citizens, that most men do not appear as candidates before you for an office, and conduct themselves in it when they have obtained it, under the same character; that they are at first industrious, humble, and modest, but afterwards lead a life of indolence and arrogance. But to me it appears that the contrary should be the case; for as the whole state is of greater consequence than the single office of consulate or praetorship, so its interests ought to be managed with greater solicitude than these magistracies are sought. Nor am I insensible how great a weight of business I am, through your kindness, called upon to sustain. To make preparations for war, and yet to be sparing of the treasury; to press those .into the service whom I am unwilling to offend; to direct everything at home and abroad; and to discharge these duties when surrounded by the envious, the hostile, and the factious is more difficult, my fellow-citizens, than is generally imagined: In addition to this, if others fail in their undertakings, their ancient rank, the heroic actions of their ancestors, the power of their relatives and connections, their numerous dependents, are all at hand to support them; but as for me, my whole hopes rest upon myself, which I must sustain by good conduct and integrity; for all other means are unavailing.

"I am sensible, too, my fellow-citizens, that the eyes of all men are turned upon me; that the just and good favor me, as my services are· beneficial to the state, but that the nobility seek occasion to attack me. I must therefore use the greater exertion, that you may not be deceived in me, and that their views may be rendered abortive. I have led such a life, indeed, from my boyhood to the present hour, that I am familiar with every kind of toil and danger; and that exertion which, before your kindness to me, I practiced gratuitously It is not my intention to relax after having received my reward. For those .who have pretended to be men of worth only to secure their election, It may be difficult to conduct themselves properly in office; but to me, who have passed my whole life in the most honorable occupations, to act well has from habit become nature.

"You have commanded me to carry on the war against Jugurtha; a commission at which the nobility are highly offended. Consider with yourselves, I pray you, whether it would be a change for the better, if you were to send to this, or to any other such appointment, one of yonder crowd of nobles, a man of ancient family, of innumerable statues, and. of no military experience; in order, forsooth, that in so important 'an office,. and being ignorant of everything connected With It, he may exhibit hurry and trepidation, and select one of the people to instruct him in his duty. For so it generally happens, that he whom you have chosen to direct, seeks another to direct him. I know some, my fellow-citizens, who, after they have been elected consuls, have begun to read the acts of their ancestors, and the military precepts of the Greeks; persons who invert the order of thin as; for though to discharge the duties of the office is posterior, in point of time, to election, it is, in reality and practical importance, prior to it.

"Compare now, my fellow-citizens, me, who am a new man, with those haughty nobles. What they have but heard or read, I have witnessed or performed. What they have learned from books, I have acquired in the field; and whether deeds or words are of greater estimation, it is for you to consider. They despise my humbleness of birth; I contemn their imbecility. My condition is made an objection to me; their misconduct is a reproach to them. The circumstance of birth, indeed, I consider as one and the same to all; but think that he who best exerts himself is the noblest. And could it be inquired of the fathers, of Albinus and Bestia, whether they would rather be the parents of them or of me, what do you suppose that they would answer, but that they would wish the most deserving to be their offspring? If the patricians Justly despise me, let them also despise their own ancestors, whose nobility, like mine, had its origin in merit. They envy me the honor that I have received; let them also envy me the toils, the abstinence, and the perils, by which I obtained that honor. But they, men eaten up with pride, live as if they disdained all the distinctions that ,You can bestow, and yet sue for those distinctions as if they had lived so as to merit them. Yet those are assuredly deceived who expect to enjoy, at the same time, things so incompatible as the pleasures of indolence and the rewards of honorable exertion.

"When they speak before you, or in the senate, they occupy the greatest part of their orations in extolling their ancestors; for they suppose that, by recounting the heroic deeds of their forefathers, they render themselves more illustrious. But the reverse of this is the case; for the more glorious were the lives of their ancestors, the more scandalous is their own inaction. The truth, indeed, is plainly this, that the glory of ancestors sheds a light on their posterity, which suffers neither their virtues nor their vices to be concealed. Of this light, my fellow-citizens, I have no share; but I have what confers much more distinction, the power of relating my own actions. Consider, then, how unreasonable they are; what they claim to themselves for the merit of others, they will not grant to me for my own; alleging, forsooth, that I have no statues, and that my distinction is newly acquired; but it is surely better to have acquired such distinction myself than to bring disgrace on that received from others.

"I am not ignorant that, if they were inclined to reply to me, they would make an abundant display of eloquent and artful language. Yet, since they attack both you and myself, on occasion of the great favor which you have conferred upon me, I did not think proper to be silent before them, lest anyone should construe my forbearance into a consciousness of demerit. As for myself, indeed, nothing that is said of me, I feel assured, can do me injury; for what is true must of necessity speak in my favor; what is false, my life and character will refute. But since your judgment, in bestowing on me so distinguished an honor and so important a trust, is called in question, consider, I beseech you, again and again, whether you are likely to repent of what you have done. I can not, to raise your confidence in me, boast of the statues, or triumphs, or consulships of my ancestors; but, if it be thought necessary, I can show you spears, a banner, caparisons for horses, and other military rewards; besides the scars of wounds on my breast. These are my statues; this is my nobility; honors, not left, like theirs, by inheritance, but acquired amidst innumerable toils and dangers.

"My speech, they say, is inelegant; but that I have ever thought of little importance. Worth sufficiently displays itself; it is for my detractors to use studied language, that they may palliate base conduct by plausible words. Nor have I learned Greek; for I had no wish to acquire a tongue that adds nothing to the valor of those who teach it. But I have gained other accomplishments, such as are of the utmost benefit to a state; I have learned to strike down an enemy; to be vigilant at my post; to fear nothing but dishonor; to bear cold and heat with equal endurance; to sleep on the ground; and to sustain at the same time hunger and fatigue. And with such rules of conduct I shall stimulate my soldiers, not treating them with rigor and myself with indulgence, nor making their toils my glory. Such a mode of commanding is at once useful to the state, and becoming to a citizen. For to coerce your troops with severity, while you yourself live at ease, is to be a tyrant, not a general.

"It was by conduct such as this, my fellow-citizens, that your ancestors made themselves and the republic renowned. Our nobility, relying on their forefathers' merits, though totally different from them in conduct, disparage us who emulate their virtues; and demand of you every public honor, as due, not to their personal merit, but to their high rank. Arrogant pretenders, and utterly unreasonable! For though their ancestors left them all that was at their disposal, their riches, their statues, and their glorious names, they left them not, nor could leave them, their virtue; which alone, of all their possessions, could neither be communicated nor received.

"They reproach me as being mean, and of unpolished manners, because, forsooth, I have but little skill in arranging an entertainment, and keep no actor, nor give my cook higher wages than my steward; all which charges I must, indeed, acknowledge to be just; for I learned from my father, and other venerable characters, that vain indulgences belong to women, and labor to men; that glory, rather than wealth, should be the object of the virtuous; and that arms and armor, not household furniture, are marks of honor. But let the nobility, if they please, pursue what is delightful and dear to them; let them devote themselves to licentiousness and luxury; let them pass their age as they have passed their youth, in revelry and feasting, the slaves of gluttony and debauchery; but let them leave the toil and dust of the field, and other such matters, to us, to whom they are more grateful than banquets. This, however, they will not do; for when these most infamous of men have disgraced themselves by every species of turpitude, they proceed to claim the distinctions due to the most honorable. Thus it most unjustly happens that luxury and indolence, the most disgraceful of vices, are harmless to those who indulge m them, and fatal only to the innocent commonwealth.

"As I have now replied to my calumniators, as far as my own character required, though not so fully as their flagitiousness deserved, I shall add a few words on the state of public affairs. In the first place, my fellow-citizens, be of good courage with regard to Numidia; for all that hitherto protected Jugurtha, avarice, inexperience, and arrogance, you have entirely removed. There is an army in it, too, which is well acquainted with the country, though, assuredly, more brave than fortunate; for a great part of it has been destroyed by the avarice or rashness of its commanders. Such of you, then, as are of military age, co-operate with me, and support the cause of your country; and let no discouragement, from the ill-fortune of others, or the arrogance of the late commanders, affect anyone of you. I myself shall be with you, both on the march and in the battle, both to direct your movements and to share your dangers. I shall treat you and myself on every occasion alike; and, doubtless, with the aid of the gods, all good things, victory, spoil and glory, are ready to our hands; though, even if they were doubtful or distant, it would still become every able citizen to act in defense of his country. For no man, by slothful timidity, has escaped the lot of mortals; nor has any parent wished for his children that they might live forever, but rather that they might act in life with virtue and honor. I would add more, my fellow-citizens, if words could give courage to the faint-hearted; to the brave I think that I have said enough."

APPIAN AND PLUTARCH
Mithridates Against Rome

Source: William Stearns Davis, ed., *Readings in Ancient History: Illustrative Extracts from the Sources*, 2 Vols. (Boston: Allyn and Bacon, 1912-13), *Vol. II: Rome and the West*, pp. 118-120, 123-127. Scanned by: J. S. Arkenberg, Dept. of History, Cal. State Fullerton. Prof. Arkenberg has modernized the text.

> *In Mithridates, king of Pontus (reigned 120 to 63 BCE), the Romans found their most formidable enemy, save only Hannibal. That he was a foe worthy to contend with Sulla, Lucullus, and Pompey is testified to in the following selection from Appian. In conquering Mithridates the Romans, almost against their wish, were forced to conquer most of the nearer Orient---especially all of Asia Minor and Syria---and to come face to face with Parthia. When at last Mithridates had been overthrown the Romans called the victory over him "The Great Victory" and Pompey, his conqueror, Magnus, or "The Great"—on account of the magnitude and intensity of his achievement. Lucullus (died about 56 BCE) would have conquered Mithridates had not Pompey been sent out (in 66 BCE) to supersede him. As it was, he brought back from the East enough wealth for a magnificent triumph.*

Appian, *Mithridatic Wars* 118-119

Many times Mithridates had over 400 ships of his own, 50,000 cavalry, and 250,000 infantry, with engines and arms in proportion. For allies he had the king of Armenia and the princes of the Scythian tribes around the Euxine and the Sea of Azov and beyond, as far as the Thracian Bosphorus. He held communication with the leaders of the Roman civil wars, which were then fiercely raging, and with those who were inciting insurrections in Spain. He established friendly relations with the Gauls for the purpose of invading Italy.

From Cilicia to the Pillars of Hercules he also filled the sea with pirates, who stopped all commerce and navigation between cities, and caused severe famine for a long time. In short, he left nothing within the power of man undone or untried to start the greatest possible movement, extending from the Orient to the Occident, to vex, so to speak, the whole world, which was warred

upon, tangled in alliances, harassed by pirates, or vexed by the neighborhood of the warfare. Such and so diversified was this one war against Mithridates, but in the end it brought the greatest gain to the Romans; for it pushed the boundaries of their dominion from the setting of the sun to the river Euphrates.

Plutarch, *Life of Lucullus*, xxxvii

The pomp [of Lucullus' triumph] proved not so wonderful or so wearisome with the length of the procession and the number of things carried in it, but consisted chiefly in vast quantities of arms and machines of the king's [i.e., Mithridates], with which he adorned the Flaminian circus, a spectacle by no means despicable.

In his progress there passed by a few horsemen in heavy armor, ten chariots armed with scythes, sixty friends and officers of the king's, and a hundred and ten brazen-beaked ships of war, which were conveyed along with a golden image of Mithridates six feet high, a shield set with precious stones, twenty loads of silver vessels, and thirty-two of golden cups, armor, and money, all carried by men. Besides which, eight mules were laden with golden couches, fifty-six with bullion, and a hundred and seven with coined silver, little less than two million seven hundred thousand pieces. There were tablets, also, with inscriptions, stating what moneys he gave Pompey for prosecuting the piratic war, what he delivered into the treasury, and what he gave to every soldier, which was nine hundred and fifty drachmas each [Arkenberg: about $715 in 1998 dollars]. After all which he nobly feasted the city and adjoining villages.

APPIAN
Drusus and his Enemies

Source: Appian 1.34-35. Translated by Horace White. In *Appian's Roman history: in four volumes.* Cambridge, Mass: Harvard University Press, 1913.

> *The cause of citizenship for the Italians was taken up by the otherwise pro-senate M. Livius Drusus, who was tribune of the plebs in 91 BCE.*

While they were thus occupied the so called Social War, in which many Italian peoples were engaged, broke out.[67] It began unexpectedly, grew rapidly to great proportions and extinguished the Roman sedition for a long time by a new terror. When it was ended it also gave rise to new seditions under more powerful leaders, who did not work by introducing new laws, or by the tricks of the demagogue, but by matching whole armies against each other. I have treated it in this history

---

[67] The Social War took place 91–88 BCE.

because it had its origin in the sedition in Rome and resulted in another much worse. It began in this way.

Fulvius Flaccus in his consulship first and foremost openly excited among the Italians the desire for Roman citizenship, so as to be partners in the empire instead of subjects.[68] When he introduced this idea and strenuously persisted in it, the Senate, for that reason, sent him away to take command in a war, in the course of which his consulship expired; but he obtained the tribuneship after that and contrived to have the younger Gracchus[69] for a colleague, with whose co-operation he brought forward other measures in favor of the Italians. When they were both killed, as I have previously related, the Italians were still more excited. They could not bear to be considered subjects instead of equals, or to think that Flaccus and Gracchus should have suffered such calamities while working for their political advantage.

After them the tribune Livius Drusus, a man of most illustrious birth, promised the Italians, at their urgent request, that he would bring forward a new law to give them citizenship. They especially desired this because by that one step they would become rulers instead of subjects. In order to conciliate the plebeians to this measure he led out to Italy and Sicily several colonies which had been voted some time before, but not yet planted. He endeavored to bring together by an agreement the Senate and the equestrian order, who were then in sharp antagonism to each other, in reference to the law courts. As he was not able to restore the courts to the Senate openly, he tried the following artifice to reconcile them. As the senators had been reduced by the seditions to scarcely 300 in number, he brought forward a law that an equal number, chosen according to merit, should be added to their enrolment from the knights, and that the courts of justice should be made up thereafter from the whole number. He added a clause in the law that they should make investigations about bribery, as accusations of that kind were almost unknown, since the custom of bribe-taking prevailed without restraint.

This was the plan that he contrived for both of them, but it turned out contrary to his expectations, for the senators were indignant that so large a number should be added to their enrolment at one time and be transferred from knighthood to the highest rank. They thought it not unlikely that they would form a faction in the Senate by themselves and contend against the old senators more powerfully than ever. The knights, on the other hand, suspected that, by this doctoring, the courts of justice would be transferred from their order to the Senate exclusively. Having acquired a relish for the great gains and power of the judicial office, this suspicion disturbed them. Most of them, too, fell into doubt and

distrust toward each other, discussing which of them seemed more worthy than others to be enrolled among the 300; and envy against their betters filled the breasts of the remainder. Above all the knights were angry at the revival of the charge of bribery, which they thought had been ere this entirely suppressed, so far as they were concerned.

Thus it came to pass that both the Senate and the knights, although opposed to each other, were united in hating Drusus. Only the plebeians were gratified with the colonies. Even the Italians, in whose especial interest Drusus was devising these plans, were apprehensive about the law providing for the colonies, because they thought that the Roman public domain (which was still undivided and which they were cultivating, some by force and others clandestinely) would at once be taken away from them, and that in many cases they might even be disturbed in their private holdings. The Etruscans and the Umbrians had the same fears as the Italians,[70] and when they were summoned to the city, as was thought, by the consuls, for the ostensible purpose of complaining against the law of Drusus, but actually to kill him, they cried down the law publicly and waited for the day of the comitia. Drusus learned of the plot against him and did not go out frequently, but transacted business from day to day in the atrium of his house, which was poorly lighted. One evening as he was sending the crowd away he exclaimed suddenly that he was wounded, and fell down while uttering the words. A shoemaker's knife was found thrust into his hip.

Thus was Drusus also slain while serving as tribune. The knights, in order to make his policy a ground of vexatious accusation against their enemies, persuaded the tribune Q. Varius to bring forward a law to prosecute those who should, either openly or secretly, aid the Italians to acquire citizenship, hoping thus to bring all the senators under an odious indictment, and themselves to sit in judgment on them, and that when they were out of the way they themselves would be more powerful than ever in the government of Rome. When the other tribunes interposed their veto the knights surrounded them with drawn daggers and enacted the measure, whereupon accusers at once brought actions against the most illustrious of the senators. Of these Bestia did not respond, but went into exile voluntarily rather than surrender himself into the hands of his enemies. After him Cotta went before the court, made an impressive defense of his administration of public affairs, and openly reviled the knights. He, too, departed from the city before the vote of the judges was taken. Mummius, the conqueror of Greece, was basely ensnared by the knights, who promised to acquit him,

[68] M. Fulvius Flaccus, consul 125 BCE.
[69] C. Sempronius Gracchus, tribune of the plebs 123 and 122 BCE, killed 121.

[70] Until the late Republic, the word "Italy" applied only to that part of the peninsula south of Etruria and Umbria.

but condemned him to banishment. He passed the remainder of his life at Delos.

VARIOUS

Accounts of the Roman State Religion

Source: From: William Stearns Davis, ed., Readings in Ancient History, 2 Vols. (Boston: Allyn and Bacon, 1912-13), Vol. II, pp. 9-15; 289; Livy, The History of Rome, by T. Livius, trans. D. Spillan and Cyrus Edmonds, (New York: G. Bell & Sons, 1892). Scanned by: J. S. Arkenberg, Dept. of History, Cal. State Fullerton. Prof. Arkenberg has modernized the text.

Cato the Elder: The Planting Ritual, c. 160 BCE

The offering is to be made in this way: Offer to Jupiter Dapalis a cup of wine of whatever size you wish. Observe the day as a holiday for the oxen, their drivers, and those who make the offering. When you make the offering, say as follows: "Jupiter Dapalis, since it is due and proper that a cup of wine be offered you, in my home among my family, for your sacred feast; for that reason, be honored by this feast that is offered you." Wash your hands, and then take the wine and say: "Jupiter Dapalis, be honored by this feast that is offered to you and be honored by the wine that is placed before you." If you wish, make an offering to Vesta. The feast of Jupiter consists of roasted meat and an urn of wine. Present it to Jupiter religiously, in the proper form. After the offering is made, plant millet, panic grass, garlic, and lentils.

Cato the Elder: The Harvest Ritual, c. 160 BCE

Before the harvest the sacrifice of the pig must be offered in this manner: Offer a sow as porca praecidanea to Ceres before you harvest spelt, wheat, barley, beans, and rape seed. Offer a prayer, with incense and wine, to Janus, Jupiter and Juno, before offering the sow. Offer a pile of cakes to Janus, saying, "Father Janus, in offering these cakes to you, I humbly pray that you will be propitious and merciful to me and my children, my house and my household." Then make an offering of cake to Jupiter with these words: "In offering you this cake, O Jupiter, I humbly pray that you, pleased with this offering, will be propitious and merciful to me and my children, my house and my household." Then present the wine to Janus, saying: "Father Janus, as I have prayed humbly in offering you the cakes, so may you in the same way be honored by this wine now placed before you." Then pray to Jupiter thus: "Jupiter, may you be honored in accepting this cake; may you be honored in accepting the wine placed before you." Then sacrifice the porca praecidanea. When the entrails have been removed, make an offering of cakes to Janus, and pray in the same way as you have prayed before. Offer a cake to Jupiter, praying just as before. In the same way offer wine to Janus and offer wine to Jupiter, in the same way as before in offering the pile of cakes, and in the

consecration of the cake. Afterward offer the entrails and wine to Ceres.

Cicero: The Flamen Dialis, c. 50 BCE

A great many ceremonies are imposed upon the Flamen Dialis,[71] and also many restraints, about which we read in the books On The Public Priesthoods and also in Book I of Fabius Pictor's work. Among them I recall the following: 1) It is forbidden the Flamen Dialis to ride a horse; 2) It is likewise forbidden him to view the classes arrayed outside the pomerium,[72] i.e., armed and in battle order—hence only rarely is the Flamen Dialis made a Consul, since the conduct of wars is entrusted to the Consuls; 3) It is likewise forbidden for him ever to take an oath by Jupiter; 4) It is likewise forbidden for him to wear a ring, unless it is cut through and empty; 5) It is also forbidden to carry out fire from the flaminia, i.e., the Flamen Dialis' house, except for a sacral purpose; 6) if a prisoner in chains enters the house he must be released and the chains must be carried up through the opening in the roof above the atrium or living room onto the roof tiles and dropped down from there into the street;

7) He must have no knot in his head gear or in his girdle or in any other part of his attire; 8) If anyone is being led away to be flogged and falls at his feet as a suppliant, it is forbidden to flog him that day; 9) The hair of the Flamen Dialis is not to be cut, except by a freeman; 10) It is customary for the Flamen neither to touch nor even to name a female goat, or raw meat, ivy, or beans; 11) He must not walk under a trellis for vines; 12) The feet of the bed on which he lies must have a thin coating of clay, and he must not be away from this bed for three successive nights, nor is it lawful for anyone else to sleep in this bed; 13) At the foot of his bed there must be a box containing a little pile of sacrificial cakes; 14) The nail trimmings and hair of the Dialis must be buried in the ground beneath a healthy tree; 15) Every day is a holy day for the Dialis; 16) He must not go outdoors without a head-covering—this is now allowed indoors, but only recently by decree of the pontiffs, as Masurius Sabinus has stated; it is also said that some of the other ceremonies have been remitted and cancelled; 17) It is not lawful for him to touch bread made with yeast; 18) His underwear cannot be taken off except in covered places, lest he appear nude under the open sky, which is the same as under the eye of Jove; 19) No one else outranks him in the seating at a banquet except the Rex Sacrorum; 20) If he loses his wife, he must resign his office; 21) His marriage cannot be dissolved except by death; 21) He never enters a burying ground, he never touches a corpse—he is, however, permitted to attend a funeral.

---

[71] The priest of Jupiter (see page 4 above).
[72] The sacred boundary of Rome.

Almost the same ceremonial rules belong to the Flaminica Dialis.[73] They say that she observes certain other and different ones, for example, that she wears a dyed gown, and that she has a twig from a fruitful tree tucked in her veil, and that it is forbidden for her to ascend more than three rungs of a ladder and even that when she goes to the Argei Festival[74] she must neither comb her head nor arrange her hair.

Livy: History of Rome, c. 10 CE

There is an ancient instruction written in archaic letters which runs: "Let him who is the Praetor Maximus fasten a nail on the Ides of September." This notice was fastened up on the right side of the Temple of Jupiter Optimus Maximus, next to the chapel of Minerva. This nail is said to have marked the number of the year— written records being scarce in those days—and was for that reason placed under the protection of Minerva because she was the inventor of numbers. Cincius, a careful student of monuments of this kind, asserts that at Volsinii also nails were fastened in the Temple of Nortia, an Etruscan goddess, to indicate the number of the year. It was in accordance with this direction that the consul Horatius dedicated the Temple of Jupiter Optimus Maximus in the year following the expulsion of the kings; from the Consuls the ceremony of fastening the nails passed to the Dictators, because they possessed greater authority. As the custom had been subsequently dropped, it was felt to be of sufficient importance to require the appointment of a Dictator. L. Manlius was accordingly nominated, but, regarding his appointment as due to political rather than to religious reasons and eager to command in the war with the Hernici, he caused a very angry feeling among the men liable to serve by the inconsiderate way in which he conducted the enrolment. At last, in consequence of the unanimous resistance offered by the tribunes of the plebs, he gave way, either voluntarily or through compulsion, and laid down his Dictatorship. Since then, this rite has been performed by the Rex Sacrorum.

Plutarch: Life of Numa, c. 110 CE

The original constitution of the priests, called Pontifices, is ascribed unto Numa, and he himself was, it is said, the first of them; and that they have the name of Pontifices from pons ["bridge"], or, thus, "bridge-makers." The sacrifices performed on the bridge were among the most sacred and ancient, and the keeping and repairing of the bridge attached, like any other public sacred office, to the priesthood. It was accounted not simply unlawful, but a positive sacrilege, to pull down the wooden bridge; which moreover is said, in

obedience to an oracle, to have been built entirely of timber and fastened with wooden pins, without nails or cramps of iron. The office of Pontifex Maximus, or chief priest, was to declare and interpret the divine law….he not only prescribed rules for public ceremony, but regulated the sacrifices of private persons, not suffering them to vary from established custom, and giving information to everyone of what was requisite for purposes of worship or supplication. He was also guardian of the vestal virgins, the institution of whom, and of their perpetual fire, was attributed to Numa, who, perhaps, fancied the charge of pure and uncorrupted flames would be fitly entrusted to chaste and unpolluted persons, or that fire, which consumes but produces nothing, bears an analogy to the virgin estate.

Some are of opinion that these vestals had no other business than the preservation of this fire; but others conceive that they were keepers of other divine secrets, concealed from all but themselves. Gegania and Verenia, it is recorded, were the names of the first two virgins consecrated and ordained by Numa; Canuleia and Tarpeia succeeded; Servius Tullius afterwards added two, and the number of four has been continued to the present time. The statutes prescribed by Numa for the vestals were these: that they should take a vow of virginity for the space of thirty years, the first ten of which they were to spend in learning their duties, the second ten in performing them, and the remaining ten in teaching and instructing others. Thus the whole term being completed, it was lawful for them to marry, and leaving the sacred order, to choose any condition of life that pleased them. But, of this permission, few, as they say, made use; and in cases where they did so, it was observed that their change was not a happy one, but accompanied ever after with regret and melancholy; so that the greater number, from religious fears and scruples forbore, and continued to old age and death in the strict observance of a single life.

For this condition they were compensated by great privileges and prerogatives: as that they had power to make a will in the lifetime of their father; that they had free administration of their own affairs without guardian or tutor; when they go outside, they have the fasces carried before them; and if in their walks they chance to meet a criminal on his way to execution, it saves his life, upon oath being made that the meeting was accidental, and not concerted or of set purpose. Any one who presses upon the chair on which they are carried is put to death.

If these vestals commit any minor fault, they are punishable by the Pontifex Maximus only, who whips the offender, sometimes with her clothes off, in a dark place, with a curtain drawn between; but she that has broken her vow of chastity is buried alive near the gate called Collina, where a little mound of earth stands inside the city reaching some little distance, called in Latin agger;

---

[73] I.e., his wife.
[74] A festival; at which 24 puppets were thrown into the Tiber.

under it a narrow room is constructed, to which a descent is made by stairs; here they prepare a bed, and light a lamp, and leave a small quantity of victuals, such as bread, water, a pail of milk, and some oil; that so that body which had been consecrated and devoted to the most sacred service of religion might not be said to perish by such a death as famine. The culprit herself is put in a litter, which they cover over, and tie her down with cords on it, so that nothing she utters may be heard. They then take her to the Forum; all people silently go out of the way as she passes, and such as follow accompany the bier with solemn and speechless sorrow; and, indeed, there is not any spectacle more appalling, nor any day observed by the city with greater appearance of gloom and sadness. When they come to the place of execution, the officers loose the cords, and then the Pontifex Maximus, lifting his hands to heaven, pronounces certain prayers to himself before the act; then he brings out the prisoner, being still covered, and placing her upon the steps that lead down to the cell, turns away his face with the rest of the priests; the stairs are drawn up after she has gone down, and a quantity of earth is heaped up over the entrance to the cell, so as to prevent it from being distinguished from the rest of the mound. This is the punishment of those who break their vow of virginity.

From Numa's day also were dated twelve sacred targets of bronze, said to have the virtue of guarding the city from pestilence. The keeping of these targets was committed to the charge of certain priests, called Salii, who received their name from that jumping dance which the Salii themselves use, when in the month of March they carry the sacred targets through the city; at which procession they are habited in short frocks of purple, girt with a broad belt studded with brass; on their heads they wear a brass helmet, and carry in their hands short daggers, which they clash every now and then against the targets. But the chief thing is the dance itself. They move with much grace, performing, in quick time and close order, various intricate figures, with a great display of strength and agility. The targets are not made round, nor like proper targets, of a complete circumference, but are cut out into a wavy line, the ends of which are rounded off and turned in at the thickest part towards each other.

Numa ordered that fish which have no scales, except the scar, should not be offered to the gods. He ordered each person to draw a line around his own real property and to set stones on the boundaries, such stones being consecrated to Jupiter Terminus. But if anyone destroyed or displaced the boundary stones, the person who had done this would be sacrificed to the god. He ordained that the funeral pyre should not be sprinkled with wine, not that libations be made to the gods with wine from unpruned vines. Among other laws he made: A concubine shall not touch the Altar of Juno, and if she does, she shall sacrifice, with her hair unbound, a ewe lamb to Juno; If a man is killed by lightning, the proper burial rite shall not be performed—those who disobey this will be sacrificed to Jupiter; Priests should have their hair cut with only bronze shears.

"January" was so called from the god Janus, and precedence given to it by Numa before March, which was dedicated to the god Mars; because, as I conceive, he wished to take every opportunity of intimating that the arts and studies of peace are to be preferred before those of war. For this Janus, whether in remote antiquity he were a demi-god or a king, was certainly a great lover of civil and social unity, and one who reclaimed men from brutal and savage living; for which reason they figure him with two faces, to represent the two states and conditions out of the one of which he brought mankind to lead them into the other. His temple at Rome has two gates, which they call the Gates of War, because they stand open in the time of war, and shut in the times of peace; of which latter there was very seldom an example, for, as the Roman state was enlarged and extended, it was so encompassed with barbarous nations and enemies to be resisted that it was seldom or never at peace. Only in the time of Augustus Caesar, after he had overcome Antony, this temple was shut; as likewise once before, when M. Atilius and T. Manlius were Consuls;[75] but then it was not long before, wars breaking out, the gates were again opened.

Certificate of Having Sacrificed, 250 CE

To the Commissioners of Sacrifice of the Village of Alexander's Island:[76] From Aurelius Diogenes, the son of Satabus, of the Village of Alexander's Island, aged 72 years:—scar on his right eyebrow. I have always sacrificed regularly to the gods, and now, in your presence, in accordance with the edict, I have done sacrifice, and poured the drink offering, and tasted of the sacrifices, and I request you to certify the same. Farewell.——Handed in by me, Aurelius Diogenes.——I certify that I saw him sacrificing [signature obliterated]. Done in the first year of the Emperor, Caesar C. Messius Q. Trajanus Decius Pius Felix Augustus, second of the month Epith. [June 26, 250 CE]

---

[75] 235 BCE.
[76] The Province of Egypt.

Slavery in the Roman Republic

Source: Plautus, Pseudolus, Act. I, Sc. 2; Cato the Elder, Agriculture, chs. 56-59; Plautus, Menaechmi, Act V, Sc. 4.; Plutarch, Life of Crassus, viii-xi. From: William Stearns Davis, ed., Readings in Ancient History: Illustrative Extracts from the Sources, 2 Vols. (Boston: Allyn and Bacon, 1912-13), Vol. II: Rome and the West, pp. 90-97.The Conduct and Treatment of Slaves.

The Conduct and Treatment of Slaves:
Plautus: *Pseudolus* Act. I, Sc. 2.

A Roman playwright, Plautus, writing about the time of the end of the Second Punic War (201 BCE), gives this picture of an inconsiderate master, and the kind of treatment his slaves were likely to get. Very probably conditions grew worse rather than better for the average slave household, for at least two centuries. As the Romans grew in wealth and the show of culture they did not grow in humanity.

[Ballio, a captious slave owner, is giving orders to his servants.]

Ballio: Get out, come, out with you, you rascals; kept at a loss, and bought at a loss. Not one of you dreams minding your business, or being a bit of use to me, unless I carry on thus! [He strikes his whip around on all of them.] Never did I see men more like asses than you! Why, your ribs are hardened with the stripes. If one flogs you, he hurts himself the most: [Aside.] Regular whipping posts are they all, and all they do is to pilfer, purloin, prig, plunder, drink, eat, and abscond! Oh! they look decent enough; but they're cheats in their conduct.

[Addressing the slaves again.] Now, unless you're all attention, unless you get that sloth and drowsiness out of your breasts and eyes, I'll have your sides so thoroughly marked with thongs that you'll outvie those Campanian coverlets in color, or a regular Alexandrian tapestry, purple-broidered all over with beasts. Yesterday I gave each of you his special job, but you're so worthless, neglectful, stubborn, that I must remind you with a good basting. So you think, I guess, you'll get the better of this whip and of me—by your stout hides! Zounds! But your hides won't prove harder than my good cowhide. [He flourishes it.] Look at this, please! Give heed to this! [He flogs one slave] Well ? Does it hurt ? ... Now stand all of you here, you race born to be thrashed! Turn your ears this way! Give heed to what I say. You, fellow! that's got the pitcher, fetch the water. Take care the kettle's full instanter. You who's got the ax, look after chopping the wood.

Slave: But this ax's edge is blunted.

Ballio: Well; be it so! And so are you blunted with stripes, but is that any reason why you shouldn't work for me? I order that you clean up the house. You know your business; hurry indoors. [Exit first slave]. Now you [to another slave] smooth the couches. Clean the plate and put in proper order. Take care that when I'm back from the Forum I find things done—all swept, sprinkled, scoured, smoothed, cleaned and set in order. Today's my birthday. You should all set to and celebrate it. Take care—do you hear—to lay the salted bacon, the brawn, the collared neck, and the udder in water. I want to entertain some fine gentlemen in real style, to give the idea that I'm rich. Get indoors, and get these things ready, so there's no delay when the cook comes. I'm going to market to buy what fish is to be had. Boy, you go ahead [to a special valet], I've got to take care that no one cuts off my purse.

How to Manage Farm Slaves:
Cato the Elder: *Agriculture* 56-59

Cato the Elder passed as the incarnation of all worldly wisdom among Romans of the second century BCE The precepts here given were undoubtedly put into effect on his own farms. During the early Republic, when the estates were small, there seems to have been a fair amount of kindly treatment awarded the slaves; as the farms grew larger the whole policy of the masters, by becoming more impersonal, became more brutal. Cato does not advocate deliberate cruelty—he would simply treat the slaves according to cold regulations, like so many expensive cattle.

Country slaves ought to receive in the winter, when they are at work, four modii[77] of grain; and four modii and a half during the summer. The superintendent, the housekeeper, the watchman, and the shepherd get three modii; slaves in chains four pounds of bread in winter and five pounds from the time when the work of training the vines ought to begin until the figs have ripened.

Wine for the slaves. After the vintage let them drink from the sour wine for three months. The fourth month let them have a hemina [about half a pint] per day or two congii and a half [over seven quarts] per month. During the fifth, sixth, seventh, and eighth months let them have a sextarius [about a pint] per day or five congii per month. Finally, in the ninth, tenth, and the eleventh months, let them have three hemina [three-fourths of a quart] per day, or an amphora [about six gallons] per month. On the Saturnalia and on Compitalia each man should have a congius [something under three quarts].

To feed the slaves. Let the olives that drop of themselves be kept so far as possible. Keep too those harvested olives that do not yield much oil, and husband them, for they last a long time. When the olives have been consumed, give out the brine and vinegar. You should distribute to everyone a sextarius of oil per month. A modius of salt apiece is enough for a year.

As for clothes, give out a tunic of three feet and a half, and a cloak once in two years. When you give a tunic or

---

[77] One modius equals about a quarter bushel.

cloak take back the old ones, to make cassocks out of. Once in two years, good shoes should be given.

Winter wine for the slaves. Put in a wooden cask ten parts of must (non-fermented wine) and two parts of very pungent vinegar, and add two parts of boiled wine and fifty of sweet water. With a paddle mix all these thrice per day for five days in succession. Add one forty-eighth of seawater drawn some time earlier. Place the lid on the cask and let it ferment for ten days. This wine will last until the solstice. If any remains after that time, it will make very sharp excellent vinegar.

How a Faithful Slave should Act:
Plautus: *Menaechmi* Act V, Sc. 4

What a slave had to do in order to save himself from constant cuffs and stripes is here set forth somewhat humorously, but with a serious undercurrent of grim truth. There was no high motive for a slave to behave himself—simply a fear of cruel punishment if he did not. There might be a hope of ultimate freedom, but that depended entirely on the caprice of the master.

Messenio, a slave, soliloquizes: Well, this is the proof of a good servant: he must take care of his master's business, look after it, arrange it, think about it; when his master is away, take care of it diligently just as much as if his master were present, or be even more careful. He must take more care of his back than his appetite, his legs than his stomach—if he's got a good heart. Just let him think what those good-for-nothings get from their masters—lazy, worthless fellows that they are. Stripes, fetters, the mill, weariness, hunger, bitter cold—fine pay for idleness. That's what I'm mightily afraid of. Surely, then, it's much better to be good than to be bad. I don't mind tongue lashings, but I do hate real floggings. I'd rather eat meal somebody else grinds, than eat what I grind myself. So I just obey what my master bids me; and I execute orders carefully and diligently. My obedience, I think, is such as is most for the profit of my back. And it surely does pay! Let others do just as they think it worth while. I'll be just where I ought to be. If I stick to that, I'll avoid blunders; and I needn't be much afraid if I'm ready for my master, come what may. The time's pretty close when for this service of mine, my master will give his reward.

The Last Great Slave Revolt:
Plutarch: *Life of Crassus* 8–11

In 73 BCE the "Speaking Tools"—as the Romans called their slaves, especially those upon the great estates of Southern Italy—burst loose in a terrible insurrection, the third such in fifty years; to quell the rebellion taxed the whole power of the government. Despite the sympathy one must have for these slaves and their gallant leader, their success would have been a calamity to civilization. An army of such brutalized wretches could only destroy; they could never have erected a firm and tolerable government. After these outbreaks and the havoc and terror spread by them, the Romans out of sheer fear seem to have begun to treat their slaves less harshly than before.

The insurrection of the gladiators and the devastation of Italy, commonly called the war of Spartacus, began upon this occasion. One Lentulus Batiates trained up a great many gladiators in Capua, most of them Gauls and Thracians, who, not for any fault by them committed, but simply through the cruelty of their master, were kept in confinement for the object of fighting one with another. Two hundred of these formed a plan to escape, but their plot being discovered, those of them who became aware of it in time to anticipate their master, being seventy-eight, got out of a cook's shop chopping knives and spits, and made their way through the city, and lighting by the way on several wagons that were carrying gladiators' arms to another city, they seized upon them and armed themselves. And seizing upon a defensible place, they chose three captains, of whom Spartacus was chief, a Thracian of one of the nomad tribes, and a man not only of high spirit and valiant, but in understanding, also, and in gentleness, superior to his condition, and more of a Grecian than the people of his country usually are.

First, then, routing those that came out of Capua against them, and thus procuring a quantity of proper soldiers' arms, they gladly threw away their own as barbarous and dishonorable.[78] After many successful skirmishes with Varinus, the praetor himself, in one of which Spartacus took his lictors and his own horse, he began to be great and terrible; but wisely considering that he was not to expect to match the force of the empire, he marched his army towards the Alps, intending, when he had passed them, that every man should go to his own home, some to Thrace, some to Gaul. But they, grown confident in their numbers, and puffed up with their success, would give no obedience to him, but went about and ravaged Italy; so that now the Senate was not only moved at the indignity and baseness, both of the enemy and of the insurrection, but,

---

[78] Two praetors who were sent against them with small armies were defeated, while a third general's army was routed and he himself slain.

looking upon it as a matter of alarm and of dangerous consequence, sent out both the consuls to it, as to a great and difficult enterprise. The consul Gellius, falling suddenly upon a party of Germans, who through contempt and confidence had straggled from Spartacus, cut them all to pieces. But when Lentulus with a large army besieged Spartacus, he sallied out upon him, and, joining battle, defeated his chief officers, and captured all his baggage. As he made towards the Alps, Cassius, who was praetor of that part of Gaul that lies about the Po, met him with ten thousand men, but being overcome in battle, he had much ado to escape himself, with the loss of a great many of his men....[79]

But Spartacus retreated through Lucania toward the sea, and in the straits, meeting with some Cilician pirate ships, he had thoughts of attempting Sicily, where, by landing two thousand men, he hoped to kindle anew the war of the slaves, which was but lately extinguished, and seemed to need but a little fuel to set it burning again. But after the pirates had struck a bargain with him, and received his earnest, they deceived him and sailed away. He thereupon retired again from the sea, and established his army in the peninsula of Rhegium....[80]

Spartacus, after this discomfiture, retired to the mountains of Petelia, but Quinctius, one of Crassus's officers, and Scrofula, the quaestor, pursued and overtook him. But when Spartacus rallied and faced them, they were utterly routed and fled, and had much ado to carry off their quaestor, who was wounded. This success, however, ruined Spartacus, because it encouraged the slaves, who now disdained any longer to avoid fighting, or to obey their officers, but as they were upon their march, they came to them with their swords in their hand, and compelled them to lead them back again through Lucania, against the Romans, the very thing which Crassus was eager for. For news was already brought that Pompey[81] was at hand; and people began to talk openly that the honor of this war was reserved for him, who would come and at once oblige the enemy to fight and put an end to the war.

Crassus, therefore, eager to fight a decisive battle, encamped very near the enemy, and began to make lines of circumvallation; but the slaves made a sally, and attacked the pioneers. As fresh supplies came in on either side, Spartacus, seeing there was no avoiding it, set all his army in array, and when his horse was brought him, he drew out his sword and killed him, saying, if he got the day, he should have a great many

better horses of the enemies, and if he lost it, he should have no need of this. And so making directly towards Crassus himself, through the midst of arms and wounds, he missed him, but slew two centurions that fell upon him together. At last, being deserted by those that were about him, he himself stood his ground, and, surrounded by the enemy, bravely defending himself, was cut to pieces.

LIVY, APPIAN

Sulla's Brutality

Source: Livy *Periochae* 88-89. Translated by Jona Lendering. From Lendering's Livius.org (http://www.livius.org/li-ln/livy/periochae/periochae00.html). Appian 1.95-96, 98-99. Translated by Horace White. In *Appian's Roman history: in four volumes*. Cambridge, Mass: Harvard U. Press, 1913.

Livy: *Periochae* 88-89

> Livy describes Sulla's war against the pro-Cinna forces in Italy and Rome in 82 BCE, and its aftermath. (The source here, the Periochae, is a summary of Livy made centuries later; these chapters of Livy are lost.)

Sulla drove Carbo out of Italy,[82] having defeated his army at Clusium, Faventia, and Fidentia, and fought, with the Samnites (the only Italian nation that had not laid down its weapons yet) near the city of Rome at the Porta Collina, and having restored the state, soiled his beautiful victory with a greater cruelty than anyone had ever displayed.

In the Villa publica, he killed 8,000 people who had already surrendered, set up a proscription list, filled the city and all of Italy with slaughter, ordered the murder of all unarmed Praenestines, and killed Marius, a man of senatorial rank, after having broken his legs and arms, cutting off his ears and pulling out his eyes.

When C. Marius,[83] still besieged at Praeneste by Lucretius Ofella of the Sullan faction, wanted to escape through a tunnel that turned out to be blocked by the army, he choose death. That means that when he found out that there was no escape from the tunnel, he and Telesinus, his companion in flight, ran into each other's drawn swords; Marius killed the other, was wounded himself, and killed by his slave.

M. Brutus, sent in a fisherman's ship by Cn. Papirius Carbo from Cossyra, where they had put in, to Lilybaeum, to see if Pompey was already there, was surrounded by ships sent by Pompey; he pointed his

---

[79] The Senate in disgust now sent Crassus against the rebels. Spartacus, however, defeated Mummius, Crassus's lieutenant, and the general had to restore discipline among the demoralized Romans by executing fifty who had begun the flight; later he advanced again.
[80] Here Crassus tried to blockade him. Spartacus escaped with part of his army to Lucania, but some of Spartacus' followers mutinied, and left him. This division of malcontents was soon destroyed by Crassus.
[81] Crassus' rival for military glory.

[82] Cn. Papirius Carbo was Cinna's chief successor; he was consul (for the third time) in 82.
[83] C. Marius the Younger, son of C. Marius, was illegally (because underage) consul beside Carbo in 82.

sword against himself and bracing it on a thwart of the ship, fell upon it with all his weight.[84]

Cn. Pompey, sent to Sicily by the Senate with special powers, killed Cn. [Papirius] Carbo, who met his death crying like a woman.

Sulla was made dictator, and had twenty-four fasces carried before him, something that no one had ever done before. With new laws, he strengthened the republic, diminished the powers of the tribunes of the plebs by taking away from them the right to introduce legislation, expanded the number of priests and augurs to fifteen, enrolled members of the equestrian order into the Senate, blocked the children of those who were proscribed from obtaining office, sold their possessions, and was the first to seize the profits. The proceeds were 350,000,000 sesterces.

He had Q. Lucretius Ofella[85] murdered at the Forum because he had run for consul against his wishes, convened a meeting and explained to the angry Roman people that he had ordered the assassination.

In Africa, Cn. Pompey defeated and killed the exiled Cn. Domitius[86] and king Hierta of Numidia (who were stirring up war), and at the age of 24 celebrated his African triumph, even though he was still a Roman knight—an honor without precedent.

When C. Norbanus, an exiled former consul, was arrested in the city of Rhodes, he committed suicide.

Another exiled man, Mutilus, secretly, with his head covered, arrived at the rear entrance of his wife Bastia's residence, but was not allowed to enter because he had been proscribed. Consequently, he stabbed himself and sprayed the doorway of his wife with his blood.

Sulla recaptured Nola in Samnium. He settled forty-seven legions in the conquered country and divided it between them. He besieged Volaterrae, a town still in resistance, and accepted its surrender.

Finally, Mitylene in Asia, the only city still in arms after the defeat of Mithridates, was captured and destroyed.

Appian: 1.95-96, 98-99

Appian is describing Sulla's actions after defeating the rebel government of Carbo, the successor to Cinna.

... And now, after thus crushing Italy by war, fire, and murder, Sulla's generals visited the several cities and established garrisons at the suspected places. Pompey was dispatched to Africa against Carbo and to Sicily

against Carbo's friends who had taken refuge there. Sulla himself called the Roman people together in an assembly and made them a speech, vaunting his own exploits and making other menacing statements in order to inspire terror. He finished by saying that he would bring about a change which would be beneficial to the people if they would obey him, but of his enemies he would spare none, but would visit them with the utmost severity. He would take vengeance by strong measures on the praetors, quaestors, military tribunes, and everybody else who had committed any hostile act after the day when the consul Scipio violated the agreement made with him.[87] After saying this he forthwith proscribed about forty senators and 1600 knights. He seems to have been the first to make a formal list[88] of those whom he punished, to offer prizes to assassins and rewards to informers, and to threaten with punishment those who should conceal the proscribed. Shortly afterward he added the names other senators to the proscription. Some of these, taken unawares, were killed wherever they were caught, in their houses, in the streets, or in the temples. Others were hurled through mid-air[89] and thrown at Sulla's feet. Others were dragged through the city and trampled on, none of the spectators daring to utter a word of remonstrance against these horrors. Banishment was inflicted upon some and confiscation upon others. Spies were searching everywhere for those who had fled from the city, and those whom they caught they killed.

There was much massacre, banishment, and confiscation also among those Italians who had obeyed Carbo, or Marius, or Norbanus,[90] or their lieutenants. Severe judgments of the courts were rendered against them throughout all Italy on various charges—for exercising military command, for serving in the army, for contributing money, for rendering other service, or even giving counsel against Sulla. Hospitality, private friendship, the borrowing or lending of money, were alike accounted crimes. Now and then one would be arrested for doing a kindness to a suspect, or merely for being his companion on a journey. These accusations abounded mostly against the rich. When charges against individuals failed Sulla took vengeance on whole communities. He punished some of them by demolishing their citadels, or destroying their walls, or by imposing fines and crushing them by heavy contributions. Among most of them he placed colonies of his troops in order to hold Italy under garrisons, sequestrating their lands and houses and dividing them among his soldiers, whom he thus made true to him even after his death. As they could

---

[84] M. Junius Brutus, praetor 88. This is *not* the father of Brutus, Caesar's assassin.
[85] Sulla's loyal supporter, victor over Marius the Younger at the siege of Praeneste.
[86] Cn. Domitius Ahenobarbus, Cinna's son-in-law.

[87] L. Cornelius Scipio Asiagenus, consul 83, was captured by Sulla and agreed to support him; on being freed, Scipio immediately renounced Sulla.
[88] Latin *proscribere*, whence "proscription."
[89] Probably from windows or roofs; but the Greek may merely mean "carried" as opposed to "dragged."
[90] C. Norbanus, Scopio's colleague in the consulship.

not be secure in their own holdings unless all Sulla's system were on a firm foundation, they were his stoutest champions even after he died.

Thus Sulla became king, or tyrant, de facto, not elected, but holding power by force and violence.[91] As, however, he needed the pretence of being elected this too was managed in this way. The kings of the Romans in the olden time were chosen for their bravery, and whenever one of them died the senators held the royal power in succession for five days each, until the people should decide who should be the new king. This five-day ruler was called the Interrex, which means king for the time being. The retiring consuls always presided over the election of their successors in office, and if there chanced to be no consul at such a time an Interrex was appointed for the purpose of holding the consular comitia. Sulla took advantage of this custom. There were no consuls at this time, Carbo having lost his life in Sicily and Marius in Praeneste. So Sulla went out of the city for a time and ordered the Senate to choose an Interrex.

They chose Valerius Flaccus, expecting that he would soon hold the consular comitia. But Sulla wrote ordering Flaccus to represent to the people his own strong opinion that it was to the immediate interest of the city to revive the dictatorship, an office which had now been in abeyance 400 years.[92] He told them not to appoint the dictator for a fixed period, but until such time as he should firmly re-establish the city and Italy and the government generally, shattered as it was by factions and wars. That this proposal referred to himself was not at all doubtful, and Sulla made no concealment of it, declaring openly at the conclusion of the letter that, in his judgment, he could be most serviceable to the city in that capacity.

Such was Sulla's message. The Romans did not like it, but they had no more opportunities for elections according to law, and they considered that this matter was not altogether in their own power. So, in the general deadlock, they welcomed this pretence of an election as an image and semblance of freedom, and chose Sulla as their absolute master for as long a time as he pleased. There had been autocratic rule of the dictators before, but it was limited to short periods. But under Sulla it first became unlimited and so an absolute tyranny. All the same they added, for propriety's sake, that they chose him dictator for the enactment of such laws as he himself might deem best and for the regulation of the commonwealth. Thus the Romans, after having government by kings for above sixty Olympiads, and a democracy, under consuls chosen yearly, for 100 Olympiads, resorted to kingly government again. This was in the 175th Olympiad, according to the Greek calendar, but there were no Olympic games then except

races in the stadium, since Sulla had carried away the athletes and all the sights and shows to Rome to celebrate his victories in the Mithridatic and Italian wars, under the pretext that the masses needed a breathing-spell and recreation after their toils.

Q. CICERO

The Roman Candidate

Source: From: William Stearns Davis, ed. *Readings in Ancient History: Illustrative Extracts from the Sources*, 2 Vols. (Boston: Allyn and Bacon, 1912-1913), *Vol. II: Rome and the West*, pp. 129-135. Scanned by: J. S. Arkenberg, Dept. of History, Cal. State Fullerton.

> Q. Tullius Cicero and his brother to the famous orator were both close watchers of the Roman political scene.

Quintus Cicero, Letter to His Brother Marcus Cicero, 64 BCE

Almost every day as you go down to the Forum you must say to yourself, "I am a *novus homo* [i.e. without noble ancestry]. "I am a candidate for the consulship." "This is Rome." For the "newness" of your name you will best compensate by the brilliance of your oratory. This has ever carried with it great political distinction. A man who is held worthy of defending ex-consuls, cannot be deemed unworthy of the constitution itself. Therefore approach each individual case with the persuasion that on it depends as a whole your entire reputation. For you have, as few *novi homines* have had---all the tax-syndicate promoters, nearly the whole equestrian *ordo*, and many municipal towns, especially devoted to you, many people who have been defended by you, many trade guilds, and besides these a large number of the rising generation, who have become attached to you in their enthusiasm for public speaking, and who visit you daily in swarms, and with such constant regularity!

See that you retain these advantages by reminding these persons, by appealing to them, and by using every means to make them understand that this, and this only, is the time for those who are in your debt now, to show their gratitude, and for those who wish for your services in the future, to place you under an obligation. It also seems possible that a *novus homo* may be much aided by the fact that he has the good wishes of men of high rank, and especially of ex-consuls. It is a point in your favor that you should be thought worthy of this position and rank by the very men to whose position you are wishing to attain.

All these men must be canvassed with care, agents must be sent to them, and they must be convinced that we have always been at one with the *Optimates*, that we have never been dangerous demagogues in the very least. Also take pains to get on your side the young men

---

of high rank, and keep the friendship of those whom you already have. They will contribute much to your political position. Whosoever gives any sign of inclination to you, or regularly visits your house, you must put down in the category of friends. But yet the most advantageous thing is to be beloved and pleasant in the eyes of those who are friends on the more regular grounds of relationship by blood or marriage, the membership in the same club, or some close tie or other. You must take great pains that these men should love you and desire your highest honor.

In a word, you must secure friends of every class, magistrates, consuls and their tribunes to win you the vote of the centuries: men of wide popular influence. Those who either have gained or hope to gain the vote of a tribe or a century, or any other advantage, through your influence, take all pains to collect and to secure. So you see that you will have the votes of all the centuries secured for you by the number and variety of your friends. The first and obvious thing is that you embrace the Roman senators and *equites*, and the active and popular men of all the other orders. There are many city men of good business habits, there are many freedmen engaged in the Forum who are popular and energetic: these men try with all your might, both personally and by common friends, to make eager in your behalf. Seek them out, send agents to them, show them that they are putting you under the greatest possible obligation. After that, review the entire city, all guilds, districts, neighborhoods. If you can attach to yourself the leading men in these, you will by their means easily keep a hold upon the multitude. When you have done that, take care to have in your mind a chart of all Italy laid out according to the tribes in each town, and learn it by heart, so that you may not allow any chartered town, colony, prefecture---in a word, any spot in Italy to exist, in which you have not a firm foothold.

Trace out also individuals in every region, inform yourself about them, seek them out, secure that in their own districts they shall canvas for you, and be, as it were, candidates in your interest.

After having thus worked for the "rural vote", the centuries of the *equites* too seem capable of being won over if you are careful. And you should be strenuous in seeing as many people as possible every day of every possible class and order, for from the mere numbers of these you can make a guess of the amount of support you will get on the balloting. Your visitors are of three kinds: one consists of morning callers who come to your house, a second of those who escort you to the Forum, the third of those who attend you on your canvass. In the case of the mere morning callers, who are less select, and according to present-day fashion, are decidedly numerous, you must contrive to think that you value even this slight attention very highly. It often happens that people when they visit a number of candidates, and

observe the one that pays special heed to their attentions, leave off visiting the others, and little by little become real supporters of this man.

Secondly, to those who escort you to the Forum: since this is a much greater attention than a mere morning call, indicate clearly that they are still more gratifying to you; and with them, as far as it shall lie in your power, go down to the Forum at fixed times, for the daily escort by its numbers produces a great impression and confers great personal distinction.

The third class is that of people who continually attend you upon your canvass. See that those who do so spontaneously understand that you regard yourself as forever obliged by their extreme kindness; from these on the other hand. who *owe* you the attention for services rendered frankly demand that so far as their age and business allow they should be constantly in attendance, and that those who are unable to accompany you in person, should find relatives to substitute in performing this duty. I am very anxious and think it most important that you should always be surrounded with numbers. Besides, it confers a great reputation, and great distinction to be accompanied by those whom you have defended and saved in the law courts. Put this demand fairly before them---that since by your means, and without any fee---some have retained property, others their honor, or their civil rights, or their entire fortunes---and since there will never be any other time when they can show their gratitude, they now should reward you by this service.

Marcus Cicero, Letter to His Brother Quintus, 54 BCE

There is a fearful recrudescence of bribery. Never was there anything like it. On the 15th of July the rate of interest rose from four to eight per cent, owing to the compact made by Memmius with the consul Domitius. I am not exaggerating. They offer as much as 10,000,000 sesterces for the vote of the first century. The matter is a burning scandal. The candidates for the tribuneship have made a mutual compact; having deposited 500,000 sesterces apiece with Cato, they agree to conduct their canvass according to his directions, with the understanding that any one offending against it will be condemned to forfeit by him.

SALLUST

Life in Rome in the Late Republic

Source: Sallust, *Conspiracy of Catiline* 11–16. From: William Stearns Davis, ed., *Readings in Ancient History: Illustrative Extracts from the Sources*, 2 Vols. (Boston: Allyn and Bacon, 1912-13), Vol. II: Rome and the West, pp. 135-138. Scanned by: J. S. Arkenberg, Dept. of History, Cal. State Fullerton. Prof. Arkenberg has modernized the text.

From the pessimistic point of view of the historian Sallust, Catiline's anarchistic conspiracy of 63 BCE was only possible in a society in which there were a great number of depraved and desperate men, ready for any enterprise, however villainous. (Sallust's view of the depravity the late Republic had reached is clear from the opening sentence of this excerpt.) For such spirits Catiline was an ideal leader. In this quotation from Sallust we see how it became possible for him to find a large following, and what manner of man he was personally.

After Sulla had recovered the government by force of arms, everybody became robbers and plunderers. Some set their hearts on houses, some on lands. His victorious troops knew no restraint, no moderation, but inflicted on the citizens disgraceful and inhumane outrages. The whole period was one of debauched tastes and lawlessness. When wealth was once counted an honor, and glory, authority, and power attended it, virtue lost her influence, poverty was thought a disgrace, and a life of innocence was regarded as a life of mere ill nature. From the influence of riches, accordingly, luxury, avarice, pride came to prevail among the youth. They grew at once rapacious and prodigal. They undervalued what was their own; they set at naught modesty and continence; they lost all distinction between sacred and profane, and threw off all consideration and self-restraint.

It is a serious matter for reflection, after viewing our modern mansions and villas, extended to the veritable size of cities, to contemplate the temples which our ancestors a most devout race of men, erected to the gods. But our forefathers adorned the fanes of the deities with devotion, and their homes with their own glory, and took nothing from what they conquered but the power of doing harm; their descendants on the contrary have even wrested from their allies, with rank injustice, whatever their brave and victorious ancestors had left to their vanquished enemies—as if the only use of power was to inflict injury. Why should I mention these displays of extraordinary luxury which now set in, which can be believed only by those who have seen them; as, for example, how mountains have been leveled, and seas actually built over with edifices by many a private citizen—men whom I deem to have made a sport of their wealth, since they were impatient to squander disreputably what they might have enjoyed with honor.

But the love of irregular gratification, open debauchery, and all kinds of luxury had spread abroad with no less force. Men and women alike threw off all restraints of modesty. To gratify appetite they sought for every kind of production by land or sea. They slept before there was any natural inclination to sleep. They no longer waited to feel hunger, thirst, or fatigue, but anticipated them all by luxurious indulgence. Such propensities drove young men, when their patrimonies were run through, to criminal practices; for their minds, impregnated with evil habits, could not easily abstain from gratifying their passions, and were thus the more inordinately devoted in every way to rapacity and extravagance.

In so populous and corrupt a city Catiline easily kept about him, as a bodyguard, crowds of the lawless and desperate. All the shameless libertines and profligate rascals were his associates and intimate friends—the men who had squandered their paternal estates by gaming, luxury, sensuality, and all too who had plunged heavily into debt to buy immunity for crimes; all assassins or sacrilegious persons from every quarter, convicted, or dreading conviction for their misdeeds; all, likewise, for whom their tongue or hand won a livelihood by perjury or bloodshed; all, in short, whom wickedness, poverty, or a guilty conscience goaded were friends to Catiline.

If any man of character as yet unblemished fell into his society, he presently rendered him by daily intercourse and temptation like to and equal to the rest. But it was the young whose acquaintance he chiefly courted and easily ensnared. For as the passions of each, according to his years, were aroused, he furnished mistresses to some, bought horses and dogs for others, and spared, in a word, neither his purse nor his character, if he could make them his devoted and trustworthy supporters.

Catiline was alleged to have corrupted a Vestal Virgin, and wrought many vile crimes; at last, smitten with a passion for a certain Aurelia, he murdered his own grown-up son, because she objected to marrying him and having in the house a grown-up stepson. And this crime seems to me to have been the chief cause of hurrying forward his conspiracy. For his guilty mind, at peace neither with gods nor men, found no comfort either waking or sleeping, so utterly did conscience desolate his tortured spirit. His complexion, in consequence, was pale, his eyes haggard, his walk sometimes quick and sometimes slow, and distraction was plainly evident in every feature and look.

The young men he enticed by various methods into evil practices. From among them he furnished false witnesses and forgers of signatures; and he taught them all to regard with equal unconcern property and danger. At length when he had stripped them of all character and shame he led them to other and greater iniquities. When there was no ready motive for crime, he nevertheless stirred them up to murder quite inoffensive persons, just as if they had injured him, lest their hand or heart should grow torpid for want of employment. Trusting to such confederates and comrades, and knowing that the load of debt was everywhere great, and that the veterans of Sulla, having spent their money too freely, now were longing for a civil war, remembering their spoils and former victory, Catiline accordingly formed the design of overthrowing the government.

SALLUST

Pompey's Letter to the Senate

Source: Sallust *Histories* 2.82 [2.98M]. Translated by John Carew Rolfe. *Sallust: With an English Translation by J. C. Rolfe.* Loeb classical library, 116. Cambridge, Mass: Harvard University Press, 1965.

Pompey wrote the following letter to the Senate in 75 requesting reinforcements in the fight against Sertorius, who was holding out successfully in Spain. Pompey was at the time a mere knight, given proconsular imperium by the senate to assist Metellus Pius against Sertorius two years before. This commission was primarily a device to get Pompey's illegal private army, which he refused to disband, out of Italy.

"If I had been warring against you, against my country, and against my fathers' gods, when I endured such hardship and dangers as those amid which from my early youth the armies under my command have routed the most criminal of your enemies and insured your safety; even then, Fathers of the Senate, you could have done no more against me in my absence than you are now doing. For after having exposed me, in spite of my youth, to a most cruel war, you have, so far as in you lay, destroyed me and a faithful army by starvation, the most wretched of all deaths.

"Was it with such expectations that the Roman people sent its sons to war? Are these the rewards for wounds and for so often shedding our blood for our country? Wearied with writing letters and sending envoys, I have exhausted my personal resources and even my expectations, and in the meantime for three years you have barely given me the means of meeting a year's expenses.

"By the immortal gods! do you think that I can play the part of a treasury or maintain an army without food or pay?

"I admit that I entered upon this war with more zeal than discretion; for within forty days of the time when I received from you the empty title of commander I had raised and equipped an army and driven the enemy, who were already at the throat of Italy, from the Alps into Spain; and over those mountains I had opened for you another and more convenient route than Hannibal had taken.

"I recovered Gaul, the Pyrenees, Lacetania, and the Indigetes; with raw soldiers and far inferior numbers I withstood the first onslaught of triumphant Sertorius; and I spent the winter in camp amid the most savage of foes, not in the towns or in adding to my own popularity.

"Why need I enumerate our battles or our winter campaigns, the towns which we destroyed or captured? Actions speak louder than words. The taking of the enemy's camp at Sucro, the battle at the river Turia, and the destruction of C. Herennius, leader of the enemy, together with his army and the city of Valentia, are well enough known to you. In return for these, grateful fathers, you give me want and hunger. Thus the condition of my army and of that of the enemy is the same; for neither is paid and either can march victorious into Italy.

"Of this situation I warn you and I beg you to give it your attention; do not force me to provide for my necessities on my own responsibility.

"Hither Spain, so far as it is not in the possession of the enemy, either we or Sertorius have devastated to the point of ruin, except for the coast towns, so that it is actually an expense and a burden to us. Gaul last year supplied the army of Metellus with pay and provisions, but can now scarcely keep itself alive because of a failure of the crops; I myself have exhausted not only my means, but even my credit.

"You are our only resource; unless you come to our rescue, against my will, but not without warning from me, our army will pass over into Italy, bringing with it all the war in Spain."

This letter was read in the senate at the beginning of the following year. But the consuls distributed the provinces which had been decreed by the senate, Cotta taking Hither Gaul and Octavius taking Cilicia. Then the next consuls, L. Lucullus and M. Cotta,[93] who were greatly agitated by Pompeius' letters and messages, both because of the interests of the state and because they feared that, if he led his army into Italy, they would have neither glory nor position, used every means to provide him with money and reinforcements. And they were aided especially by the nobles, the greater number of whom were already giving expression to their confidence and adapting their conduct to their words.

---

[93] For 74 BCE.

Against Catiline

Source: Cicero, *Cat. 1*. Translated by Charles Duke Yonge.

M. Tullius Cicero, a consul for the year 63, learned of L. Sergius Catilina's plans for armed revolt and decided that only by swaying the senate against the conspirators could he take effective action to stop the plot. He delivered this oration denouncing Catiline as a revolutionary during a specially convened meeting of the senate. Much to Cicero's surprise, Catiline was in attendance; however, the story goes that the senators adjacent to Catiline slowly moved away from him during the course of the speech.

WHEN, O Catiline, do you mean to cease abusing our patience? How long is that madness of yours still to mock us? When is there to be an end of that unbridled audacity of yours, swaggering about as it does now? Do not the nightly guards placed on the Palatine Hill—do not the watches posted throughout the city—does not the alarm of the people, and the union of all good men— does not the precaution taken of assembling the senate in this most defensible place—do not the looks and countenances of this venerable body here present, have any effect upon you? Do you not feel that your plans are detected? Do you not see that your conspiracy is already arrested and rendered powerless by the knowledge which every one here possesses of it? What is there that you did last night, what the night before—where is it that you were—who was there that you summoned to meet you—what design was there which was adopted by you, with which you think that any one of us is unacquainted?

Shame on the age and on its principles! The senate is aware of these things; the consul sees them; and yet this man lives. Lives! aye, he comes even into the senate. He takes a part in the public deliberations; he is watching and marking down and checking off for slaughter every individual among us. And we, gallant men that we are, think that we are doing our duty to the republic if we keep out of the way of his frenzied attacks.

You ought, O Catiline, long ago to have been led to execution by command of the consul. That destruction which you have been long plotting against us ought to have already fallen on your own head.

What? Did not that most illustrious man, P. Scipio, the Pontifex Maximus, in his capacity of a private citizen, put to death Ti. Gracchus, though but slightly undermining the constitution? And shall we, who are the consuls, tolerate Catiline, openly desirous to destroy the whole world with fire and slaughter? For I pass over older instances, such as how C. Servilius Ahala with his own hand slew S. Mælius when plotting a revolution in the state. There was—there was once such virtue in this republic that brave men would repress mischievous citizens with severer chastisement than the most bitter enemy. For we have a resolution of the senate, a formidable and authoritative decree against you, O Catiline; the wisdom of the republic is not at fault, nor the dignity of this senatorial body. We, we alone—I say it openly,—we, the consuls, are wanting in our duty.

The senate once passed a decree that L. Opimius, the consul, should take care that the republic suffered no injury. Not one night elapsed. There was put to death, on some mere suspicion of disaffection, C. Gracchus, a man whose family had borne the most unblemished reputation for many generations. There was slain M. Fulvius, a man of consular rank, and all his children. By a like decree of the senate the safety of the republic was entrusted to C. Marius and L. Valerius, the consuls. Did not the vengeance of the republic, did not execution overtake L. Saturninus, a tribune of the people, and C. Servilius, the praetor, without the delay of one single day? But we, for these twenty days, have been allowing the edge of the senate's authority to grow blunt, as it were. For we are in possession of a similar decree of the senate, but we keep it locked up in its parchment— buried, I may say, in the sheath; and according to this decree you ought, O Catiline, to be put to death this instant. You live,—and you live, not to lay aside, but to persist in your audacity.

I wish, O conscript fathers, to be merciful; I wish not to appear negligent amid such danger to the state; but I do now accuse myself of remissness and culpable inactivity. A camp is pitched in Italy, at the entrance of Etruria, in hostility to the republic; the number of the enemy increases every day; and yet the general of that camp, the leader of those enemies, we see within the walls—aye, and even in the senate—planning every day some internal injury to the republic. If, O Catiline, I should now order you to be arrested, to be put to death, I should, I suppose, have to fear lest all good men should say that I had acted tardily, rather than that any one should affirm that I acted cruelly. But yet this, which ought to have been done long since, I have good reason for not doing as yet; I will put you to death, then, when there shall be not one person possible to be found so wicked, so abandoned, so like yourself, as not to allow that it has been rightly done. As long as one person exists who can dare to defend you, you shall live; but you shall live as you do now, surrounded by my many and trusty guards, so that you shall not be able to stir one finger against the republic; many eyes and ears shall still observe and watch you, as they have hitherto done, though you shall not perceive them.

For what is there, O Catiline, that you can still expect, if night is not able to veil your nefarious meetings in darkness, and if private houses can not conceal the voice of your conspiracy within their walls—if everything is seen and displayed? Change your mind: trust me: forget the slaughter and conflagration you are meditating. You are hemmed in on all sides; all your plans are clearer than the day to us; let me remind you of them. Do you recollect that on the 21st of October I said in the senate that on a certain day, which was to be the 27th of October, C. Manlius, the satellite and servant of your audacity, would be in arms? Was I mistaken, Catiline, not only in so important, so atrocious, so incredible a fact, but, what is much more remarkable, in the very day? I said also in the senate that you had fixed the massacre of the nobles for the 28th of October when many chief men of the senate had left Rome, not so much for the sake of saving themselves as of checking your designs. Can you deny that on that very day you were so hemmed in by my guards and my vigilance that you were unable to stir one finger against the republic; when you said that you would be content with the flight of the rest, and the slaughter of us who remained? What? when you made sure that you would be able to seize Præneste on the 1st of November by a nocturnal attack, did you not find that that colony was fortified by my order, by my garrison, by my watchfulness and care? You do nothing, you plan nothing, you think of nothing which I not only do not hear, but which I do not see and know every particular of.

Listen while I speak of the night before. You shall now see that I watch far more actively for the safety than you do for the destruction of the republic. I say that you came the night before (I will say nothing obscurely) into the Scythedealers' Street, to the house of M. Lecca; that many of your accomplices in the same insanity and wickedness came there, too. Do you dare to deny it? Why are you silent? I will prove it if you do deny it; for I see here in the senate some men who were there with you.

O ye immortal gods, where on earth are we? in what city are we living? what constitution is ours? There are here,—here in our body, O conscript fathers, in this the most holy and dignified assembly of the whole world, men who meditate my death, and the death of all of us, and the destruction of this city, and of the whole world. I, the consul, see them; I ask them their opinion about the republic, and I do not yet attack, even by words, those who ought to be put to death by the sword. You were, then, O Catiline, at Lecca's that night; you divided Italy into sections; you settled where every one was to go; you fixed whom you were to leave at Rome, whom you were to take with you; you portioned out the divisions of the city for conflagration; you undertook that you yourself would at once leave the city, and said that there was then only this to delay you,—that I was still alive. Two Roman knights were found to deliver you from this anxiety, and to promise that very night, before daybreak, to slay me in my bed. All this I knew almost before your meeting had broken up. I strengthened and fortified my house with a stronger guard; I refused admittance, when they came, to those whom you sent in the morning to salute me, and of whom I had foretold to many eminent men that they would come to me at that time.

As, then, this is the case, O Catiline, continue as you have begun. Leave the city at least; the gates are open; depart. That Manlian camp of yours has been waiting too long for you as its general. And lead forth with you all your friends, or at least as many as you can; purge the city of your presence; you will deliver me from a great fear, when there is a wall between you and me. Among us you can dwell no longer—I will not bear it, I will not permit it, I will not tolerate it. Great thanks are due to the immortal gods, and to this very Jupiter Stator, in whose temple we are, the most ancient protector of this city, that we have already so often escaped so foul, so horrible, and so deadly an enemy to the republic. But the safety of the commonwealth must not be too often allowed to be risked on one man. As long as you, O Catiline, plotted against me while I was the consul-elect, I defended myself, not with a public guard, but by my own private diligence. When, in the next consular comitia, you wished to slay me when I was actually consul, and your competitors also, in the Campus Martius, I checked your nefarious attempt by the assistance and resources of my own friends, without exciting any disturbance publicly. In short, as often as you attacked me, I by myself opposed you, and that, too, though I saw that my ruin was connected with great disaster to the republic. But now you are openly attacking the entire republic. ...

For what is there, O Catiline, that can now afford you any pleasure in this city? for there is no one in it, except that band of profligate conspirators of yours, who does not fear you,—no one who does not hate you. What brand of domestic baseness is not stamped upon your life? What disgraceful circumstance is wanting to your infamy in your private affairs? From what licentiousness have your eyes, from what atrocity have your hands, from what iniquity has your whole body ever abstained? Is there one youth, when you have once entangled him in the temptations of your corruption, to whom you have not held out a sword for audacious crime, or a torch for licentious wickedness?

What? when lately by the death of your former wife you had made your house empty and ready for a new bridal, did you not even add another incredible wickedness to this wickedness? But I pass that over, and willingly allow it to be buried in silence, that so horrible a crime may not be seen to have existed in this city, and not to have been chastised. I pass over the ruin of your fortune, which you know is hanging over you against the ides of the very next month; I come to those things which relate not to the infamy of your private vices, not to your domestic difficulties and baseness, but to the welfare of the republic and to the lives and safety of us all. ...

But now, what is that life of yours that you are leading? For I will speak to you not so as to seem influenced by the hatred I ought to feel, but by pity, nothing of which is due to you. You came a little while ago into the senate; in so numerous an assembly, who of so many friends and connections of yours saluted you? If this in the memory of man never happened to any one else, are you waiting for insults by word of mouth, when you are overwhelmed by the most irresistible condemnation of silence? Is it nothing that at your arrival all those seats were vacated? that all the men of consular rank, who had often been marked out by you for slaughter, the very moment you sat down, left that part of the benches bare and vacant? With what feelings do you think you ought to bear this? On my honor, if my slaves feared me as all your fellow citizens fear you, I should think I must leave my house. Do not you think you should leave the city? If I say that I was even undeservedly so suspected and hated by my fellow citizens, I would rather flee from their sight than be gazed at by the hostile eyes of every one. And do you, who, from the consciousness of your wickedness, know that the hatred of all men is just and has been long due to you, hesitate to avoid the sight and presence of those men whose minds and senses you offend? If your parents feared and hated you, and if you could by no means pacify them, you would, I think, depart somewhere out of their sight. Now, your country, which is the common parent of all of us, hates and fears you, and has no other opinion of you, than that you are meditating parricide in her case; and will you neither feel awe of her authority, nor deference for her judgment, nor fear of her power?

And she, O Catiline, thus pleads with you, and after a manner silently speaks to you: There has now for many years been no crime committed but by you; no atrocity has taken place without you; you alone unpunished and unquestioned have murdered the citizens, have harassed and plundered the allies; you alone have had power not only to neglect all laws and investigations, but to overthrow and break through them. Your former actions, though they ought not to have been borne, yet I did bear as well as I could; but now that I should be wholly occupied with fear of you alone, that at every sound I should dread Catiline, that no design should seem possible to be entertained against me which does not proceed from your wickedness, this is no longer endurable. Depart, then, and deliver me from this fear—that, if it be a just one, I may not be destroyed; if an imaginary one, that at least I may at last cease to fear.

If, as I have said, your country were thus to address you, ought she not to obtain her request, even if she were not able to enforce it? What shall I say of your having given yourself into custody? what of your having said, for the sake of avoiding suspicion, that you were willing to dwell in the house of M. Lepidus? And when

you were not received by him, you dared even to come to me, and begged me to keep you in my house; and when you had received answer from me that I could not possibly be safe in the same house with you, when I considered myself in great danger as long as we were in the same city, you came to Q. Metellus, the praetor, and being rejected by him, you passed on to your associate, that most excellent man, M. Marcellus, who would be, I suppose you thought, most diligent in guarding you, most sagacious in suspecting you, and most bold in punishing you; but how far can we think that man ought to be from bonds and imprisonment who has already judged himself deserving of being given into custody. ...

And yet, why am I speaking? That anything may change your purpose? that you may ever amend your life? that you may meditate flight or think of voluntary banishment? I wish the gods may give you such a mind; though I see, if alarmed at my words you bring your mind to go into banishment, what a storm of unpopularity hangs over me, if not at present, while the memory of your wickedness is fresh, at all events hereafter. But it is worth while to incur that, as long as that is but a private misfortune of my own, and is unconnected with the dangers of the republic. But we can not expect that you should be concerned at your own vices, that you should fear the penalties of the laws, or that you should yield to the necessities of the republic, for you are not, O Catiline, one whom either shame can recall from infamy, or fear from danger, or reason from madness. ...

Though why should I invite you, by whom I know men have been already sent on to wait in arms for you at the forum Aurelium; who I know has fixed and agreed with Manlius upon a settled day; by whom I know that that silver eagle, which I trust will be ruinous and fatal to you and to all your friends, and to which there was set up in your house a shrine as it were of your crimes, has been already sent forward. Need I fear that you can long do without that which you used to worship when going out to murder, and from whose altars you have often transferred your impious hand to the slaughter of citizens?

You will go at last where your unbridled and mad desire has been long hurrying you. And this causes you no grief, but an incredible pleasure. Nature has formed you, desire has trained you, fortune has preserved you for this insanity. Not only did you never desire quiet, but you never even desired any war but a criminal one; you have collected a band of profligates and worthless men, abandoned not only by all fortune but even by hope.

Then what happiness will you enjoy! with what delight will you exult! in what pleasure will you revel! when in so numerous a body of friends, you neither hear nor see one good man. All the toils you have gone through have always pointed to this sort of life; your lying on the ground not merely to lie in wait to gratify your unclean desires, but even to accomplish crimes; your vigilance, not only when plotting against the sleep of husbands, but also against the goods of your murdered victims, have all been preparations for this. Now you have an opportunity of displaying your splendid endurance of hunger, of cold, of want of everything; by which in a short time you will find yourself worn out. All this I effected when I procured your rejection from the consulship, that you should be reduced to make attempts on your country as an exile, instead of being able to distress it as consul, and that that which had been wickedly undertaken by you should be called piracy rather than war.

Now that I may remove and avert, O conscript fathers, any in the least reasonable complaint from myself, listen, I beseech you, carefully to what I say, and lay it up in your inmost hearts and minds. In truth, if my country, which is far dearer to me than my life—if all Italy—if the whole republic were to address me, "M. Tullius, what are you doing? will you permit that man to depart whom you have ascertained to be an enemy? whom you see ready to become the general of the war? whom you know to be expected in the camp of the enemy as their chief, the author of all this wickedness, the head of the conspiracy, the instigator of the slaves and abandoned citizens, so that he shall seem not driven out of the city by you, but let loose by you against the city? Will you not order him to be thrown into prison, to be hurried off to execution, to be put to death with the most prompt severity? What hinders you? ...?"

To this holy address of the republic, and to the feelings of those men who entertain the same opinion, I will make this short answer: If, O conscript fathers, I thought it best that Catiline should be punished with death, I would not have given the space of one hour to this gladiator to live in. If, forsooth, those excellent men and most illustrious cities not only did not pollute themselves, but even glorified themselves by the blood of Saturninus, and the Gracchi, and Flaccus, and many others of old time, surely I had no cause to fear lest for slaying this parricidal murderer of the citizens any unpopularity should accrue to me with posterity. And if it did threaten me to ever so great a degree, yet I have always been of the disposition to think unpopularity earned by virtue and glory not unpopularity.

Though there are some men in this body who either do not see what threatens, or dissemble what they do see; who have fed the hope of Catiline by mild sentiments, and have strengthened the rising conspiracy by not believing it; influenced by whose authority many, and they not wicked, but only ignorant, if I punished him would say that I had acted cruelly and tyrannically. But I know that if he arrives at the camp of Manlius to which he is going, there will be no one so stupid as not to see that there has been a conspiracy, no one so hardened as not to confess it. But if this man alone were put to death,

I know that this disease of the republic would be only checked for a while, not eradicated forever. But if he banishes himself, and takes with him all his friends, and collects at one point all the ruined men from every quarter, then not only will this full-grown plague of the republic be extinguished and eradicated, but also the root and seed of all future evils.

We have now for a long time, O conscript fathers, lived among these dangers and machinations of conspiracy; but somehow or other, the ripeness of all wickedness, and of this long-standing madness and audacity, has come to a head at the time of my consulship. But if this man alone is removed from this piratical crew, we may appear, perhaps, for a short time relieved from fear and anxiety, but the danger will settle down and lie hid in the veins and bowels of the republic. As it often happens that men afflicted with a severe disease, when they are tortured with heat and fever, if they drink cold water, seem at first to be relieved, but afterward suffer more and more severely; so this disease which is in the republic, if relieved by the punishment of this man, will only get worse and worse, as the rest will be still alive.

Wherefore, O conscript fathers, let the worthless be gone,—let them separate themselves from the good,—let them collect in one place,—let them, as I have often said before, be separated from us by a wall; let them cease to plot against the consul in his own house,—to surround the tribunal of the city praetor,—to besiege the senate-house with swords,—to prepare brands and torches to burn the city; let it, in short, be written on the brow of every citizen, what his sentiments are about the republic. I promise you, this, O conscript fathers, that there shall be so much diligence in us the consuls, so much authority in you, so much virtue in the Roman knights, so much unanimity in all good men that you shall see everything made plain and manifest by the departure of Catiline,—everything checked and punished.

With these omens, O Catiline, be gone to your impious and nefarious war, to the great safety of the republic, to your own misfortune and injury, and to the destruction of those who have joined themselves to you in every wickedness and atrocity. Then do you, O Jupiter, who were consecrated by Romulus with the same auspices as this city, whom we rightly call the stay of this city and empire, repel this man and his companions from your altars and from the other temples,—from the houses and walls of the city,—from the lives and fortunes of all the citizens; and overwhelm all the enemies of good men, the foes of the republic, the robbers of Italy, men bound together by a treaty and infamous alliance of crimes, dead and alive, with eternal punishments.

Pompey's Conquest of the East

Appian, *Mithridatic Wars*, 114-119. Source: William Stearns Davis, ed., *Readings in Ancient History: Illustrative Extracts from the Sources*, 2 Vols. (Boston: Allyn and Bacon, 1912-13), *Vol. II: Rome and the West*, pp. 118-120, 123-127. Scanned by: J. S. Arkenberg, Dept. of History, Cal. State Fullerton. Prof. Arkenberg has modernized the text.

Pompey is usually overshadowed in most histories by his greater rival, Caesar, but he won marked successes along certain lines. The greatest thing that he did was to consolidate and organize the Roman power in Asia Minor, Syria, and Palestine. How important this work was, and how magnificent was the triumph that Pompey celebrated in Rome (September 30th, 61 B.C.) is told by Appian.

Pompeius Magnus [i.e., Pompey], having cleaned out the robber dens, and prostrated the greatest king living [Mithridates] in one and the same war; and having fought successful battles, besides those of the Pontic war, with Colchians, Albanians, Iberians, Armenians, Medes, Arabs, Jews, and other Eastern nations, extended the Roman sway as far as Egypt. He let some of the subjugated nations go free, and made them allies. Others he placed at once under Roman rule; still others he distributed to various vassal-kings.

He founded cities also: in Lesser Armenia was Nicopolis named for his victory; in Pontus Eupatoria (which Mithridates Eupator had built and named after himself, but destroyed because it had received the Romans without a fight) Pompeius Magnus rebuilt, and named it Magnopolis. In Cappadocia he rebuilt Mazaca, which had been completely ruined by the war. He restored other towns in many places, that had been destroyed or damaged, in Pontus, Palestine, Coele Syria, and Cilicia, in which he settled the greater part of the pirates he had conquered, and where the city formerly called Soli is now known as Pompeiopolis. The city of Talauri [in Pontus] Mithridates had used as a store house of furniture. Here were found 2000 drinking cups made of onyx welded with gold, and many cups, wine coolers, and drinking horns, bridles for horses, etc....all ornamented in like manner with gold and precious stones The quantity of this store was so great that the inventory of it occupied thirty days. These things had been inherited from Darius the Great of Persia and other mighty rulers.

At the end of the winter [63-62 BCE] Pompey distributed rewards to the army, 1500 Attic drachmas [Arkenberg: about $3857 in 1998 dollars] to each soldier, and in like proportion to the officers, the whole, it was said, amounting to 16,000 talents [Arkenberg: about $229 million in 1998 dollars]. Then he marched to Ephesus, embarked for Italy, and hastened to Rome, having dismissed his soldiers at Brundisium to their

homes, by which act his popularity was greatly increased among the Romans.

As he approached the city he was met by successive processions, first of youths, farthest from the city; then bands of men of different ages came out as far as they severally could walk; last of all came the Senate, which was lost in wonder at his exploits, for no one had ever before vanquished so powerful an enemy and at the same time brought so many great nations under subjection and extended the Roman rule to the Euphrates.

He was awarded a triumph exceeding in brilliancy any that had gone before. It occupied two successive days; and many nations were represented in the procession from Pontus, Armenia, Cappadocia, Cilicia, all the peoples of Syria, besides Albanians, Heniochi, Achaeans, Scythians, and Eastern Iberians; 700 complete ships were brought into the harbor; in the triumphal procession were two-horse carriages and litters laden with gold or with other ornaments of various kinds, also the couch of Darius [the Great], the son of Hystaspes, the throne and scepter of Mithridates Eupator himself, and his image, eight cubits high, made of solid gold, and 75,000,000 drachmae of silver coin [Arkenberg: about $193 million in 1998 dollars]. The number of wagons carrying arms was infinite and the number of prows of ships. After these came the multitude of captives and pirates, none of them bound, but all arrayed in their native costume.

Before Pompey himself were led the satraps, sons and generals of the kings against whom he had fought, who were present---some having been captured, some given as hostages---to the number of three hundred and twenty-four. Among them were five sons of Mithridates, and two daughters; also Aristobulus, king of the Jews; the tyrants of the Cilicians, and other potentates. There were carried in the procession images of those who were not present, of Tigranes king of Armenia, and of Mithridates, representing them as fighting, as vanquished, and as fleeing. Even the besieging of Mithridates and his silent flight by night were represented. Finally, it was shown how he died, and the daughters who perished with him were pictured also, and there were figures of the sons and daughters who died before him, and images of the barbarian gods decked out in the fashion of their countries. ...

Pompey himself was borne in a chariot studded with gems, wearing, it is said, the cloak of Alexander the Great, if any one can believe that. This was supposed to have been found among the possessions of Mithridates....His chariot was followed by the officers who had shared the campaigns with him, some on horseback, and others on foot. When he reached the Capitol, he did not put any prisoners to death, as had been customary at other triumphs, but sent them all home at the public expense, except the kings. Of these

Aristobulus alone was shortly put to death, and Tigranes son of Tigranes the king of Armenia some time later.

ASCONIUS

The Murder of Clodius

Source: Asconius, *Commentary on Pro Milone* 30C-36C. Translated by John Paul Adams (http://www.csun.edu/~hcfll004/asconius.htm). In *Orationum Ciceronis*. Oxford: At the Clarendon Press, 1966.

P. Clodius Pulcher, a populist, gave up his patrician status in order to qualify for the office of tribune of the plebs, which he achieved for 58 BCE. He and his enemy, Milo, tribune of the plebs in 57, continued to clash until the year they both ran for magistracies in 53. The context of this document is Asconius's commentary on Cicero's unsuccessful defense of Milo after Milo was accused of Clodius's murder.

T. Annius Milo [Papianus], P. Plautius Hypsaeus, and Q. Metellus Scipio sought the consulship[94] not only by spreading largesse openly but also accompanied by crews of armed men. There was the greatest possible personal hostility between Milo and Clodius, both because Milo was very close to Cicero and he had used his weight as tribune of the plebs in bringing Cicero back from exile;[95] and because P. Clodius was exceedingly hostile to Cicero once he had been brought back and was on that account very zealously supporting the candidacies of Hypsaeus and Scipio. Milo and Clodius also often engaged in violence with each other with their gangs in Rome. The chutzpah was equally outrageous on both sides, but Milo generally took the side of the 'better interests'. Besides that, in the same year Milo decided to stand for the consulship, and Clodius for the Praetorship (which he knew perfectly well would be less influential, if Milo were consul). In addition, when the electoral assemblies for consul went on for a long time, and were not able to produce a winner due to the very same riotous activities of the candidates, and for that reason in the month of January there were no consuls and no praetors at all, while the assemblies were being drug out just exactly as before—though Milo wanted the election to be completed as quickly as possible and was expecting that they would be thanks to the efforts of the aristocracy because he was standing in the way of Clodius, and also in the way of the populace on account of the 'gifts' which had been showered on them and the staggeringly huge costs of the theatrical spectacles and gladiatorial fight (on which Cicero remarks he had poured out three patrimonies).

His competitors wanted to drag things out, and so for that reason Pompeius, the son-in-law of [Metellus] Scipio, and T. Munatius [Plancus] tribune of the people had not allowed the question to be brought before the Senate as to the summoning of the Patricians to choose an Interrex, although a decree had been passed to name an interrex—on January 18 (the Decree and the oration itself, which agrees with the decree, ought to be followed as to the date, I think, rather than Fenestella, who gives January 17); on that day Milo made his official departure for Lanuvium, of which town he was at the time Dictator,[96] for the purpose of choosing a flamen on the next day.

Clodius, who was returning from Aricia (he had been addressing the Town Council of Aricia), ran into him around 3 p.m. a little beyond Bovillae, near the place where the shrine of the Bona Dea is located. Clodius was riding a horse. Approximately 30 mounted slaves carrying swords were following him, as was the custom at the time with people making a trip. Clodius also had three traveling companions with him: a Roman knight C. Causinius Schola and two well-known plebeians P. Pomponius and C. Clodius. Milo was being carried in a carriage with his wife Fausta, the daughter of L. Cornelius Sulla the Dictator, and with his close friend M. Fufius. A large contingent of slaves accompanied them, including gladiators; two of them were the famous Eudamus and Birria. These were riding at the end of the column and made a charge on the slaves of Clodius. When Clodius looked back at this disturbance with a threatening aspect, Birria wounded his shoulder with a thrust. Thereupon, when the battle had been begun, several of Milo's men rushed up. The wounded Clodius was carried to the nearest wine shop, in Bovillae. When Milo heard that Clodius had been wounded, while he realized that things would be even more dangerous for himself if Clodius were to survive, but, with him dead, he would have considerable peace of mind, even if he had to undergo some sort of punishment, he ordered him to be hustled out of the inn. M. Saufeius identified [Clodius] in advance to [Milo's] slaves. And so Clodius, though in hiding, was drug out and done away with, with many wounds. His dead body was left at the side of the road, because Clodius' slaves either had already been killed or were themselves in hiding with serious wounds. Sex. Teidius, a Senator, who by chance was making his return to the city from the countryside, picked it up and ordered it to be carried to Rome in his own sedan. He himself went back to where he had started from.

Clodius' corpse was brought back before 6:00 p.m., and a very large crowd of the lowest class of plebs and of slaves, with great lamentation, took up their positions around the corpse, when it was placed in the atrium of his house. Fulvia, the wife of Clodius, added to the appalling nature of the deed, however, when she kept pointing out his wounds, while pouring out her grief.

---

[94] in 53, for 52.
[95] During his tribunate Clodius had engineered the exile of the senatorial leader Cicero.

---

[96] In this case, dictator = "chief magistrate."

Next day, at dawn, an even greater crowd of the same composition assembled, and several gentlemen of note were seen. The house of Clodius, on the Palatine, had been bought a few months earlier from M. Scaurus: there came to this place T. Munatius Plancus (the brother of the speechifier L. Plancus) and Q. Pompeius Rufus (the grandson of Sulla the Dictator through his daughter), the tribunes of the plebs. At the urging of these men, the common people carried down into the Forum and placed on the Rostra Clodius' nude and barefoot body, unprepared for burial, just as it had been put into the sedan, so that the wounds could be seen.

There, in front of a public meeting, Plancus and Pompeius, who were partisans of Milo's electoral opponents, roused hatred against Milo. Under the direction of Sex. Clodius the scribe, the Populus carried the corpse of P. Clodius into the Senate House and cremated it, using the benches and risers and tables and books of the stenographers; thanks to this fire the Curia itself also burned down, and also the Basilica Porcia, which was attached to it, was fired. Also that same Clodian multitude attacked the residence of M. [Aemilius] Lepidus, the interrex, for he had been named the curule magistrate, and the absent Milo's too, but they were driven off from there by arrows. Then the crowd brought the fasces which had been snatched from the grove of Libitina to the residence of Scipio and of Hypsaeus, and then to the gardens of Cn. Pompeius, shouting repeatedly that he should be (if he wished) consul, or (if he preferred) dictator.

The burning down of the Senate House raised a greater indignation by far in the city than the slaughter of Clodius. And so Milo, whom general opinion believed to have gone into exile, encouraged by the hatred toward his adversaries returned to Rome the night that the Senate House had burned down. And not in the least deterred, he began to campaign for the consulship. Quite openly he gave to individuals tribe by tribe thousands of asses. After some days M. Caelius, tribune of the plebs, turned over a public meeting to him, and Cicero himself also supported his cause to the populace. Both of them kept saying that an assassination plot had been laid for Milo by Clodius.

Meanwhile one interrex succeeded another, because the electoral assemblies for consuls were not able to be held thanks to the same disorders on the part of the candidates and the same armed bands. And so, first of all, a Decree of the Senate was passed, ordering the interrex and the tribunes of the plebs and Cn. Pompeius (who was right outside the City as proconsul) 'to see to it that the Republic should suffer no harm', and that Pompeius should hold a military recruitment drive throughout the whole of Italy. When he put together a guard with extreme urgency, the two young aristocrats, the Appius Claudius brothers, demanded in his presence that the slaves belonging to Milo and likewise those belonging to his wife Fausta be produced. These Appii were the sons of C. Claudius, who had been the brother of Clodius, and on this account they were beginning the prosecution for the murder of their paternal uncle, in the name of their father, as it were. The two Valerii, Valerius Nepos and Valerius Leo, demanded the same slaves of Fausta and Milo. L. Herennius Balbus demanded the slaves of P. Clodius too, and those of his traveling companions. At the same time Caelius demanded the slaves of Hypsaeus and of Q. Pompeius. Q. Hortensius, M. [Tullius] Cicero, M. [Claudius] Marcellus, M. Calidius, M. Cato, and Faustus [Cornelius] Sulla supported Milo. Q. Hortensius spoke a few words to the effect that those persons were free men who were being demanded as though they were slaves. For immediately after the slaughter Milo had liberated them, using as his reason that they had saved his life. These affairs took up the intercalary month.

On approximately the 30th day after Clodius had been killed, Q. Metellus Scipio complained in a meeting of the Senate against Q. Caepio concerning this slaughter of P. Clodius. He stated that it was a lie that Milo was defending himself, but that Clodius was accompanied by 26 slaves when he had set off to give a speech to the Town Council of Aricia. But suddenly, after 10:00 a.m., when the Senate meeting ended, Milo rushed off after him with more than 300 armed slaves, and attacked him unawares during his journey, beyond Bovillae. At that point, P. Clodius, having suffered three wounds, was carried to Bovillae. The tavern in which he had taken refuge was attacked by Milo. Clodius was drug out semiconscious and killed on the Appian Way. His ring was pried off his finger as he lay dying. Then when Milo heard that Clodius' little son was in the Alban villa, he came to the villa, and after the boy had previously dragged off, he was asked permission by the slave Halicor to hack [Clodius] limb from limb; he strangled the steward and two servants besides. Of the slaves of Clodius who were defending their master 11 had been killed, of Milo's only two had been wounded. On account of this, next day Milo gave freedom to 12 slaves who had taken the greatest part, and he distributed to the populace, tribe by tribe, 1000 sesterces each in order to kill the rumors about himself. Milo was said to have sent people to Pompeius who were particularly friendly to Hypsaeus because Hypsaeus had been Pompeius's quaestor to say that Milo would quit his campaign for the consulship if Pompeius thought it a good idea. Pompeius replied that he did not authorize anybody either to seek the office or to quit seeking it, and that he had no intention of interfering with the power of the Roman Populus either with his advice (*consilium*) or his official opinion (*sententia*). Then, through C. Lucilius, who was Milo's friend because of his familiarity with M. Cicero, he is said to have ordered them as well not to burden him down with hostility by asking his advice about this affair.

In the midst of all this, as the rumor flew fast and thick that Cn. Pompeius ought to be created dictator and that the ills of the state could not otherwise be put to rest, it seemed to the optimates that it was safer for him to be named consul without colleague. When the matter had been introduced in the Senate, by an act proposed by M. Bibulus, Pompeius was named consul by the Interrex Ser. Sulpicius on the fifth day before the 1st of March in the intercalary month. He immediately entered upon his consulship. Next, two days later, he introduced the topic of making new laws: he promulgated two laws in accordance with senatorial decree, one *de vi* ('on violence') in which it remarked using names that a slaughter had taken place on the Via Appia, and the Senate House had been burned, and the house of the Interrex M. Lepidus had been attacked, and the other *de ambitu* ('on electoral corruption'): the penalty was to be heavier and the forms of trial briefer.

CICERO

Scipio's Dream

From *De Republica* Book VI. Source: Oliver J. Thatcher, ed., *The Library of Original Sources* (Milwaukee: University Research Extension Co., 1907), *Vol. III: The Roman World*, pp. 216-241. Scanned by: J. S. Arkenberg, Dept. of History, Cal. State Fullerton. Prof. Arkenberg has modernized the text..

> Cicero's "Dream of Scipio" (Latin, Somnium Scipionis) is from the sixth book of his treatise on the history, laws, and polity of the Roman republic, De re publica. It describes a fictional dream vision of the Roman general Scipio Aemilianus, set two years before he commanded at the destruction of Carthage in 146 BCE.

9. When I had arrived in Africa, where I was, as you are aware, military tribune of the fourth legion under the consul Manilius, there was nothing of which I was more earnestly desirous than to see King Massinissa, who, for very just reasons, had been always the especial friend of our family. When I was introduced to him, the old man embraced me, shed tears, and then, looking up to heaven, exclaimed I thank thee, O supreme Sun, and you also, you other celestial beings, that before I departed from this life I behold in my kingdom, and in my palace, P. Cornelius Scipio, by whose mere name I seem to be reanimated; so complete and indelibly is the recollection of that best and most invincible of men, Africanus, imprinted in my mind.

After this, I inquired of him concerning the affairs of his kingdom. He, on the other hand, questioned me about the condition of our commonwealth, and in this mutual interchange of conversation we passed the whole of that day.

10. In the evening, we were entertained in a manner worthy the magnificence of a king, and carried on our discourse for a considerable part of the night. And during all this time the old man spoke of nothing but Africanus, all whose actions, and even remarkable sayings, he remembered distinctly. At last, when we retired to bed, I fell in a more profound sleep than usual, both because I was fatigued with my journey, and because I had sat up the greatest part of the night.

Here I had the following dream, occasioned, as I verily believe, by our preceding conversation---for it frequently happens that the thoughts and discourses which have employed us in the daytime, produce in our sleep an effect somewhat similar to that which Ennius writes happened to him about Homer, of whom, in his waking hours, he used frequently to think and speak.

Africanus, I thought, appeared to me in that shape, with which I was better acquainted from his picture, than from any personal knowledge of him. When I perceived it was he, I confess I trembled with consternation; but he addressed me, saying, Take courage, my Scipio, be not afraid, and carefully remember what I am saying to you.

11. Do you see that city Carthage, which, though brought under the Roman yoke by me, is now renewing former wars, and cannot live in peace? (and he pointed to Carthage from a lofty spot, full of stars, and brilliant and glittering;) to attack which city you are this day arrived in a station not much superior to that of a private soldier. Before two years, however, are elapsed, you shall be consul, and complete its overthrow; and you shall obtain, by your own merit, the surname of Africanus, which, as yet, belongs to you no otherwise than as derived from me. And when you have destroyed Carthage, and received the honor of a triumph, and been made censor, and, in quality of ambassador, visited Egypt, Syria, Asia, and Greece, you shall be elected a second time consul in your absence, and by utterly destroying Numantia, put an end to a most dangerous war.

But when you have entered the Capitol in your triumphal car, you shall find the Roman commonwealth all in a ferment, through the intrigues of my grandson Tiberius Gracchus.

12. It is on this occasion, my dear Africanus, that you show your country the greatness of your understanding, capacity and prudence. But I see that the destiny, however, of that time is, as it were, uncertain; for when your age shall have accomplished seven times eight revolutions of the sun, and your fatal hours shall be marked out by the natural product of these two numbers, each of which is esteemed a perfect one, but for different reasons,---then shall the whole city have recourse to you alone, and place its hopes in your auspicious name. On you the senate, all good citizens, the

allies, the people of Latium, shall cast their eyes; on you the preservation of the state shall entirely depend. In a word, if you escape the impious machinations of your relatives, you will, in the quality of dictator, establish order and tranquility in the commonwealth.

When on this Laelius made an exclamation, and the rest of the company groaned loudly, Scipio, with a gentle smile, said---I entreat you, do not wake me out of my dream, but have patience, and hear the rest.

13. Now, in order to encourage you, my dear Africanus, continued the shade of my ancestor, to defend the state with the greater cheerfulness, be assured that for all those who have in any way conduced to the preservation, defense, and enlargement of their native country, there is a certain place in heaven, where they shall enjoy an eternity of happiness. For nothing on earth is more agreeable to God, the Supreme Governor of the universe, than the assemblies and societies of men united together by laws, which are called States. It is from heaven their rulers and preservers came, and there they return.

14. Though at these words I was extremely troubled, not so much at the fear of death, as at the perfidy of my own relations; yet I recollected myself enough to inquire, whether he himself, my father Paulus, and others whom we look upon as dead, were really living. Yes, truly, replied he, they all enjoy life who have escaped from the chains of the body as from a prison. But as to what you call life on earth, that is no more than one form of death. But see, here comes your father Paulus towards you! And as soon as I observed him, my eyes burst out into a flood of tears; but he took me in his arms, and bade me not weep.

15. When my first transports subsided, and I regained the liberty of speech, I addressed my father thus: You best and most venerable of parents, since this, as I am informed by Africanus, is the only substantial life, why do I linger on earth, and not rather hasten to come hither where you are? That, replied he, is impossible; unless that God, whose temples is all that vast expanse you behold, shall free you from the fetters of the body, you can have no admission into this place. Mankind have received their being on this very condition, that they should labor for the preservation of that globe, which is situated, as you see, in the midst of this temple, and is called earth.

Men are likewise endowed with a soul, which is a portion of the eternal fires, which you call stars and constellations; and which, being round, spherical bodies, animated by divine intelligence, perform their cycles and revolutions with amazing rapidity. It is your duty, there fore, my Publius, and that of all who have any veneration for the gods, to preserve this wonderful union of soul and body; nor without the express command of him who gave you a soul, should the least thought be entertained of quitting human life, lest you seem to desert the post assigned to you by God himself.

But rather follow the example of your grandfather here, and of me, your father, in paying a strict regard to justice and piety; which is due in a great degree to parents and relations, but most of all to our country. Such a life as this is the true way to heaven, and to the company of those, who, after having lived on earth and escaped from the body, inhabit the place which you now behold.

16. This was the shining circle, or zone, whose remarkable brightness distinguishes it among the constellations, and which, after the Greeks, you call the Milky Way. From thence, as I took a view of the universe, everything appeared beautiful and admirable; for there, those stars are to be seen that are never visible from our globe, and everything appears of such magnitude as we could not have imagined. The least of all the stars, was that removed furthest from heaven, and situated next to earth; I mean our moon, which shines with a borrowed light. Now the globes of the stars far surpass the magnitude of our earth, which at that distance appeared so exceedingly small, that I could not but he sensibly affected on seeing our whole empire no larger than if we touched the earth with a point.

17. And as long as I continued to observe the earth with great attention, How long, I pray you, said Africanus, will your mind be fixed on that object; why don't you rather take a view of the magnificent temples among which you have arrived? The universe is composed of nine circles, or rather spheres, one of which is the heavenly one, and is exterior to all the rest, which it embraces; being itself the Supreme God, and bounding and containing the whole. In it are fixed those stars which revolve with never-varying courses. Below this are seven other spheres, which revolve in a contrary direction to that of the heavens. One of these is occupied by the globe which on earth they call Saturn. Next to that is the star of Jupiter, so benign and salutary to mankind. The third in order, is that fiery and terrible planet called Mars. Below this again, almost in the middle region, is the Sun---the leader, governor, the prince of the other luminaries; the soul of the world, which it regulates and illumines, being of such vast size that it pervades and gives light to all places. Then follow Venus and Mercury, which attend, as it were, on the Sun. Lastly, the Moon, which shines only in the reflected beams of the Sun, moves in the lowest sphere of all. Below this, if we except that gift of the gods, the soul, which has been given by the liberality of the gods to the human race, every thing is mortal, and tends to dissolution, but above the moon all is eternal. For the Earth, which is in the ninth globe, and occupies the center, is immoveable, and being the lowest, all others gravitate towards it.

18. When I had recovered myself from the astonishment occasioned by such a wonderful prospect,

I thus addressed Africanus Pray what is this sound that strikes my ears in so loud and agreeable a manner? To which he replied It is that which is called the music of the spheres, being produced by their motion and impulse; and being formed by unequal intervals, but such as are divided according to the most just proportion, it produces, by duly tempering acute with grave sounds, various concerts of harmony. For it is impossible that motions so great should be performed without any noise; and it is agreeable to nature that the extremes on one side should produce sharp, and on the other flat sounds. For which reason the sphere of the fixed stars, being the highest, and being carried with a more rapid velocity, moves with a shrill and acute sound; whereas that of the moon, being the lowest, moves with a very flat one. As to the Earth, which makes the ninth sphere, it remains immovably fixed in the middle or lowest part of the universe. But those eight revolving circles, in which both Mercury and Venus are moved with the same celerity, give out sounds that are divided by seven distinct intervals, which is generally the regulating number of all things.

This celestial harmony has been imitated by learned musicians, both on stringed instruments and with the voice, whereby they have opened to themselves a way to return to the celestial regions, as have likewise many others who have employed their sublime genius while on earth in cultivating the divine sciences.

By the amazing noise of this sound, the ears of mankind have been in some degree deafened, and indeed, hearing is the dullest of all the human senses. Thus, the people who dwell near the cataracts of the Nile, which are called Catadupa, are, by the excessive roar which that river makes in precipitating itself from those lofty mountains, entirely deprived of the sense of hearing. And so inconceivably great is this sound which is produced by the rapid motion of the whole universe, that the human ear is no more capable of receiving it, than the eye is able to look steadfastly and directly on the sun, whose beams easily dazzle the strongest sight.

While I was busied in admiring the scene of wonders, I could not help casting my eyes every now and then on the earth.

19. On which Africanus said, I perceive that you are still employed in contemplating the seat and residence of mankind. But if it appears to you so small, as in fact it really is, despise its vanities, and fix your attention for ever on these heavenly objects. Is it possible that you should attain any human applause or glory that is worth the contending for? The earth, you see, is peopled but in a very few places, and those too of small extent; and they appear like so many little spots of green scattered through vast uncultivated deserts. And those who inhabit the earth are not only so remote from each other as to be cut off from all mutual correspondence, but their situation being in oblique or contrary parts of the globe,

or perhaps in those diametrically opposite to yours, all expectation of universal fame must fall to the ground.

20. You may likewise observe that the same globe of the earth is girt and surrounded with certain zones, whereof those two that are most remote from each other, and lie under the opposite poles of heaven, are congealed with frost; but that one in the middle, which is far the largest, is scorched with the intense heat of the sun. The other two are habitable, one towards the south---the inhabitants of which are your Antipodes, with whom you have no connection---the other, towards the north, is that which you inhabit, whereof a very small part, as you may see, falls to your share. For the whole extent of what you see, is as it were but a little island, narrow at both ends and wide in the middle, which is surrounded by the sea which on earth you call the great Atlantic ocean, and which, notwithstanding this magnificent name, you see is very insignificant. And even in these cultivated and well-known countries, has yours, or any of our names, ever passed the heights of the Caucasus, or the currents of the Ganges? In what other parts to the north or the south, or where the sun rises and sets, will your names ever be heard? And if we leave these out of the question, how small a space is there left for your glory to spread itself abroad? and how long will it remain in the memory of those whose minds are now full of it?

21. Besides all this, if the progeny of any future generation should wish to transmit to their posterity the praises of any one of us which they have heard from their forefathers, yet the deluges and combustions of the earth which must necessarily happen at their destined periods will prevent our obtaining, not only an eternal, but even a durable glory. And after all, what does it signify, whether those who shall hereafter be born talk of you, when those who have lived before you, whose number was perhaps not less, and whose merit certainly greater, were not so much as acquainted with your name?

22. Especially since not one of those who shall hear of us is able to retain in his memory the transactions of a single year. The bulk of mankind, indeed, measure their year by the return of the sun, which is only one star. But, when all the stars shall have returned to the place whence they set out, and after long periods shall again exhibit the same aspect of the whole heavens, that is what ought properly to be called the revolution of a year, though I scarcely dare attempt to enumerate the vast multitude of ages contained in it. For as the sun in old time was eclipsed, and seemed to be extinguished, at the time when the soul of Romulus penetrated into these eternal mansions, so, when all the constellations and stars shall revert to their primary position, and the sun shall at the same point and time be again eclipsed, then you may consider that the grand year is completed. Be

assured, however, that the twentieth part of it is not yet elapsed.

23. Why, if you have no hopes of returning to this place, where great and good men enjoy all that their souls can wish for, of what value, pray, is all that human glory, which can hardly endure for a small portion of one year?

If, then, you wish to elevate your views to the contemplation of this eternal seat of splendor, you will not be satisfied with the praises of your fellow-mortals, nor with any human rewards that your exploits can obtain; but Virtue herself must point out to you the true and only object worthy of your pursuit. Leave to others to speak of you as they may, for speak they will. Their discourses will be confined to the narrow limits of the countries you see, nor will their duration be very extensive, for they will perish like those who utter them, and will be no more remembered by their posterity.

24. When he had ceased to speak in this manner, I said Oh, Africanus, if indeed the door of heaven is open to those who have deserved well of their country, although, indeed, from my childhood, I have always followed yours and my father's steps, and have not neglected to imitate your glory, still I will from henceforth strive to follow them more closely.

Follow them, then, said he, and consider your body only, not yourself, as mortal. For it is not your outward form which constitutes your being, but your mind; not that substance which is palpable to the senses, but your spiritual nature. Know, then, that you are a god---for a god it must be which flourishes, and feels, and recollects, and foresees, and governs, regulates and moves the body over which it is set, as the Supreme Ruler does the world which is subject to him. For as that Eternal Being moves whatever is mortal in this world, so the immortal mind of man moves the frail body with which it is connected.

25. For whatever is always moving must be eternal, but that which derives its motion from a power which is foreign to itself, when that motion ceases must itself lose its animation. That alone, then, which moves itself can never cease to be moved, because it can never desert itself. Moreover, it must be the source, and origin, and principle of motion in all the rest. There can be nothing prior to a principle, for all things must originate from it, and it cannot itself derive its existence from any other source, for if it did it would no longer be a principle. And if it had no beginning it can have no end, for a beginning that is put an end to will neither be renewed by any other cause, nor will it produce anything else of itself. All things, therefore, must originate from one source. Thus it follows, that motion must have its source in something which is moved by itself, and which can neither have a beginning nor an end. Otherwise all the heavens and all nature must perish, for it is impossible that they can of

themselves acquire any power of producing motion in themselves.

26. As, therefore, it is plain that what is moved by itself must be eternal, who will deny that this is the general condition and nature of minds? For, as everything is inanimate which is moved by an impulse exterior to itself, so what is animated is moved by an interior impulse of its own; for this is the peculiar nature and power of mind. And if that alone has the power of self-motion it can neither have had a beginning, nor can it have an end.

Do you, therefore, exercise this mind of yours in the best pursuits. And the best pursuits are those which consist in promoting the good of your country. Such employments will speed the flight of your mind to this its proper abode; and its flight will be still more rapid, if, even while it is enclosed in the body, it will look abroad, and disengage itself as much as possible from its bodily dwelling, by the contemplation of things which are external to itself.

This it should do to the utmost of its power. For the minds of those who have given themselves up to the pleasures of the body, paying as it were a servile obedience to their lustful impulses, have violated the laws of God and man; and therefore, when they are separated from their bodies, flutter continually round the earth on which they lived, and are not allowed to return to this celestial region, till they have been purified by the revolution of many ages.

Thus saying he vanished, and I awoke from my dream.

SUETONIUS

On Julius Caesar

Source: Suet. *Div. Jul.* 1, 2, 10, 14, 20, 25, 31–36. Translated by Alexander Thompson and T. Forrester. In Kevin Guinagh and Alfred P. Dorjahn (eds.). *Latin Literature in Translation*. New York: Longmans, Green and Co, 1942.

Suetonius wrote The Twelve Caesars *around 121 CE, in the time of the emperor Hadrian. This work is important not only for details about the early emperors not preserved elsewhere, but also for the attitudes toward these men, their followers, and their accomplishments that obtained among Roman aristocrats a few generations later.*

Julius Caesar, the divine, lost his father when he was in the sixteenth year of his age; and the year following, being nominated to the office of high-priest of Jupiter, he repudiated Cossutia, who was very wealthy, although her family belonged only to the equestrian order, and to whom he had been contracted when he was a mere boy. He then married Cornelia, the daughter of Cinna, who was four times consul; and had by her, shortly afterwards, a daughter named Julia. Resisting all the efforts of the dictator Sulla to induce him to divorce Cornelia, he suffered the penalty of being stripped of his sacerdotal office, his wife's dowry, and his, own patrimonial estates; and, being identified with the adverse faction, was compelled to withdraw from Rome. After changing his place of concealment nearly every night, although he was suffering from a quartan ague, and having effected his release by bribing the officers who had tracked his footsteps, he at length obtained a pardon through the intercession of the vestal virgins, and of Mam. Aemilius and Aurelius Cotta, his near relatives. We are assured that when Sulla, having withstood for a while the entreaties of his own best friends, persons of distinguished rank, at last yielded to their importunity, he exclaimed- either by a divine impulse, or from a shrewd conjecture: "Your suit is granted, and you may take him among you; but know," he added, "that this man, for whose safety you are so extremely anxious, will, some day or other, be the ruin of the party of the nobles, in defense of which you are leagued with me; for in this one Caesar, you will find many a Marius."

His first campaign was served in Asia, on the staff of the praetor, M. Thermus; and being dispatched into Bithynia, to bring thence a fleet, he loitered so long at the court of Nicomedes, as to give occasion to reports of a criminal intercourse between him and that prince; which received additional credit from his hasty return to Bithynia, under the pretext of recovering a debt due to a freedman, his client. The rest of his service was more favorable to his reputation, and when Mitylene was taken by storm, he was presented by Thermus with the civic crown....

In his aedileship, he not only embellished the Comitium, and the rest of the Forum, with the adjoining halls, but adorned the Capitol also, with temporary piazzas, constructed for the purpose of displaying some part of the superabundant collections he had made for the amusement of the people. He entertained them with the hunting of wild beasts, and with games, both alone and in conjunction with his colleague. On this account, he obtained the whole credit of the expense to which they had jointly contributed; insomuch that his co]league, M. Bibulus, could not forbear remarking, that he was served in the manner of Pollux. For as the temple erected in the Forum to the two brothers went by the name of Castor alone, so his and Caesar's joint munificence was imputed to the latter only. To the other public spectacles exhibited to the people, Caesar added a fight of gladiators, but with fewer pairs of combatants than he had intended. For he had collected from all parts so great a company of them, that his enemies became alarmed; and a decree was made, restricting the number of gladiators which anyone was allowed to retain at Rome....

After he was chosen praetor, the conspiracy of Catiline was discovered; and while every other member of the senate voted for inflicting capital punishment on the accomplices in that crime, he alone proposed that the delinquents should be distributed for safe custody among the towns of Italy, their property being confiscated. He even struck such terror into those who were advocates for greater severity, by representing to them what universal odium would be attached to their memories by the Roman people, that Decius Silanus, consul elect, did not hesitate to qualify his proposal, it not being very honorable to change it, by a lenient interpretation; as if it had been understood in a harsher sense than he intended, and Caesar would certainly have carried his point, having brought over to his side a great number of the senators, among whom was Cicero, the consul's brother, had not a speech by M. Cato infused new vigor into the resolutions of the senate. He persisted, however, in obstructing the measure, until a body of the Roman knights, who stood under arms as a guard, threatened him with instant death, if he continued his determined opposition. They even thrust at him with their drawn swords, so that those who sat next him moved away; and a few friends, with no small difficulty, protected him, by throwing their arms round him, and covering him with their togas. At last, deterred by this violence, he not only gave way, but absented himself from the senate-house during the remainder of that year....

[At the end of his praetorship, Caesar drew Farther Spain. After quieting his creditors, he hurried off to his province. When peace was restored there, he hastened back to Rome to stand for the consulship. To this office he was elected with Bibulus.]

Having entered upon his office, he introduced a new regulation, that the daily acts both of the senate and people should be committed to writing, and published. He also revived an old custom, that an officer should precede him, and his lictors follow him, on the alternate months when the fasces were not carried before him. Upon preferring a bill to the people for the division of some public lands, he was opposed by his colleague, whom he violently drove out of the forum. Next day the insulted consul made a complaint in the senate of this treatment; but such was the consternation, that no one having the courage to bring the matter forward or move a censure, which had been often done under outrages of less importance, he was so much dispirited, that until the expiration of his office he never stirred from home, and did nothing but issue edicts to obstruct his colleague's proceedings. From that time, therefore, Caesar had the sole management of public affairs; insomuch that some wags, when they signed any instrument as witnesses, did not add "in the consulship of Caesar and Bibulus," but, "of Julius and Caesar;" putting the same person down twice, under his name and surname. The .following verses likewise were currently repeated on this occasion:

Non Bibulo quidquam nuper, sed Caesare factum est;
Nam Bibulo fieri consule nil memini.

Nothing was done in Bibulus's year:
No; Caesar only then was consul here.

The land of Stellas, consecrated by our ancestors to the gods, with some other lands in Campania left subject to tribute, for the support of the expenses of the government, he divided, but not by lot, among upwards of twenty thousand freemen, who had each of them three or more children. He eased the 'publicans, upon their petition, of a third part of the sum which they had engaged to pay into the public treasury; and openly admonished them not to bid so extravagantly upon the next occasion. He made various profuse grants to meet the wishes of others, no one opposing him; or if any such attempt was made, it was soon suppressed. M. Cato, who interrupted him in his proceedings, he ordered to be dragged out of the senate house by a lictor, and carried to prison. L. Lucullus, likewise, for opposing him with some warmth, he so terrified with the apprehension of being criminated, that to deprecate the consul's resentment, he fell on his knees. And upon Cicero's lamenting in some trial the miserable condition of the times, he the very same day, by nine o'clock, transferred his enemy, P. Clodius, from a patrician to a plebeian family; a change which he had long solicited in vain. At last, effectually to intimidate all those of the opposite party, he by great rewards prevailed upon Vettius to declare, that he had been solicited by certain persons to assassinate Pompey; and when he was brought before the rostra to name those who had been concerted between them, after naming one or two to no purpose, not without great suspicion of subornation, Caesar, despairing of success in this rash stratagem, is supposed to have taken off his informer by poison....

During nine years in which he held the government of the province, his achievements were as follows: he reduced all Gaul, bounded by the Pyrenean forest, the Alps, mount Gebenna, and the two rivers, the Rhine and the Rhone, and being about three thousand two hundred miles in compass, into the form of a province, excepting only the nations in alliance with the republic, and such as had merited his favor; imposing upon this new acquisition an 'annual tribute of forty millions of sesterces. He was the first of the Romans who, crossing the Rhine by a bridge, attacked the Germanic tribes inhabiting the country beyond that river, whom he defeated in several engagements. He also invaded the Britons, a people formerly unknown, and having vanquished them, exacted from them contributions and hostages. Amidst such a series of successes, he experienced thrice only any signal disaster; once in Britain, when his fleet was nearly wrecked in a storm; in Gaul, at Gergovia, where one of his legions was put to the rout; and in the territory of the Germans, his lieutenants Titurius and Aurunculeius were cut off by an ambuscade....

The Civil War

When intelligence, therefore, was received, that the interposition of the tribunes in his favor had been utterly rejected, and that they themselves had fled from the City, he Immediately sent forward some cohorts, but privately, to prevent any Suspicion of his design; and, to keep up appearances, attended at a public spectacle, examined the model of a fencing-school which he proposed to build, and as usual sat down to table with a numerous party of his friends. But after sun-set, mules being put to his carriage from a neighboring mill, he set forward on his journey with all possible privacy, and a small retinue. The lights g0ing out, he lost his way, and wandered about a long' time, until at length, by the help of a guide, whom he found towards day-break, he proceeded on foot through some narrow paths, and again reached the road. Coming up with his troops on the banks of the Rubicon, which was the boundary of his province, he halted for a while, and, revolving in his mind the importance of the step he was on the point of taking, he turned to those about him, and said: "We may still retreat; but if we pass this little bridge, nothing is left for us but to fight it out in arms."

While he was thus hesitating, the following incident occurred. A person remarkable for his noble mien and graceful aspect, appeared close at hand, sitting and playing upon a pipe. When, not only the shepherds, but a number of soldiers also flocked from their posts to listen to him, and some trumpeters among them, he snatched a trumpet from one of them, ran to the river with it, and sounding the advance with a piercing blast, crossed to the other Side. Upon this Caesar exclaimed, "Let us go whither the omens of the Gods and 'the iniquity of our enemies call us. The die is now cast."

Accordingly, having marched his army over the river, he showed them the tribunes of the people, who, upon their being driven from the city, had come to meet him; and, in the presence of that assembly, called upon the troops to pledge him their fidelity, with tears in his eyes, and his garment rent from his bosom. It has been supposed, that upon this occasion he promised to every soldier a knight's estate; but that opinion is founded on a mistake. For when, in his harangue to them, he frequently held out a finger of his left hand and declared, that to recompense those who should support him in the defense of his honor, he would willingly part even with his ring; the soldiers at a distance, who could more easily see than hear him while he spoke, formed their conception of what he said, by the eye, not by the ear; and accordingly gave out, that he had promised to each of them the privilege of wearing the gold ring, and an estate of four hundred thousand sesterces.

Of his subsequent proceedings I shall give a cursory detail, in the order in which they occurred. He took possession of Picenurn, Umbria, and Etruria; and having obliged L. Domitius, who had been tumultuously nominated his successor, and held Corsinium with a garrison, to surrender, and dismissed him, he marched along the coast of the Upper Sea, to Brundusium, to which place the consuls and Pompey were fled with the intention of crossing the sea as soon as possible. After vain attempts, by all the obstacles he could oppose, to prevent their leaving the harbor, he turned his steps towards Rome, where he appealed to the senate on the present state of public affairs; and then set out for Spain, in which province Pompey had a numerous army, under the command of three lieutenants, M. Petreius, L. Afranius, and M. Varro; declaring amongst his friends, before he set forward, "That he was going against an army without a general, and should return thence against a general without an army." Though his progress was retarded both by the siege of Marseilles, which shut her gates against him, and a very great scarcity of corn, yet in a short time he bore down all before him.

Thence he returned to Rome, and crossing the sea to Macedonia, blocked up Pompey during almost four months, within a line of ramparts of prodigious extent; and at last defeated him in the battle of Pharsalia. Pursuing him in his flight to Alexandria, where he was informed of his murder, he presently found himself also engaged, under all the disadvantages of time and place, in a very dangerous war, with king Ptolemy, who, he saw, had treacherous designs upon his life. It was winter, and he, Within the walls of a well-provided and subtle enemy, was destitute of everything, and wholly unprepared for such a conflict. He succeeded, however, in his enterprise, and put the kingdom of Egypt into the hands of Cleopatra and her younger brother; being afraid to make it a province, lest, under an aspiring prefect, it might become the centre of revolt. From Alexandria he went into Syria, and thence to Pontus, induced by intelligence which he had received respecting Pharnaces. This prince, who was son of the great Mithridates, had seized the opportunity which the distraction of the times offered for making war upon his neighbors, and his insolence and fierceness had grown with his success. Caesar, however, within five days after entering his country, and four hours after coming in sight of him, overthrew him in one decisive battle. Upon which, he frequently remarked to those about him the good fortune of Pompey, who had obtained his military reputation, chiefly, by victory over so feeble an enemy. He afterwards defeated Scipio and Juba, who were rallying the remains of the party in Africa, and Pompey's sons in Spain.

During the whole course of the civil war, he never once suffered any defeat, except in the case of his lieutenants; of whom C. Curio fell in Africa, C. Antonius was made prisoner in Illyricum, P. Dolabella lost a fleet in the same Illyricum, and Cneius Domitius Calvrnus, an army in Pontus. In every encounter With the enemy where he himself commanded, he came off with complete success; nor was the issue ever doubtful, except on two occasions; once at Dyrrachium, when, being obliged to give ground, and Pompey not pursuing his advantage, he said that "Pompey knew not how to conquer;" the other instance occurred in his last battle in Spain, when, despairing of the event, he even had thoughts of killing himself.

PLUTARCH

The Assassination of Julius Caesar

Source: Plutarch. Lives, from *Marcus Brutus* (excerpts). translated by John Dryden

The assassination of Julius Caesar is told here in the context of the biography of one of his assassins, M. Junius Brutus.

From this time they tried the inclinations of all their acquaintances that they durst trust, and communicated the secret to them, and took into the design not only their familiar friends, but as many as they believed bold and brave and despisers of death. For which reason they concealed the plot from Cicero, though he was very much trusted and as well beloved by them all, lest, to his own disposition, which was naturally timorous, adding now the weariness and caution of old age, by his weighing, as he would do, every particular, that he might not make one step without the greatest security, he should blunt the edge of their forwardness and resolution in a business which required all the dispatch imaginable.

As indeed there were also two others that were companions of Brutus, Statilius the Epicurean, and Favonius the admirer of Cato, whom he left out for this reason: as he was conversing one day with them, trying them at a distance, and proposing some such question to be disputed of as among philosophers, to see what opinion they were of, Favonius declared his judgment to be that a civil war was worse than the most illegal monarchy; and Statilius held, that to bring himself into troubles and danger upon the account of evil or foolish men did not become a man that had any wisdom or discretion. But Labeo, who was present, contradicted them both and Brutus, as if it had been an intricate dispute, and difficult to be decided, held his peace for that time, but afterwards discovered the whole design to Labeo, who readily undertook it. The next thing that was thought convenient was to gain the other Brutus surnamed Albinus, a man of himself of no great bravery or courage, but considerable for the number of gladiators that he was maintaining for a public show, and the great confidence that Caesar put in him. When Cassius and Labeo spoke with him concerning the matter, he gave them no answer; but, seeking an interview with Brutus himself alone, and finding that he was their captain, he readily consented to partake in the action. And among the others, also, the most and best were gained by the name of Brutus. And, though they neither gave nor took any oath of secrecy, nor used any other sacred rite to assure their fidelity to each other, yet all kept their design so close, were so wary, and held it so silently among themselves that, though by prophecies and apparitions and signs in the sacrifices the gods gave warning of it, yet could it not be believed.

But a meeting of the senate being appointed, at which it was believed that Caesar would be present, they agreed to make use of that opportunity; for then they might appear all together without suspicion; and, besides, they hoped that all the noblest and leading men of the commonwealth, being then assembled as soon as the great deed was done, would immediately stand forward and assert the common liberty. The very place too where the senate was to meet seemed to be by divine appointment favorable to their purpose. It was a portico, one of those joining the theatre, with a large recess, in which there stood a statue of Pompey, erected to him by the commonwealth, when he adorned that part of the city with the porticos and the theatre. To this place it was that the senate was summoned for the middle of March (the Ides of March is the Roman name for the day); as if some more than human power were leading the man thither, there to meet his punishment for the death of Pompey.

As soon as it was day, Brutus, taking with him a dagger, which none but his wife knew of, went out. The rest met together at Cassius's house, and brought forth his son that was that day to put on the manly gown, as it is called, into the forum; and from thence, going all to Pompey's porch, stayed there, expecting Caesar to come without delay to the senate. Here it was chiefly that any one who had known what they had purposed, would have admired the unconcerned temper and the steady resolution of these men in their most dangerous undertaking; for many of them, being praetors, and called upon by their office to judge and determine causes, did not only hear calmly all that made application to them and pleaded against each other before them, as if they were free from all other thoughts, but decided causes with as much accuracy and judgment as they had heard them with attention and patience. And when one person refused to stand to the award of Brutus, and with great clamor and many attestations appealed to Caesar, Brutus, looking round about him

upon those that were present, said, "Caesar does not hinder me, nor will he hinder me, from doing according to the laws."...

For now news was brought that Caesar was coming, carried in a litter. For, being discouraged by the ill-omens that attended his sacrifice, he had determined to undertake no affairs of any great importance that day, but to defer them till another time, excusing himself that he was sick. As soon as he came out of his litter, Popilius Laenas, he who but a little before had wished Brutus good success in his undertaking, coming up to him, conversed a great while with him, Caesar standing still all the while, and seeming to be very attentive. The conspirators (to give them this name), not being able to hear what he said, but guessing by what themselves were conscious of that this conference was the discovery of their treason, were again disheartened, and, looking upon one another, agreed from each others countenances that they should not stay to be taken, but should all kill themselves. And now when Cassius and some others were laying hands upon their daggers under their robes, and were drawing them out, Brutus, viewing narrowly the looks and gesture of Laenas, and finding that he was earnestly petitioning and not accusing, said nothing, because there were many strangers to the conspiracy mingled amongst them: but by a cheerful countenance encouraged Cassius. And after a little while, Laenas, having kissed Caesars hand, went away, showing plainly that all his discourse was about some particular business relating to himself.

Now when the senate was gone in before to the chamber where they were to sit, the rest of the company placed themselves close about Caesars chair, as if they had some suit to make to him, and Cassius, turning his face to Pompey's statue, is said to have invoked it, as if it had been sensible of his prayers. Trebonius, in the meanwhile, engaged Antony's attention at the door, and kept him in talk outside. When Caesar entered, the whole senate rose up to him. As soon as he was sat down, the men all crowded round about him, and set Tillius Cimber, one of their own number, to intercede in behalf of his brother that was banished; they all joined their prayers with his, and took Caesar by the hand, and kissed his head and his breast. But he putting aside at first their supplications, and afterwards, when he saw they would not desist, violently rising up, Tillius with both hands caught hold of his robe and pulled it off from his shoulders, and Casca, that stood behind him, drawing his dagger, gave him the first, but a slight wound, about the shoulder. Caesar snatching hold of the handle of the dagger, and crying out aloud in Latin, "Villain Casca, what do you?" he, calling in Greek to his brother, bade him come and help. And by this time, finding himself struck by a great many hands, and looking around about him to see if he could force his way out, when he saw Brutus with his dagger drawn against him, he let go

Casca's hand, that he had hold of and covering his head with his robe, gave up his body to their blows. And they so eagerly pressed towards the body, and so many daggers were hacking together, that they cut one another; Brutus, particularly, received a wound in his hand, and all of them were besmeared with the blood.

Caesar being thus slain, Brutus, stepping forth into the midst, intended to have made a speech, and called back and encouraged the senators to stay; but they all affrighted ran away in great disorder, and there was a great confusion and press at the door, though none pursued or followed. For they had come to an express resolution to kill nobody beside Caesar, but to call and invite all the rest to liberty. It was indeed the opinion of all the others, when they consulted about the execution of their design, that it was necessary to cut off Antony with Caesar, looking upon him as an insolent man, an affecter of monarchy, and one that, by his familiar intercourse, had gained a powerful interest with the soldiers. And this they urged the rather, because at that time to the natural loftiness and ambition of his temper there was added the dignity of being counsel and colleague to Caesar. But Brutus opposed this consul, insisting first upon the injustice of it, and afterwards giving them hopes that a change might be worked in Antony. For he did not despair but that so highly gifted and honorable a man, and such a lover of glory as Antony, stirred up with emulation of their great attempt, might, if Caesar were once removed, lay hold of the occasion to be joint restorer with them of the liberty of his country. Thus did Brutus save Antony's life.

CICERO

On the Rise of Augustus

Cicero, *Letters* DCCCXVI (F X, 28); DCCCXXXIX (BRUT. II, 5), DCCCXLI (BRUT. I, 3, §§ 1-3), CMIX (BRUT. I, 15). In *The Letters of Cicero; the whole extant correspondence in chronological order*, in four volumes. Evelyn S. Shuckburgh. London. George Bell and Sons. 1908-1909.

> *These letters were written in 43 BCE, after the assassination of Julius Caesar, whom Cicero regarded as a tyrant and a danger to Roman liberty. Cicero here shows that he regards the 19-year-old Octavian, usually referred to as young Caesar (after Caesar's death he was adopted via the dictator's will, becoming C. Julius Caesar Octavianus, or Octavian in modern histories), as a defender of the state against Caesar's ambitious lieutenant, M. Antonius, and—most tellingly—as a protégé of Cicero himself.*

To C. Trebonius (In Asia): Rome, 2 February

How I could wish that you had invited me to that most glorious banquet on the Ides of March! We should have had no leavings! While, as it is, we are having such a trouble with them, that the magnificent service which you men then did the state leaves room for some grumbling. In fact, for Antony's having been taken out of the way by you—the best of men—and that it was by your kindness that this pest still survives, I sometimes do feel, though perhaps I have no right to do so, a little angry with you. For you have left behind an amount of trouble which is greater for me than for everyone else put together.

For as soon as a meeting of the senate could be freely held, after Antony's very undignified departure,[97] I returned to that old courage of mine, which along with that gallant taking over the province, as though he were "succeeding" to the governorship, without allowing his predecessor even the thirty days beyond his year given him by the Julian law. citizen, your father, you ever had upon your lips and in your heart. For the tribunes having summoned the senate for the 20th of December, and having brought a different piece of business before it, I reviewed the situation as a whole, and spoke with the greatest fire, and tried all I could to recall the now languid and wearied senate to its ancient and traditional valor, more by an exhibition of high spirit than of eloquence.[98]

This day and this earnest appeal from me were the first things that inspired the Roman people with the hope of recovering its liberty. And had not I supposed that a gazette of the city and of all acts of the senate was transmitted to you, I would have written you out a copy with my own hand, though I have been overpowered with a multiplicity of business. But you will learn all that from others. From me you shall have a brief narrative, and that a mere summary. Our senate is courageous, but the consulars are partly timid, partly disaffected.[99] We have had a great loss in Servius.[100] L. Caesar entertains the most loyal sentiments, but, being Antony's uncle, he refrains from very strong language in the senate. The consuls are splendid. D. Brutus is covering himself with glory. The youthful Caesar is behaving excellently, and I hope he will go on as he has begun. You may at any rate be sure of this—that, had he not speedily enrolled the veterans, and had not the two legions transferred themselves from Antony's army to his command, and

---

[97] When Antony had met the legions from Macedonia at Brundisium, he preceded them with a strong detachment to Rome, arriving between the 15th and 22nd of November, his main body of troops being ordered to muster at Tibur. He ordered in an edict a meeting of the senate un the 23rd, but did not appear, having put off the meeting by another edict to the 28th. He, however, only transacted some formal business—a supplicatio in honour of Lepidus, and a sortitio of the provinces—and then hurriedly left the city for Tibur, probably on hearing of the desertion of the two legions.

[98] This is the speech known as the third Philippic.

[99] Cicero had advocated in the senate on the 1st and following days of January the most uncompromising hostility to Antony, the fullest recognition of Octavian and of the action of the two legions, and of D. Brutus. But he could not get his motion passed, the embassy to Antony being voted on the 7th, as a tentative measure before proceeding to extremities.

[100] Ser. Sulpicius Rufus, who died while on the mission in Antony's camp, near Mutina.

had not Antony been confronted with that danger, there is no crime or cruelty which he would have omitted to practice. Though I suppose these facts to have been told you, yet I wished you to know them still better. I will write more when I get more leisure.

To M. Junius Brutus (At Dyrrachium): Rome, 16 April

I believe that your friends—to not one of whom do I yield in affection to you—have written to tell you what dispatches were read in the senate on the 13th of April from you, and at the same time from Antony. But though there was no need for us all to repeat the same story, yet it is necessary that I should write and tell you my feeling, deliberate opinion, and sentiments as to the nature of this war generally. My object, Brutus, in imperial politics has always been the same as your own: my policy in certain points-not in all-has perhaps been somewhat more drastic. You know that it was always my opinion that the Republic should be delivered not only from a tyrant but from a tyranny also.[101] You took a more indulgent view-to your own undying honor, no doubt. But which was the better course we have felt to our bitter sorrow, and are still feeling to our grave peril. More recently you have directed all your efforts to secure peace—which could not be brought about by mere words—I to secure liberty, which is impossible without peace.[102] But my view was that peace itself could be brought about by war and arms. There was no want of enthusiasts who were eager to fight, but we checked their enthusiasm and damped their ardor. And so it had come to such a pass that, had not some god inspired Caesar Octavianus with that resolution, we must necessarily have fallen under the power of M. Antonius, the most abandoned and depraved of men, with whom you see at this very moment in what a desperate contest we are engaged. Now that, of course, would never have occurred if Antony had not been spared at that time.[103] But I pass over these reflections: for the deed which you performed-ever memorable and all but divine-disarms all criticism, for it is one which can never be even praised in terms adequate to its merit....

To M. Junius Brutus (At Dyrrachium): Rome, 21 April

Our cause seems in a better position: for I feel sure that you have had letters telling you what has happened.[104] The consuls[105] have shown themselves to be the sort of men I have often described them in my letters. In the youthful Caesar indeed there is a surprising natural strain of virtue. Pray heaven we may govern him in the flush of honors and popularity as easily as we have held him up to this time. That is certainly a more difficult thing, but nevertheless I have no mistrust. For the young man has been convinced, and chiefly by my arguments, that our safety is his work, and that at least, if he had not diverted Antony from the city, all would have been lost.[106] Three or four days indeed before this glorious news, the city, struck by a sudden panic,[107] was for pouring out with wives and children to seek you. The same city on the 20th of April, with its fears all dispelled, would rather that you came here than go to you. On that day in very truth I reaped the most abundant harvest of my great labors and my many sleepless nights—that is, at least, if there is a harvest in genuine and well-grounded glory. For I was surrounded by a concourse of people as great as our city can contain, by whom I was escorted to the Capitol and placed upon the rostra[108] amidst the loudest cheers and applause. I have no vanity in me—and indeed I ought to have none: yet after all a unanimous feeling of all orders, thanks, and congratulations do move my heart, because it is a thing to be proud of that in the hour of the people's preservation I should be the people's hero. But these things I would rather you heard from others. Pray inform me of your own doings and plans with the greatest exactness; and do be careful that your generosity does not bear the appearance of weakness.[109] This is the sentiment of the senate, and of the people, that no enemies ever more richly deserved condign punishment than those citizens who have taken up arms against their country in this war. Indeed in every speech I make in the senate I call for vengeance upon them and attack them amidst the applause of all loyal citizens. What your view of this is I must leave you to judge for yourself: my opinion is that all three brothers stand on one and the same ground.

---

[101] That is, that Antony should have shared the fate of Caesar. See pp. 174, 214, etc.
[102] Cicero puts the converse in Phil. 2.113, when he says that "peace is liberty without war," pax est tranquilla libertas.
[103] That is, when Caesar was murdered. Cicero still labours under the delusion that the revolution all depended on one man. If Antony had been murdered on the Ides of March, were there no others ready to play his part, and still more ably? Augustus is the best answer. It is well to observe how little mere assassination has ever been able to effect in political movements.
[104] The victory of Forum Gallorum over Antony's troops, let in part by Octavian.
[105] C. Vibius Pansa Caetronianus and A. Hirtius, whom Octavian assisted as a private citizen.
[106] Cicero argues that Octavian's consciousness of having done the loyalists a good service will attach him the more to them. He will be unwilling to forfeit the good opinion he has earned. He little knew Octavian and his secret purposes.
[107] This appears to have been caused by the action of the praetor Ventidius Bassus, who enrolled two legions of veterans, and was supposed to be coming to Rome to seize Cicero and the leading opponents of Antony. He, however, marched to Ariminum, and succeeded in joining Antony after the battle by a splendid march across country to Vado (Appian, BCE 3.66).
[108] The rostra of course was not on the Capitol, and this has been put forward as an argument against the genuineness of the letter. I think Cicero may be putting the story shortly. The procession first went to the Capitol to offer thanks to Iupiter, and then came down to the forum to be addressed from the rostra.
[109] That is, in sparing C. Antonius.

To M. Junius Brutus (In Macedonia): Rome (mid-July)

...But what has been my aim during this war in the motions I have made in the senate I think it will not be out of place to explain. After the death of Caesar and your ever memorable Ides of March, Brutus, you have not forgotten what I said had been omitted by you and your colleagues, and what a heavy cloud I declared to be hanging over the Republic. A great pest had been removed by your means, a great blot on the Roman people wiped out, immense glory in truth acquired by yourselves: but an engine for exercising kingly power had been put into the hands of Lepidus and Antony, of whom the former was the more fickle of the two, the latter the more corrupt, but both of whom dreaded peace and were enemies to quiet. Against these men, inflamed with the ambition of revolutionizing the state, we had no protecting force to oppose. For the fact of the matter was this: the state had become roused as one man to maintain its liberty; I at the time was even excessively warlike; you, perhaps with more wisdom, quitted the city which you had liberated, and when Italy offered you her services declined them. Accordingly, when I saw the city in the possession of parricides, and that neither you nor Cassius could remain in it with safety, and that it was held down by Antony's armed guards, I thought that I too ought to leave it: for a city held down by traitors, with all opportunity of giving aid cut off, was a shocking spectacle. But the same spirit as always had animated me, staunch to the love of country, did not admit the thought of a departure from its dangers. Accordingly, in the very midst of my voyage to Achaia, when in the period of the Etesian gales a south wind—as though remonstrating against my design—had brought me back to Italy, I saw you at Velia and was much distressed: for you were on the point of leaving the country, Brutus—leaving it, I say, for our friends the Stoics deny that wise men ever "flee."

As soon as I reached Rome I at once threw myself in opposition to Antony's treason and insane policy: and having roused his wrath against me, I began entering upon a policy truly Brutus-like—for this is the distinctive mark of your family—that of freeing my country. The rest of the story is too long to tell, and must be passed over by me, for it is about myself. I will only say this much: that this young Caesar, thanks to whom we still exist, if we would confess the truth, was a stream from the fountain-head of my policy. To him I voted honors, none indeed, Brutus, that were not his due, none that were not inevitable. For directly we began the recovery of liberty, when the divine excellence of even D. Brutus had not yet bestirred itself sufficiently to give us an indication of the truth, and when our sole protection depended on the boy who had shaken Antony from our shoulders, what honor was there that he did not deserve to have decreed to him? However, all I then proposed for him was a complimentary vote. of thanks, and that too expressed with moderation. I also proposed a decree conferring imperium on him, which, although it seemed too great a compliment for one of his age, was yet necessary for one commanding an army—for what is an army without a commander with imperium?[110] Philippus proposed a statue; Servius at first proposed a license to stand for office before the regular time. Servilius afterwards proposed that the time should be still farther curtailed. At that time nothing was thought too good for him.

But somehow men are more easily found who are liberal at a time of alarm, than grateful when victory has been won. For when that most joyful day of D. Brutus's relief from blockade had dawned on the Republic and happened also to be his birthday, I proposed that the name of Brutus should be entered in the fasti under that date. And in that I followed the example of our ancestors, who paid this honor to the woman Laurentia, at whose altar in the Velabrum you pontiffs are accustomed to offer sacrifice. And when I proposed this honor to Brutus I wished that there should be in the fasti an eternal memorial of a most welcome victory: and yet on that very day I discovered that the ill-disposed in the senate were somewhat in a majority over the grateful. In the course of those same days I lavished honors—if you like that word-upon the dead Hirtius, Pansa, and even Aquila. And who has any fault to find with that, unless he be one who, no sooner an alarm is over, forgets the past danger? There was added to this grateful memorial of a benefit received some consideration of what would be for the good of posterity also; for I wished that there should exist some perpetual record of the popular execration of our most ruthless enemies. I suspect that the next step does not meet with your approbation. It was disapproved by your friends, who are indeed most excellent citizens, but inexperienced in public business. I mean my proposing an ovation for Caesar. For myself; however—though I am perhaps wrong, and I am not a man who believes his own way necessarily right—I think that in the course of this war I never took a more prudent step. The reason for this I must not reveal, lest I should seem to have a sense of favors to come rather than to be grateful for those received. I have said too much already: let us look at other points....

---

[110] This is founded on *Phil.* 5.45.

CATULLUS

Selections

Translated by John Porter, University of Saskatchewan, 1995.

> *Catullus (fl. 57 BCE) represents a social as well as a literary phenomenon, providing us with a glimpse of the life and concerns of a wealthy and talented member of the equestrian class in the midst of the turmoil of the Late Republic. In this sense Catullus's poetry serves as a useful corrective to the gloomy picture conveyed by the violent and chaotic politics of this period: it is clear that, despite the uncertainties of the times, for many people life went along its usual course.*
>
> *A word of warning: Some of Catullus' poems are "earthy" in the extreme. If you are easily offended by obscene or politically incorrect poetry, you might want to skip this selection.*

Poem 29

Who can see this? Who can endure it,

except for the depraved, the gluttonous, the gamblers—

Mamurra[111] holding in his possession all the sleek
  wealth that Gallia Comata[112]

used to have, and that of farthest Britain?

Pathic Romulus, will you see this and endure it?

And now will that fellow do the rounds of all

the bedrooms, proud and prodigal,

like a white little dove or an Adonis?

Pathic Romulus, will you see this and endure it?

You're depraved, a glutton, and a gambler.

Was it for this, o sole commander,

that you busied yourself on the farthest island of the
  setting sun,

that this fucked-out prick of yours might

devour twenty or thirty million sesterces?

What is misguided generosity but this?

Had he plowed through too few fortunes? Not gobbled
  down enough?

First he demolished his paternal wealth,

then the Pontic plunder;[113] third came that from

Spain—all the riches gold-bearing Tagus knew,[114]

and now there's fear for Gaul and Britain.

Why, dammit, do you cherish this fellow so? What skill's
  he got,

other than wolfing down rich patrimonies?

Was it for this, o most pius men of Rome,

father and son-in-law, that you wrought havoc on the
  world?

---

[111] A Roman eques who served under both Pompey and Caesar and was one of Caesar's chief administrators in Gaul.
[112] I.e. Transalpine Gaul.
[113] The spoils from Pompey's defeat of Mithridates (63 BCE).
[114] From Caesar's campaign as propraetor in Spain in 61 BCE.

Poem 93

I have no real desire, Caesar, to wish to seek your favor,

or to know whether you are white or black.[115]

Poem 10

My friend Varus had taken me from the forum

(I had nothing going on) to visit his latest love—

a little tart, so she struck me at first sight,

not at all without charm and wit.

When we got there we fell into conversation

on a variety of topics, among which was the question of

what Bithynia was like these days, how things were
  going there,

and whether it had proved at all beneficial to my
  purse.[116]

I told them the truth—that there was nothing there,
  either for the locals

or for the praetors or for the praetor's cohort

that would cause anyone to carry a sleeker head—

especially for those who had an irrumator[117] for a
  praetor,

one who didn't give a straw for his cohort.

"But at the very least," they said, "you must certainly

have acquired what they say is the native custom,

some slaves to bear your litter?" I (thinking I would
  increase

my standing in the girl's eyes)

replied, "Things weren't so bad for me that,

just because I'd landed a lousy province,

I wasn't able to acquire eight good strong men."

(Yet in fact I had no one, neither here nor there,

who might carry on his neck the

fractured foot of my ancient little cot.)

At this point she said—as you'd expect from a little
  tramp—

"Please, my dear Catullus: lend them to me

just for a short while. I want to be carried to Serapis'
  temple[118]

in style." "Hold on!" I said to her.

"That which I said I had a moment ago—

What was I thinking? My friend,

Gaius Cinna,[119] he acquired them.

But, really, whether they're his or mine, what's that to
  me?

I have the use of them, just as if I bought them.

But you, with your wicked wit, are a downright plague,

---

[115] A colloquial way of indicating complete ignorance and indifference about somebody.
[116] Catullus evidently has just returned from Bithynia, where he served on the staff of the propraetor C. Memmius in 57-56 BCE.
[117] An irrumator is someone who practices the activity described below in poem 28, lines 9-10.
[118] An Egyptian divinity popular with women.
[119] C. Helvius Cinna, tribune in 44 BCE and another of the neoteric poets.

who allow no one the slightest latitude of speech."

Poem 28

Piso's companions,[120] empty-handed cohort,

rigged out with your tiny packs, emptied of
    unessentials—

Veranius, my friend, and you, Fabullus,

how are things going? Have you enjoyed enough

chilly starvation with that good-for-nothing?

Any profit to record—as lost?

My case is much the same: having followed my

praetor, I now set down my very expenses as gain.

O Memmius, you held me flat and at your leisure
    jammed

that log of yours down my throat good and long.

But, as far as I can see, your luck was much the same—

stuffed by no less formidable a prick.

Oh yes! "Seek out noble friends"!

But you two[121] may the gods and goddesses grant

many evils, you sources of shame to Romulus and
    Remus.

Poem 47

Porcius and little Socrates, Piso's two

left hand men, blight and bane of the earth—

have that Priapus[122] and his hard-on placed you ahead in
    favor

to my little Veranius and Fabullus?

Do you hold lavish drinking parties with all the finery

in the middle of the day, while my friends

stand on the public streets seeking dinner invitations?

Poem 16

I'll jam it up your ass and down your throat,

fairy Aurelius and queen Furius,

you who've deduced from my little poems,

because they're somewhat soft and sensual, that I'm not
    quite proper.

I'll admit that the godly poet ought to be modest of
    behavior himself,

but there's no need for his poems to be—

those only have wit and charm

if they are somewhat soft and sensual and not quite
    proper

and have something in them that might incite an itch,

not in boys, but in those shaggy gray-beards

who can scarcely rouse their sluggish members.

You two, because of what you read about those

many thousands of kisses, do you think me less than a
    man?

I'll jam it up your ass and down your throat.

Poem 79

Lesbius is pretty,[123] who denies it? He whom Lesbia
    loves

more than you and your whole family line together,
    Catullus.

But all the same, that "pretty" Lesbius would sell off
    Catullus and his line[124]

for just three kisses from his friends.[125]

HORACE

The Secular Hymn

Horace, *The Secular Hymn*. From: William Stearns Davis, ed., *Readings in Ancient History: Illustrative Extracts from the Sources*, 2 Vols. (Boston: Allyn and Bacon, 1912-13), Vol. II: Rome and the West, pp. 174-179.

In 17 BCE Augustus celebrated the "Secular Games," a peculiarly solemn event, supposedly permitted only once in a century. The occasion was one of general jubilation over the notable peace and prosperity of the age. The "Secular Hymn" by the court poet Horace is perhaps the most successful poem of occasion ever written. It fits admirably into the spirit of the occasion with its references to the old divinities and the contemporary rulers and their triumphs. It was probably sung on the third day of the festival at the temple of Apollo on the Palatine by a choir of twenty-seven noble boys and maidens.

Phoebus! and Dian, you whose sway,

Mountains and woods obey!

Twin glories of the skies, forever worshiped, hear!

Accept our prayer this sacred year

When, as the Sibyl's voice ordained

For ages yet to come,

Pure maids and youths unstained

Invoke the Gods who love the sevenfold hills of Rome.

All bounteous Sun!

Forever changing, and forever one!

Who in your lustrous car bear'st forth light,

And hid'st it, setting, in the arms of Night,

Look down on worlds outspread, yet nothing see

Greater than Rome, and Rome's high sovereignty.

You Ilithyia, too, whatever name,

Goddess, you do approve,

Lucina, Genitalis, still the same

---

[120] L. Calpurnius Piso: father-in-law of Caesar and governor of Macedonia in 57-55 BCE.

[121] I.e. Memmius and Piso.

[122] A Roman vegetation deity commonly portrayed with a large erect penis.

[123] Latin—Pulcher.

[124] I.e. into slavery.

[125] I.e. for any petty motive, without a thought. (The Romans commonly greeted one another with a kiss.)

Aid destined mothers with a mother's love;

Prosper the Senate's wise decree,
Fertile of marriage faith and countless progeny!
As centuries progressive wing their flight
For you the grateful hymn shall ever sound;
Thrice by day, and thrice by night
For you the choral dance shall beat the ground.

Fates! whose unfailing word
Spoken from lips Sibylline shall abide,
Ordained, preserved and sanctified
By Destiny's eternal law, accord
To Rome new blessings that shall last
In chain unbroken from the Past.
Mother of fruits and flocks, prolific Earth!
Bind wreaths of spiked corn round Ceres's hair:
And may soft showers and Jove's benignant air
Nurture each infant birth!

Lay down your arrows, God of day!
Smile on your youths elect who singing pray.
You, Crescent Queen, bow down your star-crowned head
And on your youthful choir a kindly influence shed.
If Rome be all your work—if Troy's sad band
Safe sped by you attained the Etruscan strand,
A chosen remnant, vowed
To seek new Lares, and a changed abode—
Remnant for whom thro Ilion's blazing gate
Aeneas, orphan of a ruined State,
Opened a pathway wide and free
To happier homes and liberty:—
Ye Gods! If Rome be yours, to placid Age
Give timely rest: to docile Youth
Grant the rich heritage
Of morals, modesty, and truth.
On Rome herself bestow a teaming race
Wealth, Empire, Faith, and all befitting Grace.

Vouchsafe to Venus' and Anchises' heir,
Who offers at your shrine
Due sacrifice of milk-white kine,
Justly to rule, to pity and to dare,
To crush insulting hosts, the prostrate foeman spare
The haughty Mede has learned to fear
The Alban axe, the Latian spear,
And Scythians, suppliant now, await
The conqueror's doom, their coming fate.
Honor and Peace, and Pristine Shame,
And Virtue's oft dishonored name,
Have dared, long exiled, to return,
And with them Plenty lifts her golden horn.

Augur Apollo! Bearer of the bow!
Warrior and prophet! Loved one of the Nine!
Healer in sickness! Comforter in woe!
If still the templed crags of Palatine
And Latium's fruitful plains to you are dear,
Perpetuate for cycles yet to come,
Mightier in each advancing year,
The ever growing might and majesty of Rome.
You, too, Diana, from your Aventine,
And Algidus deep woods, look down and hear
The voice of those who guard the books Divine,
And to your youthful choir incline a loving ear.

Return we home! We know that Jove
And all the Gods our song approve
To Phoebus and Diana given;
The virgin hymn is heard in Heaven.

VELLEIUS PATERCULUS

The Battle of Teutoburg Forest

Source: Book 2, chapters 117-120, of Paterculus' Roman History are presented here in the translation by F.W. Shipley.

> *In his* Roman History, *the Roman officer-historian Velleius Paterculus (20 BCE–after 30 CE) has included a description of the battle in the Teutoburg Forest (September 9 CE). The author was active in the Germanic wars and knew many of the actors personally. His account is the oldest surviving description of the battle and relies on eyewitness accounts; the battlefield has been discovered at Kalkriese.*

Scarcely had Tiberius put the finishing touch upon the Pannonian and Dalmatian war,[126] when, within five days of the completion of this task, dispatches from Germania brought the baleful news of the death of Varus, and of the slaughter of three legions,[127] of as many divisions of cavalry, and of six cohorts—as though fortune were granting us this indulgence at least, that such a disaster should not be brought upon us when our commander was occupied by other wars. The cause of this defeat and the personality of the general require of me a brief digression.

Varus Quintilius, descended from a famous rather than a high-born family, was a man of mild character and of a quiet disposition, somewhat slow in mind as he was in body, and more accustomed to the leisure of the camp than to actual service in war. That he was no despiser of money is demonstrated by his governorship of Syria: he entered the rich province a poor man, but

---

[126] Fought in the years 6-9 CE.
[127] The Seventeenth, Eighteenth, and Nineteenth legions.

left it a rich man and the province poor. When placed in charge of the army in Germania, he entertained the notion that the Germans were a people who were men only in limbs and voice, and that they, who could not be subdued by the sword, could be soothed by the law. With this purpose in mind he entered the heart of Germania[128] as though he were going among a people enjoying the blessings of peace, and sitting on his tribunal he wasted the time of a summer campaign in holding court and observing the proper details of legal procedure.

But the Germans, who with their great ferocity combine great craft, to an extent scarcely credible to one who has had no experience with them, and are a race to lying born, by trumping up a series of fictitious lawsuits, now provoking one another to disputes, and now expressing their gratitude that Roman justice was settling these disputes, that their own barbarous nature was being softened down by this new and hitherto unknown method, and that quarrels which were usually settled by arms were now being ended by law, brought Quintilius to such a complete degree of negligence, that he came to look upon himself as a city praetor administering justice in the forum, and not a general in command of an army in the heart of Germania.

Thereupon appeared a young man of noble birth, brave in action and alert in mind, possessing an intelligence quite beyond the ordinary barbarian; he was, namely, Arminius, the son of Segimer, a prince of that nation, and he showed in his countenance and in his eyes the fire of the mind within. He had been associated with us constantly on private campaigns, and had even attained the dignity of equestrian rank. This young man made use of the negligence of the general as an opportunity for treachery, sagaciously seeing that no one could be more quickly overpowered than the man who feared nothing, and that the most common beginning of disaster was a sense of security. At first, then, he admitted but a few, later a large number, to a share in his design; he told them, and convinced them too, that the Romans could be crushed, added execution to resolve, and named a day for carrying out the plot.

This was disclosed to Varus through Segestes, a loyal man of that race and of illustrious name, who also demanded that the conspirators be put in chains. But fate now dominated the plans of Varus and had blindfolded the eyes of his mind. Indeed, it is usually the case that heaven perverts the judgment of the man whose fortune it means to reverse, and brings it to pass - and this is the wretched part of it- that that which happens by chance seems to be deserved, and accident passes over into culpability. And so Quintilius refused to believe the story, and insisted upon judging the apparent friendship of the Germans toward him by the standard

of his merit. And, after this first warning, there was no time left for a second.

The details of this terrible calamity, the heaviest that had befallen the Romans on foreign soil since the disaster of Crassus in Parthia,[129] I shall endeavor to set forth, as others have done, in my larger work. Here I can merely lament the disaster as a whole. An army unexcelled in bravery, the first of Roman armies in discipline, in energy, and in experience in the field, through the negligence of its general, the perfidy of the enemy, and the unkindness of fortune was surrounded, nor was as much opportunity as they had wished given to the soldiers either of fighting or of extricating themselves, except against heavy odds; nay, some were even heavily chastised for using the arms and showing the spirit of Romans.

Hemmed in by forests and marshes and ambuscades, it was exterminated almost to a man by the very enemy whom it had always slaughtered like cattle, whose life or death had depended solely upon the wrath or the pity of the Romans. The general had more courage to die than to fight, for, following the example of his father and grandfather, he ran himself through with his sword. Of the two prefects of the camp, L. Eggius furnished a precedent as noble as that of Ceionius was base, who, after the greater part of the army had perished, proposed its surrender, preferring to die by torture at the hands of the enemy than in battle.

Vala Numonius, lieutenant of Varus, who, in the rest of his life, had been an inoffensive and an honorable man, also set a fearful example in that he left the infantry unprotected by the cavalry and in flight tried to reach the Rhine with his squadrons of horse. But fortune avenged his act, for he did not survive those whom he had abandoned, but died in the act of deserting them. The body of Varus, partially burned, was mangled by the enemy in their barbarity; his head was cut off and taken to Maroboduus[130] and was sent by him to Caesar; but in spite of the disaster it was honored by burial in the tomb of his family.[131]

On hearing of this disaster, Tiberius flew to his father's side. The constant protector of the Roman empire again took up his accustomed part. Dispatched to Germania, he reassured the provinces of Gaul, distributed his armies, strengthened the garrison towns, and then, measuring himself by the standard of his own greatness, and not by the presumption of an enemy who threatened Italy with a war like that of the Cimbri and Teutones,[132] he took the offensive and crossed the Rhine with his army. He thus made aggressive war upon the

[128] In the year 6.

[129] A reference to the battle at Carrhae, where the Romans were defeated by the Parthian commander Surena, in 53 BCE.
[130] King of the Marcomanni, living in Bohemia.
[131] I.e., the tomb of the imperial family, the Mausoleum of Augustus.
[132] Germanic tribes that had invaded the Mediterranean world in the last decade of the second century BCE.

enemy when his father and his country would have been content to let him hold them in check, he penetrated into the heart of the country, opened up military roads, devastated fields, burned houses, routed those who came against him, and, without loss to the troops with which he had crossed, he returned, covered with glory, to winter quarters.

Due tribute should be paid to L. Asprenas, who was serving as lieutenant under Varus his uncle, and who, backed by the brave and energetic support of the two legions under his command,[133] saved his army from this great disaster, and by a quick descent to the quarters of the army in Germania Inferior strengthened the allegiance of the races even on the hither side of the Rhine who were beginning to waver. There are those, however, who believed that, though he had saved the lives of the living, he had appropriated to his own use the property of the dead who were slain with Varus, and that inheritances of the slaughtered army were claimed by him at pleasure.

The valor of L. Caedicius, prefect of the camp, also deserves praise, and of those who, pent up with him at Aliso, were besieged by an immense force of Germans. For, overcoming all their difficulties which want rendered unendurable and the forces of the enemy almost insurmountable, following a design that was carefully considered, and using a vigilance that was ever on the alert, they watched their chance, and with the sword won their way back to their friends.

From all this it is evident that Varus, who was, it must be confessed, a man of character and of good intentions, lost his life and his magnificent army more through lack of judgment in the commander than of valor in his soldiers. When the Germans were venting their rage upon their captives, an heroic act was performed by Caldus Caelius, a young man worthy in every way of his long line of ancestors, who, seizing a section of the chain with which he was bound, brought down with such force upon his own head as to cause his instant death, both his brains and his blood gushing from the wound.

Acts of the Divine Augustus

Selections from the Acts of the Divine Augustus (Res Gestae Divi Augusti), Lewis Stiles, translator (with additions by John Porter).

Extracts of the things done by the Divine Augustus, the things by which he subjected the orb of the lands to the Imperium of the People of Rome, and of the money which for the Res Publica and the People of Rome he spent—the (original) is incised upon two bronze pillars set up at Rome—a copy (of his own account) follows.

At nineteen years of age [44-43 BCE] I prepared an army by (my own) personal plan and at (my own) personal expense, through which I reclaimed the Res Publica from the domination of the faction oppressing it, and set it free. In the name of that deed the Senate, by honorific decrees, into its own rank elected me,[134] at the same time giving me a consular place for giving my opinion,[135] and it gave imperium to me. The Res Publica ordered me as a praetor, along with the consuls, to see to it that it suffered nothing detrimental to itself. The People, moreover, in the same year [43 BCE] made me consul, when the consuls both had fallen in war, and Triumvir for the purpose of constituting the Res Publica.

Those who had killed my parent I drove out into exile through the legitimate courts, as the avenger of their crime; and afterwards when they were bringing war against the Res Publica I conquered them in two battles.[136]

Wars by land and by sea, civil and foreign, over the whole orb of the lands I often waged; and as victor I spared all who sought pardon as citizens. The foreign nations—those which in safety I was able to forgive—I preferred to preserve rather than to kill. Of Roman citizens bound by a (military) sacrament to me there were about 500,000; out of these I led out into colonies or sent back into their own municipalities—when they had earned a year's wages—somewhat more than 300,000, and to them all I assigned arable land or else I gave money as a reward for military service. I captured 600 ships, beyond those which were smaller than triremes.

Twice I had triumphal ovations, and three times curule triumphs; and I was called, twenty-two times, Imperator. When, however, the Senate decreed more triumphs, I sat out from them. The bay leaves from my fasces I deposited in the Capitol when my vows, which in each war I had pronounced, were fulfilled. On account of things by land and by sea successfully done by me or by

---

[133] L. Nonius Asprenas, a relative of Varus, was the commander of the army of Germania Superior. His legions, I Germanica and V Alaudae, were stationed at Mainz.

[134] C. Pansa and A. Hirtius were consuls.
[135] I.e., the right to speak and vote as one of consular rank in the senate.
[136] I.e. at Philippi—42 BCE.

my delegates under my auspices, 55 times the Senate decreed that prayers be made to the immortal gods. Of days, moreover, on which by the Senate's decree (these) prayers were made, there were 890. In triumphs of mine there were led before my chariot, of kings or king's children, nine. I had been consul 13 times, when I wrote this [14 CE], and was in the 37th year of my tribunician power.

Dictatorship, offered to me both when I was absent and when I was present by both the People and the Senate when M. Marcellus and L. Arruntius were consuls [22 BCE], I did not accept. I did not beg off, when there was a great shortage of grain, from the management of its supply, which I so administered that within a few days from its immediate fear and danger I freed the entire state at my own expense and by my own care. Consulship, annual and also perpetual, at that time offered to me, I did not accept [22 BCE].

When the consuls were M. Vinicius and Q. Lucretius [19 BCE], and afterwards when they were P. and Cn. Lentulus [18 BCE], and a third time when they were Paullus Fabius Maximus and Q. Tubero [11 BCE], even with the Senate and the Roman People consenting that I should be made sole curator of laws and public morals with imperium, I accepted no magistracy offered contrary to the custom of our ancestors. The things which at that time the Senate wanted done through me, I accomplished through my tribunician power; and a colleague in that power I myself, of my own accord, five times demanded from the Senate and received.

I was Triumvir for the constituting of the Res Publica throughout ten continual years [43-33 BCE]. I was Princeps of the Senate, up to the day on which I wrote this, throughout 40 years. I was Pontifex Maximus, an Augur, one of the Fifteen for making sacrifices, one of the Seven for religious feasts, an Arval brother, a Titian fellow, and a Fetial.

The Patricians' numbers I increased, as consul for the fifth time, at the bidding of the People and the Senate [29 BCE]. Three times I revised the membership of the Senate and in my sixth consulship [28 BCE] I held a census of the people, with M. Agrippa as my colleague. I conducted a lustrum after (a lapse of) 41 years; in that lustrum of Roman citizens there were counted 4,063,000 heads. Then again, with consular imperium, alone I conducted a lustrum when C. Censorinus and C. Asinius were consuls [8 BCE]; in that lustrum were counted, of Roman citizens, 4,233,000 heads. And a third time with consular imperium I conducted a lustrum, with, as colleague, Ti. Caesar my son [14 CE]; in that lustrum were counted, of Roman citizens' heads, 4,937,000. Through new laws brought forward at my instigation I reintroduced many salutary practices established by our ancestors—things that at that time were beginning to disappear from our age; and I myself handed on

examples of many things which ought to be imitated by those who come after.

That prayers for my health be undertaken by the consuls and priests every fifth year, the Senate decreed. Along with these prayers, they often held games while I was living, sometimes the four most important colleges of priests, sometimes the consuls. Also, both privately and municipally the entire body of citizens, unanimously and continuously at all the altars, for my health made supplication.

My name by the Senate's decree was included in the Saliar Hymn; and it was legislated that I be sacrosanct in perpetuity and, while I lived, that the tribunician power be given me [23 BCE]. I refused to be made Pontifex Maximus in the place of my colleague while he lived, when the people offered me that priesthood which my father had held; that priesthood some years later, upon the death at last of that man who had used the occasion of civil tumult to get it, with all Italy pouring together for my election in a multitude such as had never been reported at Rome before that time, I accepted (P. Sulpicius and C. Valgius were consuls [12 BCE]).

An altar of Fortune the Bringer-back before the shrines of Honor and Virtue at the Capene Gate, on behalf of my return, was by the Senate consecrated; in it the priests and Vestal Virgins were ordered to make anniversary sacrifice on the day on which (when Q. Lucretius and M. Vinicius were consuls [19 BCE]) I came back to the city from Syria, and the day was named the Augustalia from my cognomen.

By the Senate's decree at the same time a part of the praetors and of the tribunes of the plebs, with the consul Q. Lucretius and the principal men (of the Senate) were sent to meet me in Campania—an honor which up to that time no one except me had been decreed.

When from Spain and Gaul—matters in those provinces having been successfully managed—I came back to Rome,[137] an altar of August[138] Peace, by the Senate, in honor of my return, was ordered to be consecrated on the Field of Mars; in it the magistrates and priests and Vestal Virgins were ordered to make anniversary sacrifices.

As for the Gates of Janus Quirinus, which our ancestors wanted closed whenever through the whole area of the imperium of the Roman People, by land and by sea, peace had been secured by victories—although before I was born from the founding of the city only twice[139] in all it had been closed according to tradition— three times while I was Princeps the Senate ordered them closed.

My sons, who as youths were snatched from me by Fortune—C. and L. Caesar—for my honor's sake were by

---

[137] When Tiberius and P. Quintilius were consuls—13 BCE.
[138] *August* carries the sense of "holy, majestic."
[139] Once by King Numa and again at the conclusion of the First Punic War.

the Senate and People of Rome, when they were each fourteen, made consuls-designate, on the condition that they enter that magistracy after five years; and the Senate decreed that from the day on which they were led into the Forum they should be present at public councils. The Equites of Rome, moreover, universally named each of them Princeps of the Youth and presented them with shield and spears of silver.

For the plebs of Rome, man by man, I counted out 300 sesterces (each) from the will of my father [44 BCE], and in my own name 400 each out of the spoils of war I gave in my fifth consulship [29 BCE]; again moreover in my tenth consulship [24 BCE] from my own patrimony I counted out as a gift 400 sesterces man by man; in my eleventh consulship [23 BCE] I measured out [for each citizen] twelve rations of grain privately bought; in the twelfth year of my tribunician power [12 BCE] I gave 400 sesterces for the third time, man by man. These gifts of mine never came through to fewer than 250,000 men. In the eighteenth year of my tribunician power, in my twelfth consulship [5 BCE], I gave 240 sesterces, man by man, to 320,000 members of the urban plebs. And to the colonists chosen from my soldiers in my fifth consulship [29 BCE] I gave out of war-spoils 1,000 sesterces each; in the colonies about 12,000 men received this gift during my triumph. In my thirteenth consulship [2 BCE] I gave 60 denarii [each] to the plebs who then were receiving grain rations; they were a few more than 200,000 men.[140]

For the lands which in my fourth consulship [30 BCE] and afterwards when M. Crassus and Cn. Lentulus the Augur were consuls [14 BCE] I assigned to the soldiers, I paid money to the municipalities; this sum was about 600,000,000 sesterces which I counted out for the war-spoils in Italy and about 260,000,000 which I paid for land in the provinces....

Four times from my own money I helped out the Public Treasury....[141]

I built the Curia [the Senate house] and the Chalcidicum which adjoins it, the temple of Apollo on the Palatine with its porticoes, the temple of the Divine Julius, the Lupercal, the portico near the Flaminian Circus (which I suffered to be named the Octavian Portico, after the man who had built the earlier one at that same site), the shrine near the Circus Maximus, the temples of Jupiter Feretrius[142] and Jupiter the Thunderer[143] on the Capitoline, the temple of Quirinus, the temples of Minerva and of Queen Juno and of Jupiter

of Liberty on the Aventine, the temple of the Lares at the top of the Sacred Way, the temple of the Divine Penates in the Velian district, the temple of Youth, the temple of the Great Mother on the Palatine.

At great expense I rebuilt both the Capitoline temple and the theater of Pompey, without inscribing my name on either. In many areas I repaired water channels which had fallen into disrepair with age, and I doubled the output of the Marcian aqueduct by introducing a new water source to its channel. I completed the Julian forum and the Julian basilica—the one between the temple of Castor and the temple of Saturn—both of which were begun and nearly completed by my father, and when this same basilica was destroyed by fire I enlarged its foundations and began to rebuild it in the name of my sons, with commands that, should I not have lived to complete the work, it should be completed by my heirs. In my sixth consulship [28 BCE], on the authority of the senate, I rebuilt 82 temples of the gods in the city, with none omitted which at that time were in need of repair. In my seventh consulship [27 BCE] I rebuilt the Flaminian Way from the city to Arminum [modern Rimini] and all the bridges with the exception of the Mulvian and Minucian bridges.

On private ground I built the temple of Mars the Avenger and the Forum of Augustus [2 CE], out of war-spoils....

Three gladiatorial games I gave in my own name and five in my sons' or grandsons' names; in these games there fought around 10,000 men.... I gave hunts of beasts from Africa in my name or in that of my sons or grandsons in the circus or forum or amphitheater 26 times; in these were used up around 3,500 beasts.

I gave the spectacle of a naval battle to the People, across the Tiber in the place where now is the Grove of the Caesars, having excavated a piece of ground 1,800 feet in length and 1,200 in width; in this 30 beaked triremes or biremes and even more smaller ships fought amongst themselves; in these fleets fought—besides the rowers—around 3,000 men.

In the temples of all the cities of the province of Asia I as victor put back the ornaments which, when he had despoiled the temples, the one against whom I waged the war had possessed privately. Statues of myself—on foot, on horse, or in chariots—silver ones, stood in the city, around 80 of them; these I myself took up, and from that money I put golden gifts in the temple of Apollo in my own name and in the names of those who had done me the honor of [commissioning] the statues.

The sea I pacified, (freeing it) from pirates. In that war of the slaves who had fled their masters and against the Res Publica had taken up arms,[144] I captured about 30,000 and gave them to their masters for punishment.

---

[140] 1 denarius = 4 sesterces; 900 sesterces was the annual gross income of a soldier under Augustus.
[141] In this section Augustus claims to have contributed 150 million sesterces to the Roman treasury.
[142] Livy 1.10: victory of Romulus over forces of Caenina; kills leader of opposing forces and thereby wins "spoils of victory." Rome's first temple, according to Livy: probably c. 650-550 BCE.
[143] Commemorating escape from lightning bolt while on Cantaberian campaign (27 BCE?).

---

[144] I.e., against Sex. Pompeius, Pompey's son in Spain [38-37 BCE.].

There swore allegiance to me all of Italy of its own will, and demanded me as leader of the war in which I was victor at Actium; the Gallic Provinces and the Spanish ones, and Africa, Sicily and Sardinia swore the same allegiance. Of those who under my standards then campaigned there were more than 700 Senators, among whom those who either before or later became consuls [to the day on which this was written] were 83, and (those who became) priests were around 170.

Of all of the provinces of the People of Rome on whose borders were races which did not obey our imperium, I extended the borders. The Gallic and Spanish provinces, and also Germany—the part which Ocean encloses from Cadiz to the north of the Elbe river—I pacified. The Alps, from the region which is nearest to the Adriatic Sea to the Tuscan one I pacified—to no race bringing a war through an unjust cause. My fleet through Ocean from the mouth of the Rhine to the region of the rising sun, to the borders of the Cimbri, sailed; to a place where neither by land nor by sea any Roman before that time had gone. And the Cimbri and Charydes and Semnones and the other Germanic peoples of that area through delegates sought my friendship and that of the Roman People. At my order and under my auspices two armies were led at almost the same time into Ethiopia and into the part of Arabia called the Blessed; and great forces of the enemy of both races were cut down on the battle-field, and many towns were captured. Into Ethiopia as far as the town of Nabata [our army] went through—to the place nearest to Meroe; into Arabia so far within the borders of the Sabaeans proceeded the army as to the town of Mariba.

Egypt to the imperium of the Roman People I added. As for Greater Armenia, when its king, Artaxes, had been killed, although I could have made it a province I preferred—following our ancestors' example—to give over that kingdom to Tigranes, king Artavasdes' son and grandson moreover of Tigranes the king, through (the agency of) Tiberius Nero, who was then my stepson. And when then that same race after withdrawing and rebelling had been tamed through [the agency of] Gaius my son, I gave it over to king Ariobarzanes, son of Artabazus king of the Medes, for him to rule, and after his death to his son Artavasdes; when he was killed I sent [yet another] Tigranes, who was of the royal house of the Armenians born, into that kingdom. The provinces, all those across the Adriatic Sea which verge on the East, and Cyrenae—at that time the greater part of them was possessed by kings—and before that Sicily and Sardinia when they were occupied during the slave war, I recovered.

Colonies in Africa, Sicily, Macedonia, both Spains, Achaia, Asia, Syria, Gallia Narbonensis and Psidia, out of my soldiers I founded. Italy also has 28 colonies which in my lifetime were very densely populated and which under my authority were founded.

Several standards, by other leaders lost, when the enemies were conquered I recovered—out of Spain and Gaul and from the Dalmatians. I compelled the Parthians to give back the spoils and the standards of three Roman armies[145] to me, and as suppliants to beg the friendship of the Roman People. Those standards moreover in the innermost shrine which is in the temple of Mars the Avenger I deposited.

The Pannonian races, which before I was Princeps an army of the Roman People had never gone to, were conquered through (the agency of) Tiberius Nero, who was then my stepson and delegate; to the imperium of the Roman People I subjected them, and I carried forward the borders of Illyricum to the banks of the river Danube. To our side of that river a Dacian army crossed—under my auspices it was defeated and routed, and afterwards my army was led across the Danube and compelled the Dacian races to submit to the imperium of the Roman People.

To me from India's kings delegates often were sent, men not seen before that time in attendance on any Roman leader....

In my sixth and seventh consulships [28-27 BCE], after I had extinguished the civil wars, being by universal consent in control of all affairs, I transferred the Res Publica out of my power and (put it) under the judgment of the Senate and People of Rome. In return for this deserving act of mine, by the Senate's decree I was named "Augustus" and with bay leaves the door-posts of my dwelling were wreathed, publicly; a civic crown over my door was fixed, and a golden shield put in the Curia Julia, which the Senate and People of Rome gave to me for the sake of my courage, clemency, justice and piety, as witnessed by that shield's inscription. After that time in authority before all men I stood, but of actual power I had no more than did the others who were my colleagues in each magistracy.

While I held my thirteenth consulship [2 BCE] the Senate and the Equestrian class and the People of Rome universally named me Father of our Fatherland, and resolved that this should in the porch of my dwelling be inscribed and in the Curia Julia and in the Forum of Augustus under the chariot which for me by the Senate's decree had been placed there.

When I wrote this my age was seventy-six.

---

[145] The armies of Crassus (defeated at Carrhae in 53) and Antony (in Asia Minor in 40 and in Armenia in 36).

The Death of Augustus and the Accession of Tiberius Nero

Source: Tac. *Ann.* I.1-44. Translated by A. J. Church and W. J. Brodribb. In Kevin Guinagh and Alfred P. Dorjahn (eds.). *Latin Literature in Translation.* New York: Longmans, Green and Co, 1942.

> *The first paragraph below is the famous opening to Tacitus's* Annals, *which cover the period from Augustus's death in 14 CE to the fall of Nero in 68. Tacitus's dark depiction of Tiberius was influential in both ancient and modern times (he was neglected in the middle ages), in part because of the brilliant concision of his Latin.*
>
> *Take note of how Tacitus opens his story of Tiberius's time as emperor: "The first crime of the new reign..."*

Rome at the beginning was ruled by kings. Freedom and the consulship were established by L. Brutus. Dictatorships were held for a temporary crisis. The power of the decemvirs did not last beyond two years, nor was the consular. jurisdiction of the military tribunes of long duration. The despotisms of Cinna and Sulla were brief; the rule of Pompeius and of Crassus soon yielded before Caesar—the arms of Lepidus and Antonius before Augustus; who, when he world was wearied by civil strife, subjected it to empire under the title of "Prince." But the successes and reverses of the old Roman people have been recorded by famous historians; and fine intellects were not wanting to describe the times of Augustus, till growing sycophancy scared them away. The histories of Tiberius, Gaius, Claudius, and Nero, while they were in power, were falsified through terror, and after their death were written under the irritation of a recent hatred. Hence my purpose is to relate a few facts about Augustus—more particularly his last acts, then the reign of Tiberius, and all which follows, without either· bitterness or partiality, from any motives to which I am far removed....

Thus the State had been revolutionized, and there was not a vestige left of the old sound morality. Stripped of equality, all looked up to the commands of a sovereign without the least apprehension for the present, while Augustus in the vigor of life, could maintain his own position, that of his house, and the general tranquility. When in advanced old age, he was worn out by a sickly frame, and the end was near and new prospects opened, a few spoke in vain of the blessings of freedom, but most people dreaded and some longed for war....

The infirmities of Augustus increased, and some suspected guilt on his wife's part. For a rumor bad gone abroad that a few months before he had sailed to Planasia on a visit to Agrippa with the knowledge of some chosen friends, and with one companion, Fabius Maximus; that many tears were shed on both sides, with expressions of affection, and that thus there was a hope of the young man being restored to the home of his grandfather. This, it was said, Maximus had divulged to his wife Marcia, she again to Livia. All was known to Caesar, and when Maximus soon afterwards died, by a death some thought to be self-inflicted, there was heard at his funeral wailings from Marcia, in which she reproached herself for having been the cause of her husband's destruction. Whatever the fact was, Tiberius as he was just entering Illyria was summoned home by an urgent letter from his mother, and it has not been thoroughly ascertained whether at the city of Nola he found Augustus still breathing or quite lifeless. For Livia had surrounded the house and its approaches with a strict watch, and favorable bulletins were published from time to time, till, provision having been made for the demands of the crisis, one and the same report told men that Augustus was dead and that Tiberius Nero was master of the State.

The first crime of the new reign was the murder of P. Agrippa. Though he was surprised and unarmed, a centurion of the firmest resolution dispatched him with difficulty. Tiberius gave no explanation of the matter to the Senate; he pretended that there were directions from his father ordering the tribune in charge of the prisoner not to delay the slaughter of Agrippa, whenever he should himself have breathed his last. Beyond a doubt, Augustus had often complained of the young man's character, and had thus succeeded in obtaining the sanction of a decree of the Senate for his banishment. But he never was hard-hearted enough to destroy any of his kinsfolk, nor was it credible that death was to be the sentence of the grandson in order that the stepson might feel secure. It was more probable that Tiberius and Livia, the one from fear, the other from a stepmother's enmity, hurried on the destruction of a youth whom they suspected and hated.

On the first day of the Senate he allowed nothing to be discussed but the funeral of Augustus, whose will, which was brought in by the Vestal Virgins, named as his heirs Tiberius and Livia. The latter was to be admitted into the Julian family with the name of Augusta; next in expectation were the grand and great-grandchildren. In the third place, he had named the chief men of the State, most of whom he hated, simply out of ostentation and to win credit with posterity. His legacies were not beyond the scale of a private citizen, except a bequest of forty-three million five hundred thousand sesterces "to the people and populace of Rome," of one thousand to every praetorian soldier, and of three hundred to every man in the legionary cohorts composed of Roman citizens.

Next followed a deliberation about funeral honors. Of these the most imposing were thought fitting. The procession was to be conducted through "the gate of triumph," on the motion of Gallus Asinius; the titles of the laws passed, the names of the nations conquered by

Augustus were to be borne in front, on that of L. Arruntius. Messala Valerius further proposed that the oath of allegiance to Tiberius should be yearly renewed, and when Tiberius asked him whether it was at his bidding that he had brought forward this motion, he replied that he had proposed it spontaneously, and that in whatever concerned the State he would use only his own discretion, even at the risk of offending. This was the only style of adulation which yet remained. The Senators unanimously exclaimed that the body ought to be borne on their shoulders to the funeral pile. The emperor left the point to them with disdainful moderation, and he then admonished the people by a proclamation not to indulge in that tumultuous enthusiasm which had distracted the funeral of the Divine Julius, or express a wish that Augustus should be burnt in the Forum instead of in his appointed resting place in the Campus Martius.

On the day of the funeral soldiers stood round as a guard, amid much ridicule from those who had either themselves witnessed or who had heard from their parents of the famous day when slavery was still something- fresh, and freedom had been resought in vain, when the slaying of Caesar, the Dictator, seemed to some the vilest, to others, the most glorious of deeds. "Now," they said, "an aged sovereign, whose power had lasted long, who had provided his heirs with abundant means to coerce the State, requires forsooth the defense of soldiers that his burial may be undisturbed."

Then followed much talk about Augustus himself, and many expressed an idle wonder that the same day marked the beginning of his assumption of empire and the close of his life, and, again, that he had ended his days at Nola in the same house and room as his father Octavius. People extolled too the number of his consulships, in which he had equaled Valerius Corvus and C. Marius combined, the continuance for thirty-seven years of the tribunician power, the title of Imperator twenty-one times earned, and his other honors which had been either frequently repeated or were wholly new. Sensible men, however, spoke variously of his life with praise and censure. Some said "that dutiful feeling towards a father, and the necessities of the State in which laws had then no place, drove him into civil war, which can neither be planned nor conducted on any right principles. He had often yielded to Antonius, while he was taking vengeance on his father's murderers, often also to Lepidus. When the latter sank into feeble dotage and the former had been ruined by his profligacy, the only remedy for his distracted country was the rule of a single man. Yet the State had been organized under the name neither of a kingdom nor a dictatorship, but under that of a prince. The ocean and remote rivers were the boundaries of the empire; the legions, provinces, fleets, all things were linked together; there was law for the citizens; there was

respect shown to the allies. The capital had been embellished on a grand scale; only in a few instances had he resorted to force, simply to secure general tranquility."

It was said, on the other hand, "that filial duty and State necessity were merely assumed as a mask. It was really from a lust of sovereignty that he had excited the veterans by bribery, had, when a young man and a subject, raised an army, tampered with the Consul's legions, and feigned an attachment to the faction of Pompeius. Then, when by a decree of the Senate he had usurped the high functions and authority of Praetor, when Hirtius and Pansa were slain.- whether they were destroyed by the enemy, or Pansa by poison infused into a wound, Hirtius by his own soldiers and Caesar's treacherous machinations—he at once possessed himself of both their armies, wrested the consulate from a reluctant Senate, and turned against the State the arms with which he had been entrusted against Antonius. Citizens were proscribed lands divided, without so much as the approval of those who executed these deeds. Even granting that the deaths of Cassius and of the Bruti were sacrifices to a hereditary enmity (though duty requires us to waive private feuds for the sake of the public welfare), still Pompeius had been deluded by the phantom of peace, and Lepidus by the mask of friendship. Subsequently, Antonius had been lured op by the treaties of Tarentum and Brundusium, and by his marriage with the sister, and paid by his death the penalty of a treacherous alliance. No doubt, there was peace after all this but it was a peace stained with blood; there were the disasters of Lollius and Varus, the murders at Rome of the Varros, Egnatii, and Juli."

The domestic life too of Augustus was not spared. "Nero's wife had been taken from him,[146] and there had been the farce of consulting the pontiffs, whether, with a child conceived and not yet born, she could properly marry. There were the excesses of Q. Tedius and Vedius Pollio; last of all, there was Livia, terrible to the State as a mother, terrible to the house of the Caesars as a stepmother. No honor was left for the gods, when Augustus chose to be himself worshipped with temples and statues, like those of the deities, and with flamens and priests. He had not even adopted Tiberius as his successor out of affection or any regard to the State, but, having thoroughly seen his arrogant and savage temper, he had sought glory for himself by a contrast of extreme wickedness." For, in fact, Augustus, a few years before, when he was a second time asking from the Senate the tribunician power for Tiberius, though his speech was complimentary, had thrown out certain hints as to his manners, style, and habits of life, which he meant as

---

[146] Augustus induced Livia's first husband, Ti. Claudius Nero, to give her up and let her marry Augustus. Nero's sons were D. Claudius Drusus (usually called Drusus) and Tiberius Claudius Nero, who became Augustus's step-son and, in the end, his heir.

reproaches, while he seemed to excuse. However, when his obsequies had been duly performed, a temple with a religious ritual was decreed him.

After this all prayers were addressed to Tiberius. He, on his part, urged various considerations, the greatness of the empire, his distrust of himself. "Only," he said, "the intellect of the Divine Augustus was equal to such a burden. Called as he had been by him to share his anxieties, he had learnt by experience how exposed to fortune's caprices was the task of universal rule. Consequently, in a state which had the support of so many great men, they should not put everything on one man, as many, by uniting their efforts would more easily discharge public functions." There was more grand sentiment than good faith in such words. Tiberius's language, even in matters which he did not care to conceal, either from nature or habit, was always hesitating and obscure, and now that he was struggling to hide his feelings completely, it was all the more involved in uncertainty and doubt. The Senators, however, whose only fear was lest they might seem to understand him, burst into complaints, tears, and prayers. They raised their hands to the gods, to the statue of Augustus, and to the knees of Tiberius, when he ordered a document to be produced and read. This contained a description of the resources of the State, of the number of citizens and allies under arms, of the fleets, subject kingdoms, provinces, taxes, direct and indirect, necessary expenses and customary bounties. All these details Augustus had written with his own hand, and had added a counsel, that the empire should be confined to its present limits, either from fear or out of jealousy...

Meantime, while the Senate stooped to the most abject supplication, Tiberius happened to say that although he was not equal to the whole burden of the State, yet he would undertake the charge of whatever part of it might be entrusted to him. Thereupon Asinius Gallus said, "I ask you, Caesar, what part of the State you wish to have entrusted to you?" Confounded by the sudden inquiry he was silent for a few moments; then, recovering his presence of mind, he replied that it would by no means become his modesty to choose or to avoid in a case where he would prefer to be wholly excused. Then Gallus again, who had inferred anger from his looks, said that the question had not been asked with the intention of dividing what could not be separated, but to convince him by his own admission that the body of the State was one, and must be directed .by a single mind. He further spoke in praise of Augustus, and reminded Tiberius himself of his victories, and of his admirable deeds for many years as a civilian. Still, he did not thereby soften the emperor's resentment, for he had long been detested from an impression that, as he had married Vipsania, daughter of M. Agrippa, who had once been the wife of Tiberius, he aspired to be more than a citizen, and kept up the arrogant tone of his father, Asinius Pollio.

Next, L. Arruntius, who differed but little from the speech of Gallus, gave like offence, though Tiberius had no old grudge against him, but simply mistrusted him, because he was rich and daring, had brilliant accomplishments, and corresponding popularity. For Augustus, when in his last conversations he was discussing who would refuse the highest place, though sufficiently capable, who would aspire to it without being equal to it, and who would unite both the ability and ambition, had described M. Lepidus as able but contemptuously indifferent, Gallus Asinius as ambitious and incapable, L. Arruntius as not unworthy of it, and, should the chance be given him, sure to make the venture. About the two first there is a general agreement, but instead of Arruntius some have mentioned Cneius Piso, and all these men, except Lepidus, were soon afterwards destroyed by various charges through the contrivance of Tiberius. Q. Haterius too and Mam. Scaurus ruffled his suspicious temper, Haterius by having said—"How long, Caesar, will you suffer the State to be without a head?" Scaurus by the remark that there was a hope that the Senate's prayers would not be fruitless, seeing that he had not used his right as Tribune to negative the motion of the Consuls. Tiberius instantly broke out into invective against Haterius; Scaurus, with whom he was far more deeply displeased, he passed over in silence. Wearied at last by the assembly's clamorous importunity and the urgent demands of individual Senators, he gave way by degrees, not admitting that he undertook empire, but yet ceasing to refuse it and to be entreated. It is known that Haterius having entered the palace to ask pardon, and thrown himself at the knees of Tiberius as he was walking, was almost killed by the soldiers, because Tiberius fell forward, accidentally or from being entangled by the suppliant's hands. Yet the peril of so great a man did not make him relent, till Haterius went with entreaties to Augusta, and was saved by her very earnest intercessions.

Great too was the Senate's sycophancy to Augusta. Some would have her styled "parent;" others "mother of the country," and a majority proposed that to the name of Caesar should be added "son of Julia." The emperor repeatedly asserted that there must be a limit to the honors paid to women, and that he would observe similar moderation in those bestowed on himself, but annoyed at the invidious proposal, and indeed regarding a woman's elevation as a slight to himself, he would not allow so much as a lictor to be assigned her, and forbade the erection of an altar in memory of her adoption, and any like distinction.

A Speech on Incorporating the Gauls

Source: From: William Stearns Davis, ed., Readings in Ancient History: Illustrative Extracts from the Sources, 2 Vols. (Boston: Allyn and Bacon, 1912-13), Vol. II: Rome and the West, pp. 186-188,

Claudius, the third successor of Augustus (41 to 54 CE), had a reputation as a pedantic and long-winded individual. He was not without abilities as a ruler, however, and did much to equalize the condition of the Italians and the Provincials.

The following speech of his in the Senate (preserved on an inscription) illustrates at once the nature of an imperial harangue before the Conscript Fathers (the members of the Senate), the interruptions that seem to have been allowed even in the speech of an Emperor, the broad personalities in which Claudius indulged, and his liberal policy withal, especially to the Gauls. A version of the speech is also reported by Tacitus; it is presented below.

Claudius: "It is surely an innovation of the divine Augustus, my great-uncle, and of Tiberius Caesar, my uncle, to desire that particularly the flower of the colonies and of the municipal towns, that is to say, all those that contain men of breeding and wealth, should be admitted to this assembly."

[Interruption, seemingly by a senator]: "How now? Is not an Italian senator to be preferred to a provincial senator!?"

Claudius: "I will soon explain this point to you, when I submit that part of my acts which I performed as censor, but I do not conceive it needful to repel even the provincials who can do honor to the Senate House. Here is this splendid and powerful colony of Vienna;[147] is it so long since it sent to us senators? From that colony comes L. Vestinus, one of the glories of the equestrian order, my personal friend, whom I keep close to myself for the management of my private affairs. Let his sons be suffered—I pray you—to become priests of the lowest rank, while waiting until, with the lapse of years, they can follow the advancement of their dignity. As for that robber, Valerius Asiaticus from Vienna, I will pass over his hateful name. For I detest that hero of the gymnasium, who brought the consulship into his family before even his colony had obtained the full rights of Roman citizenship. I could say as much of his brother, stamped as unworthy by this unlucky relationship, and incapable henceforth of being a useful member of your body."

[Interrupting shout]: "Here now, Tiberius Caesar Germanicus! It's time to let the Conscript Fathers understand what your talk is driving at—already you've reached the very limits of Narbonnese Gaul!"

Claudius: "All these young men of rank, on whom I cast my glance, you surely do not regret to see among the number of the senators; any more than Persicus, that most high-born gentleman and my friend, is ashamed when he meets upon the images of his ancestors the name Allobrogius. And if such is your thought, what would you desire more? Do I have to point it out to you? Even the territory which is located beyond the province of Gallia Narbonensis, has it not already sent you senators? For surely we have no regrets in going clear up to Lugdunum[148] for the members of our order. Assuredly, Conscript Fathers, it is not without some hesitation that I cross the limits of the provinces which are well known and familiar to you, but the moment is come when I must plead openly the cause of Further Gaul. It will be objected that Gaul sustained a war against the divine Julius for ten years. But let there be opposed to this the memory of a hundred years of steadfast fidelity, and a loyalty put to the proof in many trying circumstances. My father, Drusus, was able to force Germany to submit, because behind him reigned a profound peace assured by the tranquility of the Gauls. And note well, that at the moment he was summoned to that war, he was busy instituting the census in Gaul, a new institution among them, and contrary to their customs. And how difficult and perilous to us is this business of the census, although all we require is that our public resources should be known, we have learned by all too much experience."

✳   ✳   ✳

Source: Tacitus: Annals, Book 11., Translated by Alfred John Church and William Jackson Brodribb. Full text online at http://classics.mit.edu/Tacitus/annals.html

In the consulship of A. Vitellius and L. Vipstanus the question of filling up the Senate was discussed, and the chief men of Gallia Comata, as it was called, who had long possessed the rights of allies and of Roman citizens, sought the privilege of obtaining public offices at Rome. There was much talk of every kind on the subject, and it was argued before the emperor with vehement opposition. "Italy," it was asserted, "is not so feeble as to be unable to furnish its own capital with a senate. Once our native-born citizens sufficed for peoples of our own kin, and we are by no means dissatisfied with the Rome of the past. To this day we cite examples, which under our old customs the Roman character exhibited as to valor and renown. Is it a small thing that Veneti and Insubres have already burst into the Senate-house, unless a mob of foreigners, a troop of captives, so to say, is now forced upon us? What distinctions will be left for the remnants of our noble houses, or for any impoverished senators from Latium? Every place will be

---

[147] Modern Vienne in the South of France (not Vienna, Austria).

[148] Modern Lyons in France, Claudius's birthplace.

crowded with these millionaires, whose ancestors of the second and third generations at the head of hostile tribes destroyed our armies with fire and sword, and actually besieged the divine Julius at Alesia. These are recent memories. What if there were to rise up the remembrance of those who fell in Rome's citadel and at her altar by the hands of these same barbarians! Let them enjoy indeed the title of citizens, but let them not vulgarize the distinctions of the Senate and the honors of office."

These and like arguments failed to impress the emperor. He at once addressed himself to answer them, and thus harangued the assembled Senate. "My ancestors, the most ancient of whom was made at once a citizen and a noble of Rome, encourage me to govern by the same policy of transferring to this city all conspicuous merit, wherever found. And indeed I know, as facts, that the Julii came from Alba, the Coruncanii from Camerium, the Porcii from Tusculum, and not to inquire too minutely into the past, that new members have been brought into the Senate from Etruria and Lucania and the whole of Italy, that Italy itself was at last extended to the Alps, to the end that not only single persons but entire countries and tribes might be united under our name. We had unshaken peace at home; we prospered in all our foreign relations, in the days when Italy beyond the Po was admitted to share our citizenship, and when, enrolling in our ranks the most vigorous of the provincials, under color of settling our legions throughout the world, we recruited our exhausted empire. Are we sorry that the Balbi came to us from Spain, and other men not less illustrious from Narbon Gaul? Their descendants are still among us, and do not yield to us in patriotism.

"What was the ruin of Sparta and Athens, but this, that mighty as they were in war, they spurned from them as aliens those whom they had conquered? Our founder Romulus, on the other hand, was so wise that he fought as enemies and then hailed as fellow-citizens several nations on the very same day. Strangers have reigned over us. That freedmen's sons should be entrusted with public offices is not, as many wrongly think, a sudden innovation, but was a common practice in the old commonwealth. But, it will be said, we have fought with the Senones. I suppose then that the Volsci and Aequi never stood in array against us. Our city was taken by the Gauls. Well, we also gave hostages to the Etruscans, and passed under the yoke of the Samnites. On the whole, if you review all our wars, never has one been finished in a shorter time than that with the Gauls. Thenceforth they have preserved an unbroken and loyal peace. United as they now are with us by manners, education, and intermarriage, let them bring us their gold and their wealth rather than enjoy it in isolation. Everything, Senators, which we now hold to be of the highest antiquity, was once new. Plebeian magistrates came after patrician; Latin magistrates after plebeian; magistrates of other Italian peoples after Latin. This practice too will establish itself, and what we are this day justifying by precedents, will be itself a precedent."

The emperor's speech was followed by a decree of the Senate, and the Aedui were the first to obtain the right of becoming senators at Rome. This compliment was paid to their ancient alliance, and to the fact that they alone of the Gauls cling to the name of brothers of the Roman people.

SENECA

The Pumpkinification of Claudius

Source: L. Annaeus Seneca: *Divi Claudii Apocolocyntosis*. Translation by W.H.D. Rouse. 1920.

'Pumpkinification,' in Latin 'Apocolocyntosis,' is a pun on 'apotheosis,' the transition to heaven for divine spirits. Emperors (and, on occasion, those close to them like Caligula's sister Drusilla) were expected to be observed upon their death rising to the heavens. Tradition ascribes authorship of this satire to Seneca; it is impossible to prove that it is his, and impossible to prove that it is not. In the matters of style and of sentiment much may be said on both sides.

Many of Claudius's attributes are satirized here—not only his physical infirmities, but also his gambling at dice and his tendency to produce windy speech.

I wish to place on record the proceedings in heaven October 13 last, of the new year which begins this auspicious age. It shall be done without malice or favor. This is the truth. Ask if you like how I know it? To begin with, I am not bound to please you with my answer. Who will compel me? I know the same day made me free, which was the last day for him who made the proverb true—One must be born either a Pharaoh or a fool. If I choose to answer, I will say whatever trips off my tongue. Who has ever made the historian produce witness to swear for him? But if an authority must be produced, ask of the man who saw Drusilla translated to heaven: the same man will aver he saw Claudius on the road, making shorter steps.[149] Willy-nilly, all that happens in heaven he needs must see. He is the custodian of the Appian Way; by that route, you know, both Tiberius and Augustus went up to the gods. Question him, he will tell you the tale when you are alone; before company he is dumb. You see he swore in the Senate that he beheld Drusilla mounting heavenwards, and all he got for his good news was that everybody gave him the lie: since when he solemnly

---

[149] Virgil Aeneid, ii. 724

swears he will never bear witness again to what he has seen, not even if he had seen a man murdered in open market. What he told me I report plain and clear, as I hope for his health and happiness.

Now had the sun with shorter course drawn in his risen light,
And by equivalent degrees grew the dark hours of night:
Victorious Cynthia now held sway over a wider space,
Grim winter drove rich autumn out, and now usurped his place;
And now the fiat had gone forth that Bacchus must grow old,
The few last clusters of the vine were gathered ere the cold:

I shall make myself better understood, if I say the month was October, the day was the thirteenth. What hour it was I cannot certainly tell; philosophers will agree more often than clocks; but it was between midday and one after noon. "Clumsy creature!" you say. "The poets are not content to describe sunrise and sunset, and now they even disturb the midday siesta. Will you thus neglect so good an hour?"

Now the sun's chariot had gone by the middle of his way;
Half wearily he shook the reins, nearer to night than day,
And led the light along the slope that down before him lay.

Claudius began to breathe his last, and could not make an end of the matter. Then Mercury, who had always been much pleased with his wit, drew aside one of the three Fates, and said: "Cruel beldame, why do you let the poor wretch be tormented? After all this torture cannot he have a rest? Four and sixty years it is now since he began to pant for breath. What grudge is this you bear against him and the whole empire? Do let the astrologers tell the truth for once; since he became emperor, they have never let a year pass, never a month, without laying him out for his burial. Yet it is no wonder if they are wrong, and no one knows his hour. Nobody ever believed he was really quite born. Do what has to be done: 'Kill him, and let a better man rule in empty court.'"[150]

Clotho replied: "Upon my word, I did wish to give him another hour or two, until he should make Roman citizens of the half dozen who are still outsiders. (He made up his mind, you know, to see the whole world in the toga, Greeks, Gauls, Spaniards, Britons, and all.) But since it is your pleasure to leave a few foreigners for seed, and since you command me, so be it." She opened her box and out came three spindles. One was for Augurinus, one for Baba, one for Claudius. "These three," she says, "I will cause to die within one year and at no great distance apart, and I will not dismiss him unattended. Think of all the thousands of men he was wont to see following after him, thousands going before, thousands all crowding about him, and it would never do to leave him alone on a sudden. These boon companions will satisfy him for the nonce." ...

At once he bubbled up the ghost, and there was an end to that shadow of a life. He was listening to a troupe of comedians when he died, so you see I have reason to fear those gentry. The last words he was heard to speak in this world were these. When he had made a great noise with that end of him which talked easiest, he cried out, "Oh dear, oh dear! I think I have made a mess of myself." Whether he did or no, I cannot say, but certain it is he always did make a mess of everything.

What happened next on earth it is mere waste of time to tell, for you know it all well enough, and there is no fear of your ever forgetting the impression which that public rejoicing made on your memory. No one forgets his own happiness. What happened in heaven you shall hear: for proof please apply to my informant. Word comes to Jupiter that a stranger had arrived, a man well set up, pretty grey; he seemed to be threatening something, for he wagged his head ceaselessly; he dragged the right foot. They asked him what nation he was of; he answered something in a confused mumbling voice: his language they did not understand. He was no Greek and no Roman, nor of any known race. On this Jupiter bids Hercules go and find out what country he comes from; you see Hercules had traveled over the whole world, and might be expected to know all the nations in it. But Hercules, the first glimpse he got, was really much taken aback, although not all the monsters in the world could frighten him; when he saw this new kind of object, with its extraordinary gait, and the voice of no terrestrial beast, but such as you might hear in the leviathans of the deep, hoarse and inarticulate, he thought his thirteenth labor had come upon him. When he looked closer, the thing seemed to be a kind of man.

Up he goes, then, and says what your Greek finds readiest to his tongue: "Who art thou, and what thy people? Who thy parents, where thy home?" [151]

Claudius was delighted to find literary men up there, and began to hope there might be some corner for his own historical works. So he caps him with another Homeric verse, explaining that he was Caesar: "Breezes wafted me from Ilion unto the Ciconian land."[152]

But the next verse was more true, and no less Homeric: "Thither come, I sacked a city, slew the people every one."

He would have taken in poor simple Hercules, but that Our Lady of Malaria was there, who left her temple and came alone with him: all the other gods he had left at Rome. Quoth she, "The fellow's tale is nothing but lies. I have lived with him all these years, and I tell you, he was born at Lyons. You behold a fellow-burgess of Marcus. As I say, he was born at the sixteenth milestone from Vienna, a native Gaul. So of course he took Rome, as a good Gaul ought to do. I pledge you my word that in

---

[150] Virgil *Georgius*, iv. 90.

---

[151] Homer, *Odyssey*, i. 17.
[152] Homer, *Odyssey*, ix. 39

Lyons he was born, where Licinus was king so many years. But you that have trudged over more roads than any muleteer that plies for hire, you must have come across the people of Lyons, and you must know that it is a far cry from Xanthus to the Rhone." At this point Claudius flared up, and expressed his wrath with as big a growl as he could manage. What he said nobody understood; as a matter of fact, he was ordering my lady of Fever to be taken away, and making that sign with his trembling hand (which was always steady enough for that, if for nothing else) by which he used to decapitate men. He had ordered her head to be chopped off. For all the notice the others took of him, they might have been his own freedmen.

Then Hercules said, "You just listen to me, and stop playing the fool. You have come to the place where the mice nibble iron. Out with the truth, and look sharp, or I'll knock your quips and quiddities out of you."...

Claudius, seeing a mighty man before him, saw things looked serious and understood that here he had not quite the same pre-eminence as at Rome, where no one was his equal: the Gallic cock was worth most on his own dunghill. So this is what he was thought to say, as far as could be made out: "I did hope, Hercules, bravest of all the gods, that you would take my part with the rest, and if I should need a voucher, I meant to name you who know me so well. Do but call it to mind, how it was I used to sit in judgment before your temple whole days together during July and August. You know what miseries I endured there, in hearing the lawyers plead day and night. If you had fallen amongst these, you may think yourself very strong, but you would have found it worse than the sewers of Augeas: I drained out more filth than you did. But since I want..."

[...][153]

"No wonder you have forced your way into the Senate House: no bars or bolts can hold against you. Only do say what species of god you want the fellow to be made. An Epicurean god he cannot be: for they have no troubles and cause none. A Stoic, then? How can he be globular, as Varro says, without a head or any other projection? There is in him something of the Stoic god, as I can see now: he has neither heart nor head. Upon my word, if he had asked this boon from Saturn, he would not have got it, though he kept up Saturn's feast all the year round, a truly Saturnalian prince. A likely thing he will get it from Jove, whom he condemned for incest as far as in him lay: for he killed his son-in-law Silanus, because Silanus had a sister, a most charming girl, called Venus by all the world, and he preferred to call her Juno. Why, says he, I want to know why, his own sister? Read your books, stupid: you may go half-way at Athens, the whole way at Alexandria. Because the mice lick meal at Rome, you say.

---

[153] Some pages have fallen out, in which Hercules must have been persuaded. The gods are now discussing what Hercules tells them

Is this creature to mend our crooked ways? What goes on in his own closet he knows not; and now he searches the regions of the sky, wants to be a god. Is it not enough that he has a temple in Britain, that savages worship him and pray to him as a god, so that they may find a fool to have mercy upon them?"

At last it came into Jove's head, that while strangers were in the House it was not lawful to speak or debate. "My lords and gentlemen," said he, "I gave you leave to ask questions, and you have made a regular farmyard of the place. Be so good as to keep the rules of the House. What will this person think of us, whoever he is?" So Claudius was led out, and the first to be asked his opinion was Father Janus: he had been made consul elect for the afternoon of the next first of July, being as shrewd a man as you could find on a summer's day: for he could see, as they say, before and behind. He made an eloquent harangue, because his life was passed in the forum, but too fast for the notary to take down. That is why I give no full report of it, for I don't want to change the words he used. He said a great deal of the majesty of the gods, and how the honor ought not to be given away to every Tom, Dick, or Harry. "Once," said he, "it was a great thing to become a god; now you have made it a farce. Therefore, that you may not think I am speaking against one person instead of the general custom, I propose that from this day forward the godhead be given to none of those who eat the fruits of the earth, or whom mother earth doth nourish. After this bill has been read a third time, whosoever is made, said, or portrayed to be god, I vote he be delivered over to the bogies, and at the next public show be flogged with a birch amongst the new gladiators." ...

The meeting was divided, and it looked as though Claudius was to win the day. For Hercules saw his iron was in the fire, trotted here and trotted there, saying, "Don't deny me; I make a point of the matter. I'll do as much for you again, when you like; you roll my log, and I'll roll yours: one hand washes another."

Then arose the blessed Augustus, when his turn came, and spoke with much eloquence. "I call you to witness, my lords and gentlemen," said he, "that since the day I was made a god I have never uttered one word. I always mind my own business. But now I can keep on the mask no longer, nor conceal the sorrow which shame makes all the greater. Is it for this I have made peace by land and sea? For this have I calmed intestine wars? For this, laid a firm foundation of law for Rome, adorned it with buildings, and all that—my lords, words fail me; there are none can rise to the height of my indignation. I must borrow that saying of the eloquent Messala Corvinus, I am ashamed of my authority. This man, my lords, who looks as though he could not hurt a fly, used to chop off heads as easily as a dog sits down. But why should I speak of all those men, and such men? There is no time to lament for public disasters, when one has so many private sorrows to think of. I leave that, therefore, and say only this; for even if my sister knows no Greek, I do: The knee is nearer than the shin. This man you see, who for so many years has been masquerading under my name, has done me the favor of murdering two Julias, great-granddaughters of mine, one by cold steel and one by starvation; and one great grandson, L. Silanus—see, Jupiter, whether he had a case against him (at least it is your own if you will be fair.) Come tell me, blessed Claudius, why of all those you killed, both men and women, without a hearing, why you did not hear their side of the case first, before putting them to death? Where do we find that custom? It is not done in heaven.

Look at Jupiter: all these years he has been king, and never did more than once to break Vulcan's leg, "Whom seizing by the foot he cast from the threshold of the sky,"[154] and once he fell in a rage with his wife and strung her up: did he do any killing? You killed Messalina, whose great-uncle I was no less than yours. 'I don't know,' did you say? Curse you! that is just it: not to know was worse than to kill. Caligula he went on persecuting even when he was dead. Caligula murdered his father-in-law, Claudius his son-in-law to boot. Caligula would not have Crassus' son called Great; Claudius gave him his name back, and took away his head. In one family he destroyed Crassus, Magnus, Scribonia, the Tristionias, Assario, noble though they were; Crassus indeed such a fool that he might have been emperor. Is this he you want now to make a god? Look at his body, born under the wrath of heaven! In fine, let him say the three words quickly, and he may have me for a slave. God! who will worship this god, who will believe in him? While you make gods of such as he, no one will believe you to be gods. To be brief, my lords: if I have lived honorably among you, if I have never given plain speech to any, avenge my wrongs. This is my motion": then he read out his amendment, which he had committed to writing: "Inasmuch as the blessed Claudius murdered his father-in-law Ap. Silanus, his two sons-in-law, Pompeius Magnus and L. Silanus, Crassus Frugi his daughter's father-in-law, as like him as two eggs in a basket, Scribonia his daughter's mother-in-law, his wife Messalina, and others too numerous to mention; I propose that strong measures be taken against him, that he be allowed no delay of process, that immediate sentence of banishment be passed on him, that he be deported from heaven within thirty days, and from Olympus within thirty hours."

This motion was passed without further debate. Not a moment was lost: Mercury screwed his neck and haled him to the lower regions, to that borne "from which they say no traveler returns."

As they passed downwards along the Sacred Way, Mercury asked what was that great concourse of men?

could it be Claudius' funeral? It was certainly a most gorgeous spectacle, got up regardless of expense, clear it was that a god was being borne to the grave: tootling of flutes, roaring of horns, an immense brass band of all sorts, such a din that even Claudius could hear it. Joy and rejoicing on every side, the Roman people walking about like free men. Agatho and a few pettifoggers were weeping for grief, and for once in a way they meant it. The Barristers were crawling out of their dark corners, pale and thin, with hardly a breath in their bodies, as though just coming to life again. One of them when he saw the pettifoggers putting their heads together, and lamenting their sad lot, up comes he and says: "Did not I tell you the Saturnalia could not last for ever?"

When Claudius saw his own funeral train, he understood that he was dead. For they were chanting his dirge in anapests, with much mopping and mouthing:

"Pour forth your laments, your sorrow declare,
Let the sounds of grief rise high in the air:
For he that is dead had a wit most keen,
Was bravest of all that on earth have been.
Race-horses are nothing to his swift feet:
Rebellious Parthians he did defeat;
Swift after the Persians his light shafts go:
For he well knew how to fit arrow to bow,
Swiftly the striped barbarians fled:
With one little wound he shot them dead.
And the Britons beyond in their unknown seas,
Blue-shielded Brigantians too, all these
He chained by the neck as the Romans' slaves.
He spoke, and the Ocean with trembling waves
Accepted the axe of the Roman law.
O weep for the man! This world never saw
One quicker a troublesome suit to decide,
When only one part of the case had been tried,
(He could do it indeed and not hear either side).
Who'll now sit in judgment the whole year round?
Now he that is judge of the shades underground
Once ruler of five score cities in Crete,
Must yield to his better and take a back seat.
Mourn, mourn, pettifoggers, ye venal crew,
And you, minor poets, woe, woe is to you!
And you above all, who get rich quick
By the rattle of dice and the three card trick."

Claudius was charmed to hear his own praises sung, and would have stayed longer to see the show. But the Talthybius of the gods laid a hand on him, and led him across the Campus Martius, first wrapping his head up close that no one might know him, until betwixt Tiber and the Subway he went down to the lower regions. His freedman Narcissus had gone down before him by a short cut, ready to welcome his master. Out he comes to meet him, smooth and shining (he had just left the bath), and says he: "What make the gods among mortals?" "Look alive," says Mercury, "go and tell them we are coming." Away he flew, quicker than tongue can tell. It is

---

[154] Homer Illiad, i. 591

easy going by that road, all down hill. So although he had a touch of the gout, in a trice they were come to Dis's door. There lay Cerberus, or, as Horace puts it, the hundred-headed monster.[155] Claudius was a trifle perturbed (it was a little white bitch he used to keep for a pet) when he spied this black shag-haired hound, not at all the kind of thing you could wish to meet in the dark. In a loud voice he cried, "Claudius is coming!" All marched before him singing, "The lost is found, O let us rejoice together!" Here were found C. Silius consul elect, Juncus the ex-praetor, Sex. Traulus, M. Helvius, Trogus, Cotta, Vettius Valens, Fabius, Roman Knights whom Narcissus had ordered for execution. In the midst of this chanting company was Mnester the mime, whom Claudius for honor's sake had made shorter by a head. The news was soon blown about that Claudius had come: to Messalina they throng: first his freedmen, Polybius, Myron, Harpocras, Amphaeus, Pheronactus, all sent before him by Claudius that he might not be unattended anywhere; next two prefects, Justus Catonius and Rufrius Pollio; then his friends, Saturninus, Lusius and Pedo Pompeius and Lupus and Celer Asinius, these of consular rank; last came his brother's daughter, his sister's daughter, sons-in-law, fathers and mothers-in-law, the whole family in fact. In a body they came to meet Claudius; and when Claudius saw them, he exclaimed, "Friends everywhere, on my word! How came you all here?" To this Pedo Pompeius answered, "What, cruel man? How came we here? Who but you sent us, you, the murderer of all the friends that ever you had? To court with you! I'll show you where their lordships sit."

Pedo brings him before the judgment seat of Aeacus, who was holding court under the Lex Cornelia to try cases of murder and assassination. Pedo requests the judge to take the prisoner's name, and produces a summons with this charge: Senators killed, 35; Roman Knights, 221; others as the sands of the sea-shore for multitude. Claudius finds no counsel. At length out steps P. Petronius, an old chum of his, a finished scholar in the Claudian tongue and claims a remand. Not granted. Pedo Pompeius prosecutes with loud outcry. The counsel for the defense tries to reply; but Aeacus, who is the soul of justice, will not have it. Aeacus hears the case against Claudius, refuses to hear the other side and passes sentence against him, quoting the line: "As he did, so be he done by, this is justice undefiled."[156]

A great silence fell. Not a soul but was stupefied at this new way of managing matters; they had never known anything like it before. It was no new thing to Claudius, yet he thought it unfair. There was a long discussion as to the punishment he ought to endure. Some said that Sisyphus had done his job of porterage

long enough; Tantalus would be dying of thirst, if he were not relieved; the drag must be put at last on wretched Ixion's wheel. But it was determined not to let off any of the old stagers, lest Claudius should dare to hope for any such relief. It was agreed that some new punishment must be devised: they must devise some new task, something senseless, to suggest some craving without result. Then Aeacus decreed he should rattle dice for ever in a box with no bottom. At once the poor wretch began his fruitless task of hunting for the dice, which for ever slipped from his fingers.

"For when he rattled with the box, and thought he'd got 'em.
The little cubes would vanish thro' the perforated bottom.
Then he would pick 'em up again, and once more set a-trying:
The dice but served him the same trick: away they went a-flying.
So still he tries, and still he fails; still searching long he lingers;
And every time the tricksy things go slipping thro' his fingers.
Just so when Sisyphus at last once gets there with his boulder,
He finds the labor all in vain—it rolls down off his shoulder."

All on a sudden who should turn up but Caligula, and claims the man for a slave: brings witnesses, who said they had seen him being flogged, caned, fisticuffed by him. He is handed over to Caligula, and Caligula makes him a present to Aeacus. Aeacus delivers him to his freedman Menander, to be his law-clerk.

TACITUS

The Principle of Adoption

Source: Tacitus: *Histories*, Book 1., 15-16, translated by Alfred John Church and William Jackson Brodribb. Slightly adapted. Full text online at http://classics.mit.edu/Tacitus/histories.html

Augustus had passed on the principate to members of his own family, who formed an odd sort of dynasty. Galba initiated what was perhaps the most successful method of transfer of power—the adoption as son by a reigning emperor of an adult male, modeled on the method of the Julio-Claudians of adopting a cousin or other relation as son and heir. Tacitus describes Galba's motives. In fact in 69 CE, it was Vespasian who emerged victorious, and he was succeeded by his two sons, T. and Domitian. With Nerva's adoption of Trajan, the adoptive method was used for almost a century until M. Aurelius allowed his (natural) son Commodus to succeed him.

We are told that Galba, taking hold of Piso's hand, spoke to this effect: "If I were a private man, and were now adopting you by the Act of the Curiae before the pontiffs, as our custom is, it would be a high honor to me to introduce into my family a descendant of Cn. Pompey and M. Crassus; it would be a distinction to you to add to the nobility of your race the honors of the Sulpician and

---

[155] Horace Odes ii. 13. 34.
[156] Homer, Iliad, ix. 385

Lutatian houses. As it is, I, who have been called to the throne by the unanimous consent of gods and men, am moved by your splendid endowments and by my own patriotism to offer to you, a man of peace, that power, for which our ancestors fought, and which I myself obtained by war. I am following the precedent of the Divine Augustus, who placed on an eminence next to his own, first his nephew Marcellus, then his son-in-law Agrippa, afterwards his grandsons, and finally Tiberius Nero, his stepson. But Augustus looked for a successor in his own family, I look for one in the state, not because I have no relatives or companions of my campaigns, but because it was not by any private favor that I myself received the imperial power. Let the principle of my choice be shown not only by my connections which I have set aside for you, but by your own. You have a brother, noble as yourself, and older, who would be well worthy of this dignity, were you not worthier. Your age is such as to be now free from the passions of youth, and such your life that in the past you have nothing to excuse. Hitherto, you have only borne adversity; prosperity tries the heart with keener temptations; for hardships may be endured, whereas we are spoiled by success. You indeed will cling with the same constancy to honor, freedom, friendship, the best possessions of the human spirit, but others will seek to weaken them with their servility. You will be fiercely assailed by adulation, by flattery, that worst poison of the true heart, and by the selfish interests of individuals. You and I speak together to-day with perfect frankness, but others will be more ready to address us as emperors than as men. For to urge his duty upon a prince is indeed a hard matter; to flatter him, whatever his character, is a mere routine gone through without any heart.

"Could the vast frame of this empire have stood and preserved its balance without a directing spirit, I was not unworthy of inaugurating a republic. As it is, we have been long reduced to a position, in which my age confer no greater boon on the Roman people than a good successor, your youth no greater than a good emperor. Under Tiberius, Gaius, and Claudius, we were, so to speak, the inheritance of a single family. The choice which begins with us will be a substitute for freedom. Now that the family of the Julii and the Claudii has come to an end, adoption will discover the worthiest successor. To be begotten and born of a princely race is a mere accident, and is only valued as such. In adoption there is nothing that need bias the judgment, and if you wish to make a choice, an unanimous opinion points out the man. Let Nero be ever before your eyes, swollen with the pride of a long line of Caesars; it was not Vindex with his unarmed province, it was not myself with my single legion, that shook his yoke from our necks. It was his own profligacy, his own brutality, and that, though there had been before no precedent of an emperor condemned by his own people. We, who have been called to power

by the issues of war, and by the deliberate judgment of others, shall incur unpopularity, however illustrious our character. Do not however be alarmed, if, after a movement which has shaken the world, two legions are not yet quiet. I did not myself succeed to a throne without anxiety; and when men shall hear of your adoption I shall no longer be thought old, and this is the only objection which is now made against me. Nero will always be regretted by the thoroughly depraved; it is for you and me to take care, that he be not regretted also by the good. To prolong such advice, suits not this occasion, and all my purpose is fulfilled if I have made a good choice in you. The most practical and the shortest method of distinguishing between good and bad measures, is to think what you yourself would or would not like under another emperor. It is not here, as it is among nations despotically ruled, that there is a distinct governing family, while all the rest are slaves. You have to reign over men who cannot bear either absolute slavery or absolute freedom." This, with more to the same effect, was said by Galba; he spoke to Piso as if he were creating an emperor; the others addressed him as if he were an emperor already.

It is said of Piso that he betrayed no discomposure or excessive joy, either to the gaze to which he was immediately subjected, or afterwards when all eyes were turned upon him. His language to the Emperor, his father, was reverential; his language about himself was modest. He showed no change in look or manner; he seemed like one who had the power rather than the wish to rule.

TACITUS

The Legions Proclaim Vespasian Emperor

Source: Tacitus: Histories, Book I1., 49-51, translated by Alfred John Church and William Jackson Brodribb. Slightly adapted. Full text online at http://classics.mit.edu/Tacitus/histories.html.

Vespasian emerged victorious from the "Year of Four Emperors" (69 CE). He was created emperor by the legions, and away from Rome. Eventually this was to become a pattern.

The initiative in transferring the Empire to Vespasian was taken at Alexandria under the prompt direction of Ti. Alexander, who on the 1st of July made the legions swear allegiance to him. That day was ever after celebrated as the first of his reign, though the army of Judaea on July 3rd took the oath to Vespasian in person with such eager alacrity that they would not wait for the return of his son T., who was then on his way back from Syria, acting as the medium between Mucianus and his father for the communication of their plans. All this was done by the impulsive action of the soldiers without the preliminary of a formal harangue or any concentration of the legions.

While they were seeking a suitable time and place, and for that which in such an affair is the great difficulty, the first man to speak, while hope, fear, the chances of success or of disaster, were present to their minds, one day, on Vespasian quitting his chamber, a few soldiers who stood near, in the usual form in which they would salute their legate, suddenly saluted him as Emperor. Then all the rest hurried up, called him Caesar and Augustus, and heaped on him all the titles of Imperial rank. Their minds had passed from apprehension to confidence of success. In Vespasian there appeared no sign of elation or arrogance, or of any change arising from his changed fortunes. As soon as he had dispelled the mist with which so astonishing a vicissitude had clouded his vision, he addressed the troops in a soldier-like style, and listened to the joyful intelligence that came pouring in from all quarters. This was the very opportunity for which Mucianus had been waiting. He now at once administered to the eager soldiers the oath of allegiance to Vespasian. Then he entered the theatre at Antioch, where it is customary for the citizens to hold their public deliberations, and as they crowded together with profuse expressions of flattery, he addressed them. He could speak Greek with considerable grace, and in all that he did and said he had the art of displaying himself to advantage. Nothing excited the provincials and the army so much as the assertion of Mucianus that Vitellius had determined to remove the legions of Germany to Syria, to an easy and lucrative service, while the armies of Syria were to have given them in exchange the encampments of Germany with their inclement climate and their harassing toils. On the one hand, the provincials from long use felt a pleasure in the companionship of the soldiers, with whom many of them were connected by friendship or relationship; on the other, the soldiers from the long duration of their service loved the well-known and familiar camp as a home.

Before the 15th of July the whole of Syria had adopted the same alliance. There joined him, each with his entire kingdom, Sohemus, who had no contemptible army, and Antiochus, who possessed vast ancestral wealth, and was the richest of all the subject-kings. Before long Agrippa, who had been summoned from the capital by secret dispatches from his friends, while as yet Vitellius knew nothing, was crossing the sea with all speed. Queen Berenice too, who was then in the prime of youth and beauty, and who had charmed even the old Vespasian by the splendor of her presents, promoted his cause with equal zeal. All the provinces washed by the sea, as far as Asia and Achaia, and the whole expanse of country inland towards Pontus and Armenia, took the oath of allegiance. The legates, however, of these provinces were without troops, Cappadocia as yet having had no legions assigned to it. A council was held at Berytus to deliberate on the general conduct of the war. Thither came Mucianus with the legates and tribunes and all the most distinguished centurions and soldiers, and thither also the picked troops of the army of Judaea. Such a vast assemblage of cavalry and infantry, and the pomp of the kings that strove to rival each other in magnificence, presented an appearance of Imperial splendor.

JOSEPHUS

The Roman Army in the First Century CE

Source: Flavius Josephus: *The Jewish War*. III.5-6, trans. William Whiston. Complete works of Josephus online at CCEL.

> *Josephus, a law-observant and Hellenized Jew, recounted the Jewish revolt against Roman occupation (66–70 CE), in which he had fought as the Jewish military commander in Galilee. After the war he went to Rome, attached to the entourage of the future emperor Titus, and became a Roman citizen.*

Now here one cannot but admire at the precaution of the Romans, in providing themselves of such household servants, as might not only serve at other times for the common offices of life, but might also be of advantage to them in their wars. And, indeed, if any one does but attend to the other parts of their military discipline, he will be forced to confess that their obtaining so large a dominion hath been the acquisition of their valor, and not the bare gift of fortune; for they do not begin to use their weapons first in time of war, nor do they then put their hands first into motion, while they avoided so to do in times of peace; but, as if their weapons did always cling to them, they have never any truce from warlike exercises; nor do they stay till times of war admonish them to use them; for their military exercises differ not at all from the real use of their arms, but every soldier is every day exercised, and that with great diligence, as if it were in time of war, which is the reason why they bear the fatigue of battles so easily; for neither can any disorder remove them from their usual regularity, nor can fear affright them out of it, nor can labor tire them; which firmness of conduct makes them always to overcome those that have not the same firmness; nor would he be mistaken that should call those their exercises unbloody battles, and their battles bloody exercises. Nor can their enemies easily surprise them with the suddenness of their incursions; for as soon as they have marched into an enemy's land, they do not begin to fight till they have walled their camp about; nor is the fence they raise rashly made, or uneven; nor do they all abide ill it, nor do those that are in it take their places at random; but if it happens that the ground is uneven, it is first leveled: their camp is also four-square by measure, and carpenters are ready, in great numbers, with their tools, to erect their buildings for them.

As for what is within the camp, it is set apart for tents, but the outward circumference hath the resemblance to a wall, and is adorned with towers at equal distances, where between the towers stand the engines for throwing arrows and darts, and for slinging stones, and where they lay all other engines that can annoy the enemy, all ready for their several operations. They also erect four gates, one at every side of the circumference, and those large enough for the entrance of the beasts, and wide enough for making excursions, if occasion should require. They divide the camp within into streets, very conveniently, and place the tents of the commanders in the middle; but in the very midst of all is the general's own tent, in the nature of a temple, insomuch, that it appears to be a city built on the sudden, with its market-place, and place for handicraft trades, and with seats for the officers superior and inferior, where, if any differences arise, their causes are heard and determined. The camp, and all that is in it, is encompassed with a wall round about, and that sooner than one would imagine, and this by the multitude and the skill of the laborers; and, if occasion require, a trench is drawn round the whole, whose depth is four cubits, and its breadth equal.

When they have thus secured themselves, they live together by companies, with quietness and decency, as are all their other affairs managed with good order and security. Each company hath also their wood, and their corn, and their water brought them, when they stand in need of them; for they neither sup nor dine as they please themselves singly, but all together. Their times also for sleeping, and watching, and rising are notified beforehand by the sound of trumpets, nor is any thing done without such a signal; and in the morning the soldiery go every one to their centurions, and these centurions to their tribunes, to salute them; with whom all the superior officers go to the general of the whole army, who then gives them of course the watchword and other orders, to be by them cared to all that are under their command; which is also observed when they go to fight, and thereby they turn themselves about on the sudden, when there is occasion for making sallies, as they come back when they are recalled in crowds also.

Now when they are to go out of their camp, the trumpet gives a sound, at which time nobody lies still, but at the first intimation they take down their tents, and all is made ready for their going out; then do the trumpets sound again, to order them to get ready for the march; then do they lay their baggage suddenly upon their mules, and other beasts of burden, and stand, as at the place of starting, ready to march; when also they set

fire to their camp, and this they do because it will be easy for them to erect another camp, and that it may not ever be of use to their enemies. Then do the trumpets give a sound the third time, that they are to go out, in order to excite those that on any account are a little tardy, that so no one may be out of his rank when the army marches. Then does the crier stand at the general's right hand, and asks them thrice, in their own tongue, whether they be now ready to go out to war or not? To which they reply as often, with a loud and cheerful voice, saying, "We are ready." And this they do almost before the question is asked them: they do this as filled with a kind of martial fury, and at the same time that they so cry out, they lift up their right hands also.

When, after this, they are gone out of their camp, they all march without noise, and in a decent manner, and every one keeps his own rank, as if they were going to war. The footmen are armed with breastplates and head-pieces, and have swords on each side; but the sword which is upon their left side is much longer than the other, for that on the right side is not longer than a span. Those foot-men also that are chosen out from the rest to be about the general himself have a lance and a buckler, but the rest of the foot soldiers have a spear and a long buckler, besides a saw and a basket, a pick-axe and an axe, a thong of leather and a hook, with provisions for three days, so that a footman hath no great need of a mule to carry his burdens. The horsemen have a long sword on their right sides, axed a long pole in their hand; a shield also lies by them obliquely on one side of their horses, with three or more darts that are borne in their quiver, having broad points, and not smaller than spears. They have also head-pieces and breastplates, in like manner as have all the footmen. And for those that are chosen to be about the general, their armor no way differs from that of the horsemen belonging to other troops; and he always leads the legions forth to whom the lot assigns that employment.

This is the manner of the marching and resting of the Romans, as also these are the several sorts of weapons they use. But when they are to fight, they leave nothing without forecast, nor to be done off-hand, but counsel is ever first taken before any work is begun, and what hath been there resolved upon is put in execution presently; for which reason they seldom commit any errors; and if they have been mistaken at any time, they easily correct those mistakes. They also esteem any errors they commit upon taking counsel beforehand to be better than such rash success as is owing to fortune only; because such a fortuitous advantage tempts them to be inconsiderate, while consultation, though it may sometimes fail of success, hath this good in it, that it makes men more careful hereafter; but for the advantages that arise from chance, they are not owing to him that gains them; and as to what melancholy accidents happen unexpectedly, there is this comfort in them, that they had however taken the best consultations they could to prevent them.

Now they so manage their preparatory exercises of their weapons, that not the bodies of the soldiers only, but their souls may also become stronger: they are moreover hardened for war by fear; for their laws inflict capital punishments, not only for soldiers running away from the ranks, but for slothfulness and inactivity, though it be but in a lesser degree; as are their generals more severe than their laws, for they prevent any imputation of cruelty toward those under condemnation, by the great rewards they bestow on the valiant soldiers; and the readiness of obeying their commanders is so great, that it is very ornamental in peace; but when they come to a battle, the whole army is but one body, so well coupled together are their ranks, so sudden are their turnings about, so sharp their hearing as to what orders are given them, so quick their sight of the ensigns, and so nimble are their hands when they set to work; whereby it comes to pass that what they do is done quickly, and what they suffer they bear with the greatest patience. Nor can we find any examples where they have been conquered in battle, when they came to a close fight, either by the multitude of the enemies, or by their stratagems, or by the difficulties in the places they were in; no, nor by fortune neither, for their victories have been surer to them than fortune could have granted them. In a case, therefore, where counsel still goes before action, and where, after taking the best advice, that advice is followed by so active an army, what wonder is it that Euphrates on the east, the ocean on the west, the most fertile regions of Libya on the south, and the Danube and the Rhine on the north, are the limits of this empire? One might well say that the Roman possessions are not inferior to the Romans themselves.

This account I have given the reader, not so much with the intention of commending the Romans, as of comforting those that have been conquered by them, and for the deterring others from attempting innovations under their government. This discourse of the Roman military conduct may also perhaps be of use to such of the curious as are ignorant of it, and yet have a mind to know it. I return now from this digression....

But as Vespasian had a great mind to fall upon Galilee, he marched out of Ptolemais, having put his army into that order wherein the Romans used to march. He ordered those auxiliaries which were lightly armed, and the archers, to march first, that they might prevent any sudden insults from the enemy, and might search out the woods that looked suspiciously, and were capable of ambuscades. Next to these followed that part of the Romans which was completely armed, both footmen ,and horsemen. Next to these followed ten out of every hundred, carrying along with them their arms, and what was necessary to measure out a camp withal; and after

them, such as were to make the road even and straight, and if it were any where rough and hard to be passed over, to plane it, and to cut down the woods that hindered their march, that the army might not be in distress, or tired with their march. Behind these he set such carriages of the army as belonged both to himself and to the other commanders, with a considerable number of their horsemen for their security. After these he marched himself, having with him a select body of footmen, and horsemen, and pikemen. After these came the peculiar cavalry of his own legion, for there were a hundred and twenty horsemen that peculiarly belonged to every legion. Next to these came the mules that carried the engines for sieges, and the other warlike machines of that nature. After these came the commanders of the cohorts and tribunes, having about them soldiers chosen out of the rest. Then came the ensigns encompassing the eagle, which is at the head of every Roman legion, the king, and the strongest of all birds, which seems to them a signal of dominion, and an omen that they shall conquer all against whom they march; these sacred ensigns are followed by the trumpeters. Then came the main army in their squadrons and battalions, with six men in depth, which were followed at last by a centurion, who, according to custom, observed the rest. As for the servants of every legion, they all followed the footmen, and led the baggage of the soldiers, which was borne by the mules and other beasts of burden. But behind all the legions carne the whole multitude of the mercenaries; and those that brought up the rear came last of all for the security of the whole army, being both footmen, and those in their armor also, with a great number of horsemen.

LEGAL TEXT

Law Concerning the Power of Vespasian

Source: *Lex De Imperio Vespasiani*: ILS 244.

"The Law concerning the power of Vespasian" (69/70 CE) is an inscription in bronze; only this portion, which is the end of the document, survives.

¶1... that he shall have the right, just as the deified Augustus[157] and Ti. Julius Caesar Augustus[158] and Ti. Claudius Caesar Augustus Germanicus[159] had, to conclude treaties with whomever he wishes;

---

[157] a.k.a. Octavian, who ruled from 31 BCE to 14 CE.
[158] Tiberius, emperor from 14-31.
[159] Claudius, emperor from 41–54. Notably absent here are the emperors C. (Caligula), officially neglected; Nero, afterwards damned; and Vespasian's immediate predecessors, the other emperors of 69 CE: Galba, Otho, and Vitellius, here ignored. Only the three emperors mentioned were considered worthy examples.

¶2 And that he shall have the right, just as the deified Augustus and Ti. Julius Caesar Augustus and Ti. Claudius Caesar Augustus Germanicus had, to convene the senate, to put and refer proposals to it, and to cause decrees of the senate to be enacted by proposal and division of the house;

¶3 And that when the senate is convened [in special session] pursuant to his wish, authorization, order, or command, or in his presence, all matters transacted shall be considered and observed as fully binding as if the meeting of the senate had been regularly convoked and held;

¶4 And that at all elections especial consideration shall be given to those candidates for a magistracy, authority, imperium, or any post whom he has recommended to the Roman senate and people or to whom he has given and promised his vote;

¶5 And that he shall have the right, just as Ti. Claudius Caesar Augustus Germanicus had, to extend and advance the boundaries of the pomerium[160] whenever he deems it to be in the interest of the state;

¶6 And that he shall have the right and power, just as the deified Augustus and Ti. Julius Caesar Augustus and Ti. Claudius Caesar Augustus Germanicus had, to transact and do whatever things divine, human, public and private he deems to serve the advantage and the overriding interest of the state;

¶7 And that the Emperor Caesar Vespasian shall not be bound by those laws and plebiscites which were declared not binding upon the deified Augustus Ti. Julius Caesar Augustus or Ti. Claudius Caesar Augustus Germanicus, and the Emperor Caesar Vespasian Augustus shall have the right to do whatsoever it was proper for the deified Augustus or Ti. Julius Caesar Augustus or Ti. Claudius Caesar Augustus Germanicus to do by virtue of any law or enactment;

¶8 And that whatever was done, executed, decreed, or ordered before the enactment of this law by the Emperor Caesar Vespasian Augustus, or by anyone at his order or command, shall be as fully binding and valid as if they had been done by order of the people or plebs.

¶9 Sanction: If anyone in consequence of this law has or shall have acted contrary to laws, enactments, plebiscites, or decrees of the senate, or if he shall have failed to do in consequence of this law anything that it is incumbent on him to do in accordance with a law, enactment, plebiscite, or decree of the senate, it shall be with impunity, nor shall he on that account have to pay any penalty to the people, nor shall anyone have the right to institute suit or judicial inquiry concerning such matter, nor shall any [authority] permit proceedings before him on such matter.

PLINY THE ELDER

The Grandeur of Rome

Source: Pliny Maior, *Natural History* III.v.66-67., XXXVI.xxiv.101-110, XXXVI.xxiv.121-123. From: William Stearns Davis, ed., *Readings in Ancient History: Illustrative Extracts from the Sources*, 2 Vols. (Boston: Allyn and Bacon, 1912-13), Vol. II: Rome and the West, pp. 179-181, 232-237. Scanned by: J. S. Arkenberg, Dept. of History, Cal. State Fullerton. Prof. Arkenberg has modernized the text.

The following short sketch of Rome, its streets, buildings, etc., is given us by a careful author, writing in the reign of Vespasian (69–79 CE). While the area of Rome was far less than most great modern capitals, probably the masses of the population were so compactly housed that the inhabitants in Pliny's time numbered well up to 1,500,000, although any estimates must be very uncertain.

Romulus left the city of Rome, if we are to believe those who state the very greatest number, with only three gates, and no more. When the Vespasiani' were Emperors and Censors in the year of the building of the city 826,[161] the circumference of the walls which surrounded it was thirteen and two-fifths miles. Surrounding as it does the Seven Hills, the city is divided into fourteen districts, with 265 crossroads under the guardianship of the Lares.[162] If a straight line is drawn from the mile column placed at the entrance of the Forum to each of the gates, which are at present thirty-seven in number—taking care to count only once the twelve double gates, and to omit the seven old ones, which no longer exist—the total result will be a straight line of twenty miles and 765 paces. But if we draw a straight line from the same mile column to the very last of the houses, including therein the Praetorian camp [in the suburbs] and follow throughout the line of the streets, the result will be something over seventy miles. Add to these calculations the height of the houses, and then a person may form a fair idea of this city, and surely he must confess that no other place in the world can vie with it in size.

On the eastern side it is bounded by the mound (agger) of Tarquinius Superbus—a work of surpassing grandeur; for he raised it so high as to be on a level with the walls on the side on which the city lay most exposed to attack from the neighboring plains. On all the other sides it has been fortified either with lofty walls, or steep and precipitous hills; yet it has come to pass, that the buildings of Rome—increasing and extending beyond all bounds—have now united many outlying towns to it....

In great buildings as well as in other things the rest of the world has been outdone by us Romans. If, indeed, all the buildings in our City are considered in the aggregate, and supposing them—so to say—all thrown together in

---

[160] The official border of the city of Rome proper.

---

[161] 73 CE.
[162] I.e., a little shrine to the Lares would stand at each crossing.

one vast mass, the united grandeur of them would lead one to imagine that we were describing another world, accumulated in a single spot.

Not to mention among our great works the Circus Maximus, that was built by the Dictator Caesar—one stadium broad and three in length—and occupying with the adjacent buildings no less than four jugera[163] with room for no less than 160,000 spectators seated—am I not, however, to include in the number of our magnificent structures the Basilica of Paulus with its admirable Phrygian columns,[164] the Forum of the late Emperor Augustus, the Temple of Peace erected by the Emperor Vespasian Augustus—some of the finest work the world has ever seen? [and many others].

We behold with admiration pyramids that were built by kings, while the very ground alone that was purchased by the Dictator Caesar, for the construction of his Forum, cost 100,000,000 sesterces. If, too, an enormous expenditure has its attractions for any one whose mind is influenced by money matters, be it known that the house in which Clodius dwelt was purchased by him at a price of 14,800,000 sesterces—a thing which I for my part look upon as no less astonishing than the monstrous follies that have been displayed by kings.

Frequently praise is given to the great sewer system of Rome. There are seven "rivers" made to flow, by artificial channels, beneath the city. Rushing onward like so many impetuous torrents, they are compelled to carry off and sweep away all the sewerage; and swollen as they are by the vast accession of the rain water, they reverberate against the sides and bottoms of their channels. Occasionally too the Tiber, overflowing, is thrown backward in its course, and discharges itself by these outlets. Obstinate is the struggle that ensues between the meeting tides, but so firm and solid is the masonry that it is able to offer an effectual resistance. Enormous as are the accumulations that are carried along above, the work of the channels never gives way. Houses falling spontaneously to ruins, or leveled with the ground by conflagrations are continually battering against them; now and then the ground is shaken by earthquakes, and yet—built as they were in the days of Tarquinius Priscus, seven hundred years ago—these constructions have survived, all but unharmed.

Passing to the dwellings of the city, in the consulship of Lepidus and Catulus[165] we learn on good authority there was not in all Rome a finer house than that belonging to Lepidus himself, but yet—by Hercules!—within twenty-five years the very same house did not hold the hundredth rank simply in the City! Let anybody calculate—if he please—considering this fact, the vast masses of marble, the productions of painters, the regal treasures that must have been expended in bringing these hundred mansions to vie with one that in its day had been the most sumptuous and celebrated in all the City; and then let him reflect that, since then and down to the present, these houses had all of them been surpassed by others without number. There can be no doubt that the great fires are a punishment inflicted upon us for our luxury; but such are our habits, that in spite of such warnings, we cannot be made to understand that there are things in existence more perishable than even man himself....

But let us now turn our attention to some marvels that, if justly appreciated, may be pronounced to remain unsurpassed. Q. Marcius Rex[166] upon being commanded by the Senate to repair the Appian Aqueduct and that of the Anio, constructed during his praetorship a new aqueduct that bore his name, and was brought hither by a channel pierced through the very sides of mountains. Agrippa, during his aedileship, united the Marcian and the Virgin Aqueducts and repaired and strengthened the channels of others. He also formed 700 wells, in addition to 500 fountains, and 130 reservoirs, many of them magnificently adorned. Upon these works too he erected 300 statues of marble or bronze, and 400 marble columns, and all this in the space of a single year! In the work which he has written in commemoration of his aedileship, he also informs us that public games were celebrated for the space of fifty-seven days and 170 gratuitous bathing places were opened to the public. The number of these at Rome has vastly increased since his time.

The preceding aqueducts, however, have all been surpassed by the costly work which has more recently been completed by the Emperors Gaius [Caligula] and Claudius. Under these princes the Curtian and the Caerulean Waters with the "New Anio" were brought a distance of forty miles, and at so high a level that all the hills—whereon Rome is built—were supplied with water. The sum expended on these works was 350,000,000 sesterces. If we take into account the abundant supply of water to the public, for baths, ponds, canals, household purposes, gardens, places in the suburbs and country houses, and then reflect upon the distances that are traversed from the sources on the hills, the arches that have been constructed, the mountains pierced, the valleys leveled, we must perforce admit that there is nothing more worthy of our admiration throughout the whole universe.

---

[163] About 2 acres.
[164] Built also in Julius Caesar's day.
[165] 78 BCE.

---

[166] Praetor in 144 BCE.

Panegyric Addressed to the Emperor Trajan

Source: Pliny, Panegyric 65–80. Lewis, Naphtali, and Meyer Reinhold. Roman civilization. selected readings Vol. 2, The Empire. New York ; Chichester: Columbia University Press, 1990.

> *The Romans confined the panegyric—formal and detailed praise addressed to the subject—to the living, and reserved the funeral oration exclusively for the dead. The most celebrated example of a Latin panegyric is that delivered by the younger Pliny (100 CE) in the senate on the occasion of his assumption of the consulship, containing a somewhat fulsome eulogy of Trajan.*

You have spontaneously subjected yourself to the laws, to the laws which, Caesar, no one ever drafted to be binding upon the princeps.[167] But you desire to have no more rights than we (the Senate); and the result is that we would like you to have more. What I now hear for the first time, now learn for the first time, is not, "The princeps is above the laws," but "The laws are above the princeps, and the same restrictions apply to Caesar when consul as to others." He swears fidelity to the laws in the presence of attentive gods-for to whom should they be more attentive than to Caesar? ...

Hardly had the first day of your consulship dawned when you entered the senate house and exhorted us, now individually, now all together, to resume our liberty, to take up the duties of imperial administration shared, so to speak, between yourself and us, to watch over the public interests, to rouse ourselves. All emperors before you said about the same, but none before you was believed. People had before their eyes the shipwrecks of many men who sailed along in a deceptive calm and foundered in an unexpected storm.... But you we follow fearlessly and happily, wherever you call us. You order us to be free: we will be. You order us to express our opinions openly: we will pronounce them. It is neither through any cowardice nor through any natural sluggishness that we have remained silent until now; terror and fear and that wretched prudence born of danger warned us to turn our eyes, our ears, our minds, away from the state-in fact, there was no state altogether. But today, relying and leaning upon your right hand and your promises, we unseal our lips closed in long servitude and we loose our tongues paralyzed by so many ills....

Here is the picture of the father of our state as I for my part seem to have discerned it both from his speech and from the very manner of its presentation. What weight in his ideas, what unaffected genuineness in his words, what earnestness in his voice, what confirmation in his face, what sincerity in his eyes, bearing, gestures, in short in his whole body! He will always remember his advice to us, and he will know that we are obeying him whenever we make use of the liberty he has given us. And there is no fear that he will judge us reckless if we take advantage unhesitatingly of the security of the times, for he remembers that we lived otherwise under an evil princeps.'[168]

It is our custom to offer public prayers for the eternity of the Empire and the preservation of the emperor ... "if [he] has ruled the state well and in the interest of all." ... You reap, Caesar, the most glorious fruit of your preservation from the consent of the gods. For when you stipulate that the gods should preserve you only "if you have ruled the state well and in the interest of all," you are assured that you do rule the state well since they preserve you.'49 And so you pass in security and joy the day which tortured other emperors with worry and fear when in suspense, thunderstruck, uncertain how far they could rely on our patience, they awaited from here and there the messages of public servitude....

In judicial inquiries, what soft severity [you display], what clemency without weakness! You do not sit as judge intent on enriching your private treasury, and you want no reward for your decision other than to have judged rightly. Litigants stand before you concerned not for their fortunes, but for your good opinion, and they fear not so much what you may think of their case as what you may think of their character. O care truly that of a princeps, and even of a god, to reconcile rival cities, to calm peoples in ferment, less by imperial command than by reason, to impede the injustices of magistrates, to annul everything that ought not have been done, in fine, in the manner of the swiftest star to see all, hear all, and like a divinity be present and be helpful forthwith wherever invoked! Such, I imagine, are the things that the father of the world (i.e., Jupiter) regulates with a nod when he lets his glance fall upon the earth and deigns to count human destinies among his divine occupations. Henceforth free and released in this area he can attend to the sky alone, since he has sent you to fill his role toward the human race. You fulfill that function, and you are worthy of him who entrusted it to you, since each of your days is devoted to our greatest good, to your greatest glory.

---

[167] C.f. Justinian Digest l. iii. 31 (quoting Ulpian): "The emperor is not bound by the laws."

[168] A clear reference to Domitian, emperor 81-97 CE, cruel as C./Caligula, but much more intelligent and sane, and more dangerous.

The Correspondence of a Provincial Governor and the Emperor

Source: Pliny the Younger, *Letters* X.25 ff. From: William Stearns Davis, ed., *Readings in Ancient History: Illustrative Extracts from the Sources*, 2 Vols. (Boston: Allyn and Bacon, 1912-13), Vol. II: Rome and the West, 196-210, 215-222, 250-251, 289-290, 295-296, 298-300.

About 112 CE. Trajan appointed Pliny the Younger, a distinguished Senator and literary man, as governor of Bithynia—a province suffering from previous maladministration. The nature of the governor's problems and the obligation he was under of referring very petty matters to the Emperor appears clearly in the following letters. This correspondence of Trajan and Pliny (given here only in small part) is among the most valuable bits of historical data we have for the whole Imperial Age.

Pliny to Trajan: The people of Prusa, Sire, have a public bath in a neglected and dilapidated state. They wish—with your kind permission—to restore it; but I think a new one ought to be built, and I reckon you can safely comply with their wishes. [Then the governor names various ways to find the money, e.g. reducing the free distribution of oil.]

Trajan to Pliny: If the building of a new bath will not cripple the finances of Prusa, we can indulge their wishes; only it must be understood that no new taxes are to be raised to meet the cost, and that their contributions for necessary expenses shall not show any falling off.

Pliny to Trajan: A desolating fire broke out in Nicomedia, and destroyed a number of private houses, and two public buildings—the almshouse and the temple of Isis—although a road ran between them. The fire was allowed to spread farther than it need, first owing to the violent wind; second, to the laziness of the citizens, it being generally agreed they stood idly by without moving, and simply watched the conflagration. Besides there was not a single public fire engine or bucket in the place, and not one solitary appliance for mastering a fire. However, these will be provided upon orders I have already given. But, Sire, I would have you consider whether you think a fire company of about 150 men ought not to be formed? I will take care that no one not a genuine fireman shall be admitted, and that the guild should not misapply the charter granted it. Again there would be no trouble in keeping an eye on so small a body.

Trajan to Pliny: You have formed the idea of a possible fire company at Nicomedia on the model of various others already existing; but remember that the province of Bithynia, and especially city-states like Nicomedia, are the prey of factions. Give them the name

we may, and however good be the reasons for organization, such associations will soon degenerate into dangerous secret societies. It is better policy to provide fire apparatus, and to encourage property holders to make use of them, and if need comes, press the crowd which collects into the same service.

Pliny to Trajan: Sire, the people of Nicomedia spent 3,229,000 sesterces[169] upon an aqueduct, which was left in an unfinished state, and I may say in ruin, and they also levied taxes to the extent of 2,000,000 sesterces[170] for a second one. This, too, has been abandoned, and to get a water supply those who have wasted these vast sums must go to a new expense. I have visited a splendid clear spring, from which it seems to me the supply ought to be brought to the town [and have formed a scheme that seems practicable].

Trajan to Pliny: Steps must certainly be taken to provide Nicomedia with a water supply; and I have full confidence you will undertake the duty with all due care. But I profess it is also part of your diligent duty to find out who is to blame for the waste of such sums of money by the people of Nicomedia on their aqueducts, and whether or no there has been any serving of private interests in this beginning and then abandoning of [public] works. See that you bring to my knowledge whatever you find out.

Pliny to Trajan: The theater at Nicaea, Sire, the greater part of which has already been constructed—though it is still unfinished—has already cost over 10,000,000 sesterces[171]—at least so I am told, for the accounts have not been made out; and I am fearful lest the money has been thrown away. For the building has sunk and there are great gaping crevices to be seen, either because the ground is damp, or owing to the [bad quality] of the stone. [It is doubtful if the affair is worth completing.] Just before I came the Nicaeans also began to restore the public gymnasium, which had been destroyed by fire, on a larger scale than the old building, and they have already disbursed a considerable sum thereon, and I fear to little purpose [for it is very ill constructed]. Moreover the architect—the rival, to be sure, of the man who began the work—asserts that the walls, although twenty-two feet thick, cannot bear the weight placed upon them, because they have not been put together with cement in the middle and have not been strengthened with brickwork.

Trajan to Pliny: You are the best judge of what to do at Nicaea. It will be enough for me to be informed of the plan you adopt. All Greek peoples have a passion for gymnasia, so perhaps the people of Nicaea have set about building one on a rather lavish scale, but they must be content to cut their coat according to their cloth.

---

[169] About $1,857,000 in 1998 dollars.
[170] About $1,543,000 in 1998 dollars.
[171] About $7,500,000 in 1998 dollars.

You again must decide what advice to give the people of Claudiopolis.

Pliny to Trajan: When I asked for a statement of the expenditures of the city of Byzantium—which are abnormally high—it was pointed out to me, Sire, that a delegate was sent every year with a complimentary decree to pay his respects to you, and that he received 12,000 sesterces for so doing. Remembering your instructions I ordered him to stay at home and to forward the decree by me in order to lighten the expenses. I beg you to tell whether I have done right.

Trajan to Pliny: You have done quite right, my dear Pliny, in canceling the expenditure of the Byzantines... for that delegate. They will in the future do their duty well enough, even though the decree alone is sent me through you.

Pliny to Trajan: Sire, a person named Julius Largus of Pontus, whom I have never seen or heard of before, has entrusted me with the management of his property with which he seeks to prove his loyalty to you. For he has asked me in his will to undertake as heir the division of his property, and after keeping 50,000 sesterces, hand over all the remainder to the free cities of Heraclea and Teos. He leaves it to my discretion whether I think it better to erect public works and dedicate them to your glory, or to start an athletic festival, to be held every five years, and to be called the "Trajan Games." I have decided to lay the facts before you and ask your decision.

Trajan to Pliny: Julius Largus, in picking you out for your trustworthiness, has acted as though he knew you intimately. So do you consider the circumstances of each place, and the best means of perpetuating his memory, and follow the course you think best.

Pliny to Trajan: It is my custom, Sire, to refer to you in all cases where I am in doubt, for who can better clear up difficulties and inform me? I have never been present at any legal examination of the Christians, and I do not know, therefore, what are the usual penalties passed upon them, or the limits of those penalties, or how searching an inquiry should be made. I have hesitated a great deal in considering whether any distinctions should be drawn according to the ages of the accused; whether the weak should be punished as severely as the more robust, or whether the man who has once been a Christian gained anything by recanting? Again, whether the name of being a Christian, even though otherwise innocent of crime, should be punished, or only the crimes that gather around it?

In the meantime, this is the plan which I have adopted in the case of those Christians who have been brought before me. I ask them whether they are Christians, if they say "Yes," then I repeat the question the second time, and also a third—warning them of the penalties involved; and if they persist, I order them away to prison. For I do not doubt that—be their admitted crime what it may—their pertinacity and inflexible obstinacy surely ought to be punished.

There were others who showed similar mad folly, whom I reserved to be sent to Rome, as they were Roman citizens. Later, as is commonly the case, the mere fact of my entertaining the question led to a multiplying of accusations and a variety of cases were brought before me. An anonymous pamphlet was issued, containing a number of names of alleged Christians. Those who denied that they were or had been Christians and called upon the gods with the usual formula, reciting the words after me, and those who offered incense and wine before your image—which I had ordered to be brought forward for this purpose, along with the regular statues of the gods—all such I considered acquitted—especially as they cursed the name of Christ, which it is said bona fide Christians cannot be induced to do.

Still others there were, whose names were supplied by an informer. These first said they were Christians, then denied it, insisting they had been, "but were so no longer"; some of them having "recanted many years ago," and more than one "full twenty years back." These all worshiped your image and the god's statues and cursed the name of Christ.

But they declared their guilt or error was simply this—on a fixed day they used to meet before dawn and recite a hymn among themselves to Christ, as though he were a god. So far from binding themselves by oath to commit any crime, they swore to keep from theft, robbery, adultery, breach of faith, and not to deny any trust money deposited with them when called upon to deliver it. This ceremony over, they used to depart and meet again to take food—but it was of no special character, and entirely harmless. They also had ceased from this practice after the edict I issued—by which, in accord with your orders, I forbade all secret societies.

I then thought it the more needful to get at the facts behind their statements. Therefore I placed two women, called "deaconesses," under torture, but I found only a debased superstition carried to great lengths, so I postponed my examination, and immediately consulted you. This seems a matter worthy of your prompt consideration, especially as so many people are endangered. Many of all ages and both sexes are put in peril of their lives by their accusers; and the process will go on, for the contagion of this superstition has spread not merely through the free towns, but into the villages and farms. Still I think it can be halted and things set right. Beyond any doubt, the temples—which were nigh deserted—are beginning again to be thronged with worshipers; the sacred rites, which long have lapsed, are now being renewed, and the food for the sacrificial victims is again finding a sale—though up to recently it had almost no market. So one can safely infer how vast numbers could be reclaimed, if only there were a chance given for repentance.

Trajan to Pliny: You have adopted the right course, my dear Pliny, in examining the cases of those cited before you as Christians; for no hard and fast rule can be laid down covering such a wide question. The Christians are not to be hunted out. If brought before you, and the offense is proved, they are to be punished, but with this reservation—if any one denies he is a Christian, and makes it clear he is not, by offering prayer to our gods, then he is to be pardoned on his recantation, no matter how suspicious his past. As for anonymous pamphlets, they are to be discarded absolutely, whatever crime they may charge, for they are not only a precedent of a very bad type, but they do not accord with the spirit of our age.

STRABO, OXYRHYNCHOS PAPYRI

Egypt under the Roman Empire

Source: Strabo, *Geography*, XVII.i.52-53, ii.4-5; XVIII.i.12-13. In *The Geography of Strabo: Literally Translated, with Notes*, trans. H. C. Hamilton, esq., & W. Falconer (London: H. G. Bohn, 1854-1857), pp. 266-267, 272-274. The Oxyrhynchos Papyri. William Stearns Davis, ed., Readings in Ancient History: Illustrative Extracts from the Sources, 2 Vols. (Boston: Allyn and Bacon, 1912-13), Vol. II: Rome and the West, pp. 172-174, 244-247.

Strabo: *Geography* XVII, XVIII

Roman rule was established in Egypt after Octavian (Augustus) displaced the last ruler of the Ptolemaic line, the famous Cleopatra VII. It proved to be a great and rich province for Augustus, who organized the country not so much as a Roman Province but as the emperor's own special domain land. In Egypt, the Emperor was considered the successor of the ancient Pharaohs; his deputy—the prefect—ruled the country with an authority permitted to few other governors.

At present[172] Egypt is a Roman province, and pays considerable tribute, and is well-governed by prudent persons sent there in succession. The governor thus sent out has the rank of king. Subordinate to him is the administrator of justice, who is the supreme judge in many cases. There is another officer called the Idologus whose business is to inquire into property for which there is no claimant, and which of right falls to Caesar. These are accompanied by Caesar's freedmen and stewards, who are entrusted with affairs of more or less importance.

Three legions are stationed in Egypt, one in the city of Alexandria, the rest in the country. Besides these, there are also nine Roman cohorts quartered in the city, three on the borders of Ethiopia in Syene, as a guard to that tract, and three in other parts of the country. There are

also three bodies of cavalry distributed at convenient posts.

Of the native magistrates in the cities, the first is the "Expounder of the Law"—who is dressed in scarlet. He receives the customary honors of the land, and has the care of providing what is necessary for the city. The second is the "Writer of the Records"; the third is the "Chief Judge"; the fourth is the "Commander of the Night Guard." These officials existed in the time of the Ptolemaic kings, but in consequence of the bad administration of the public affairs by the latter, the prosperity of the city of Alexandria was ruined by licentiousness. Polybius expresses his indignation at the state of things when he was there. He describes the inhabitants of Alexandria as being composed of three classes, first the Egyptians and natives, acute in mind, but very poor citizens, and wrongfully meddlesome in civic affairs. Second were the mercenaries, a numerous and undisciplined body, for it was an old custom to keep foreign soldiers—who from the worthlessness of their sovereigns knew better how to lord it than to obey. The third were the so-called "Alexandrines," who, for the same reason, were not orderly citizens; however they were better than the mercenaries, for although they were a mixed race, yet being of Greek origin they still retained the usual Hellenic customs.

Such, then, if not worse, were the social conditions of Alexandria under the last kings. The Romans, as far as they were able, corrected—as I have said-many abuses, and established an orderly government—by setting up vice-governors, nomarchs, and ethnarchs, whose business it was to attend to the details of administration.

Herodotus and other writers trifle very much when they introduce into their histories the marvelous, like (an interlude) of music and song, or some melody; for example, by asserting that the sources of the Nile are near the numerous islands, at Syene and Elephantine, and that at this spot the river has an unfathomable depth. In the Nile there are many islands scattered about, some of which are entirely covered, others in part only, at the time of the rise of the waters. The very elevated parts are irrigated by means of screw pumps. Egypt was from the first disposed to peace, from having resources within itself, and because it was difficult of access to strangers. It was also protected on the north by a harborless coast and the Egyptian Sea; on the east and west by the desert mountains of Libya and Arabia, as I have said before. The remaining parts towards the south are occupied by Troglodytae, Blemmyes, Nubians, and Megabarzae Ethiopians above Syene. These are nomads, and not numerous nor warlike, but accounted so by the ancients, because frequently, like robbers, they attacked defenseless persons. Neither are the Ethiopians, who extend towards the south and Meroë, numerous nor collected in a body; for they inhabit a long, narrow, and winding tract of land on the riverside, such as we have

---

[172] In Augustus's time.

before described; nor are they well prepared either for war or the pursuit of any other mode of life.

At present the whole country is in the same pacific state, proof of which is that the upper country is sufficiently guarded by three cohorts, and these not complete. Whenever the Ethiopians have ventured to attack them, it has been at the risk of danger to their own country. The rest of the forces in Egypt are neither very numerous, nor did the Romans ever once employ them collected into one army. For neither are the Egyptians themselves of a warlike disposition, nor the surrounding nations, although their numbers are very large.

Cornelius Gallus, the first governor of the country appointed by Augustus Caesar, attacked the city Heroöpolis, which had revolted,[173] and took it with a small body of men. He suppressed also in a short time an insurrection in the Thebaïs which originated as to the payment of tribute. At a later period Petronius resisted, with the soldiers about his person, a mob of myriads of Alexandrines, who attacked him by throwing stones. He killed some, and compelled the rest to desist.

To what has been said concerning Egypt, we must add these peculiar products; for instance, the Egyptian bean, as it is called, from which is obtained the ciborium, and the papyrus, for it is found here and in India only; the persea [peach] grows here only, and in Ethiopia; it is a lofty tree, and its fruit is large and sweet; the sycamine, which produces the fruit called the sycomorus, or fig-mulberry, for it resembles a fig, but its flavor is not esteemed. The corsium also (the root of the Egyptian lotus) grows there, a condiment like pepper, but a little larger. There are in the Nile fish in great quantity and of different kinds, having a peculiar and indigenous character. The best known are the oxyrhynchos [the sturgeon], and the lepidotus, the latus, the alabes, the coracinus, the choerus, the phagrorius, called also the phagrus. Besides these are the silurus, the citharus, the thrissa [the shad], the cestreus [the mullet], the lychnus, the physa, the bous, and large shellfish which emit a sound like that of wailing.

The animals peculiar to the country are the ichneumon and the Egyptian asp, having some properties which those in other places do not possess. There are two kinds, one a span in length, whose bite is more suddenly mortal than that of the other; the second is nearly an orguia [six feet] in size, according to Nicander, the author of the Theriaca. Among the birds are the ibis and the Egyptian hawk, which, like the cat, is more tame than those elsewhere. The nycticorax is here peculiar in its character; for with us it is as large as an eagle, and its cry is harsh; but in Egypt it is the size of a jay, and has a different note. The tamest animal, however, is the ibis; it resembles a stork in shape and size. There are two kinds, which differ in color; one is like a stork, the other is entirely black. Every street in Alexandria is full of them. In some respects they are useful; in others troublesome. They are useful, because they pick up all sorts of small animals and the offal thrown out of the butchers= and cooks= shops. They are troublesome because they devour everything, are dirty, and with difficulty prevented from polluting in every way what is clean and what is not given to them.

Herodotus truly relates of the Egyptians that it is a practice peculiar to them to knead clay with their hands, and the dough for making bread with their feet. Caces is a peculiar kind of bread which restrains fluxes. Kiki [the castor-oil bean] is a kind of fruit sowed in furrows. An oil is expressed from it which is used for lamps almost generally throughout the country, but for anointing the body only by the poorer sort of people and laborers, both men and women. The coccina are Egyptian textures made of some plant, woven like those made of rushes, or the palm tree. Barley beer is a preparation peculiar to the Egyptians. It is common among many tribes, but the mode of preparing it differs in each. This, however, of all their usages is most to be admired—that they bring up all children that are born. They circumcise the males, as also the females,[174] as is the custom also among the Jews, who are of Egyptian origin, as I said when I was treating of them.

The Oxyrhynchos Papyri

Most of the letters here given explain themselves. They are from papyri of the Imperial period, found at the Egyptian town of Oxyrhynchos, and serve to give a curious and valuable light upon the life of an obscure provincial community, circa late third & early fourth centuries CE.

1. Dioscorides, logistes[175] of the Oxyrhynchite nome. The assault at arms by the youths will occur tomorrow, the 24th. Tradition, no less than the distinguished character of the festival, requires that they do their uttermost in the gymnastic display. The spectators will be present at the two performances.

2. At a meeting of our body a dispatch was read from Theodorus, recently chosen in place of Areion, the scribe, to proceed to his highness, the Prefect [of Egypt] and attend his immaculate court. In this dispatch he explained that he is victor in the games and exempted from inquiries. We have, therefore, nominated Aurelianus to serve and we send you word accordingly that this fact may be brought to his knowledge, and no time be lost in his departure and attendance upon the court.

---

[173] in 28 BCE.

[174] I.e., cliterodectomy.
[175] A high local magistrate in Roman Egypt.

3. To Aureleus Theon, keeper of the training school, from Aurelius Asclepiades, son of Philadelphus, president of the council of the village of Bacchias. I desire to hire from you Tisais, the dancing girl, and another, to dance for us at the above village for fifteen days from the 13th Phaophi by the old [Egyptian] calendar. You shall receive as pay 36 drachmae a day, and for the whole period three artabai of wheat, and fifteen couples of loaves; also three donkeys to fetch them and take them back.

4. Chaereman requests your company at dinner, at the table of the lord Serapis at the Serapeum, tomorrow the 15th, at 9 o'clock.

5. Herais requests your company at dinner, in celebration of the marriage of her children, in her house tomorrow, the 5th, at 9 o'clock.

6. Greeting, my dear Serenia, from Petosiris. Be sure, dear, to come upon the 20th for the birthday festival of the god, and let me know whether you are coming by boat or by donkey, in order that we may send for you accordingly. Take care not to forget. I pray for your continued health.

7. To Flavius Thennyras, logistes of the Oxyrhynchite district, from Aurelius Nilus, son of Didysus, of the illustrious and most illustrious city of Oxyrhynchos, an egg seller by trade. I hereby agree on the August, divine oath by our lord the Emperor and the Caesars to offer my eggs in the market place publicly for sale, and to supply to the said city, every day without intermission; and I acknowledge that it shall be unlawful for me in the future to sell secretly or in my house. If I am detected in so doing, I shall be liable to penalty."

8. I married a woman of my own tribe ... a free-born woman, of free parents, and have children by her. Now Tabes, daughter of Ammonios and her husband Laloi, and Psenesis and Straton their sons, have committed an act that disgraces all the chiefs of the town, and shows their recklessness; they carried off my wife and children to their own house, calling them their slaves, although they were free, and my wife has brothers living who are free. When I remonstrated, they seized me and beat me shamefully.

9. On the fourth of this month, Taorsenouphis, wife of Ammonios Phimon, an elder of the village of Bacchias although she had no occasion against me, came to my house, and made herself most unpleasant to me. Besides tearing my tunic and cloak, she carried off 16 drachmae that I had put by, the price of vegetables I had sold. And on the fifth her husband, Ammonios Phimon, came to my house, pretending he was looking for my husband, and took my lamp and went up into the house. And he went off with a pair of silver armlets, weighing forty drachmae, while my husband was away from home.

SUETONIUS

How Domitian Attempted to Amuse the Populace

Source: Suetonius, *Life of Domitian* IV. From: William Stearns Davis, ed., Readings in Ancient History: Illustrative Extracts from the Sources, 2 Vols. (Boston: Allyn and Bacon, 1912-13), Vol. II: Rome and the West. Scanned by: J. S. Arkenberg, Dept. of History, Cal. State Fullerton.

Despite their control of the army and the subservience of the Senate, the average Emperor quailed before the hoots and ill will of the Roman mob. Thus Domitian (emperor 81–96 CE), tried to win popularity by providing the idle masses of the capital with their favorite games and arena massacres.

He frequently entertained the people with the most magnificent and costly shows, not only in the amphitheater, but in the circus; where, besides the usual chariot races, with two or four horses abreast, he exhibited the imitation of a battle betwixt cavalry and infantry; and in the amphitheater a sea fight. The people too were entertained with wild-beast hunts, and gladiator fights even in the night-time, by torchlight. He constantly attended the games given by the quaestors, which had been disused for some time, but were revived by him; and upon these occasions, he always gave the people the liberty of demanding two pair of gladiators out of his own private school, who appeared last in court uniforms.

He presented the people with naval fights, performed by fleets almost as numerous as those usually employed in real engagements; making a vast lake near the Tiber, and building seats around it. And he witnessed these fights himself during a heavy rain.

Thrice he bestowed upon the people a bounty of 300 sesterces per man, and at a public show of gladiators a very plentiful feast. At the "Festival of the Seven Hills" he distributed large hampers of provisions to the Senatorial and Equestrian orders, and small baskets to the commonalty, and encouraged them to eat by setting the example. The day after he scattered among the people a variety of cakes and other delicacies to be scrambled after; and on the greater part of them falling amidst the seats of the lower classes, he ordered 500 tickets to be thrown into each range of benches belonging to the Senatorial and Equestrian orders.

VARIOUS

Roman Educational Practices

Source: Horace: Satires, I.6.xi.70-90; Pliny the Younger: Letters, IV.13; Martial: Epigrams, X.62From: William Stearns Davis, ed., Readings in Ancient History: Illustrative Extracts from the Sources, 2 Vols. (Boston: Allyn and Bacon, 1912-13), Vol. II: Rome and the West, pp. 227-230.

Horace: *Satires* I.6.xi.70-90

During the later Republic and Early Empire the craving for a good education was probably more prevalent than in any other age, barring the present. Even the lower classes were not usually illiterate (witness the numerous wall scribblings at Pompeii), although there was no system of free public schools. What one father did to give his son all possible advantages is told in this noble and touching tribute by Horace.

If I dare venture to speak in my own praise, and say that I live undefiled, innocent, and dear to my friends, let me confess that I owe all this to my father. A poor man he was, and on a lean farm, yet he was not content to send me to a local school[176] under the pedant Flavius, though boys of pretensions, sons of prominent centurions, went there with their school bags and writing tablets slung over their left arms, and carrying their teacher the fee in their hands on the Ides of eight months in the year. On the contrary, he had the spirit to bring me even as a child to Rome, to be taught those liberal arts which a senator or eques requires for his children. If anyone had seen my dress and the slaves that attended me in the big city, he would have guessed that I was maintained by some hereditary estate. My father—most faithful of guardians—was ever present at all my studies. Why need I say more? He preserved my modesty (the first point of virtue) not merely untainted, but free from the very rumor of taint. He was not afraid lest any one should reproach him[177] who turned out to be an auctioneer, or as my father was, a tax gatherer. I should not then have complained. But all the more is praise due to him, and from me the greater gratitude. As long as I keep my senses I will never be ashamed of such a father, nor apologize for my [humble] birth as do so many, asserting "it is no fault of theirs."

Pliny the Younger: *Letters* IV.13

The following letter by Pliny to the famous historian Tacitus is witness to the interest taken in education under the Empire. The school here mentioned was, of course, not a mere primary school—that existed surely already at Comum—but one of the higher learning. Pliny's munificence was by no means unique. Probably in no other age was so much money donated by wealthy men for education—especially in their home towns—until recently in America.

This letter contains a request: let me tell you why I ask it. When I was last in my native district[178] a son of a fellow townsman of mine, a youth under age, came to pay his respects to me. I said to him, "Do you keep up your studies?" "Yes," he answered. "Where?" I asked. "At Milan," was the reply. "But why not here?" I pressed. Then the lad's father, who was with him, said, "because we have no teachers here. " "How is that?" I asked. "It is a matter of urgent importance to you who are fathers," and it so chanced that luckily quite a number of fathers were listening to me, "that your children should get their education here at home."

For where can they pass their time so pleasantly as in their native town, where can they be brought up so virtuously as under their parent's eyes; or so inexpensively as at home? If you put your money together, you could hire teachers at a trifling cost, and you could add to their stipends the sum you now spend on your son's lodgings and travel money—no small sum. I have no children of my own, still, in the interests of the community—which I may consider as my child or my parent—I am ready to contribute a third part of what you may decide to club together upon. I would even promise the whole sum if I did not fear that if I did so, my generosity might be corrupted to serve private interests, as I see is the case in many places where teachers are employed at the public charge. There is only one way of preventing the evil, and that is by leaving the right of employing the teachers to the parents alone, who will be careful to make a right choice if they are obliged to find part of the money. You cannot make your children a better present than this, nor can you do your place a better turn."

And now, my friend Tacitus, since this is a serious matter, I beg you to look out for some teachers among the throng of learned men who gather around you, whom we can sound on the matter, but not in such a way as to pledge ourselves to employ any of them. For I wish to give the parents a perfectly free hand. They must judge and choose for themselves: I have only a sympathetic interest and a share in the cost. So if you find any one who thinks himself capable, let him go to

---

[176] At Venusia, his home town.
[177] For giving an education to a son.

---

[178] Comum, North Italy.

Comum, but on the express understanding that he builds upon no certainty beyond his confidence in himself. Farewell.

Martial: *Epigrams* **X.62:**

> *That the Roman schoolmasters, no less than their Greek predecessors, relied on the scourge to quicken slow wits is shown in the following from this writer of the end of the first century CE*

Sir Schoolmaster—show pity upon your simple scholars, at least if you wish to have many a long-haired boy attendant upon your lectures, and the class seated around your critical table love you. Then would no teacher of arithmetic or swift writing have a greater ring of pupils around him. Hot and bright are the days now under the flaming constellation of the lion; and fervid July is ripening the bursting harvest. So let your Scythian scourge with its dreadful thongs, such as flogged Marsyas of Celaenae, and your formidable cane—the schoolmaster's scepter—be laid aside, and sleep until the Ides of October. Surely in summer time, if the boys keep their health, they do enough.

MARCUS AURELIUS

On the Virtue of Antoninus Pius

Source: Marcus Aurelius, *Meditations* I.16. William Stearns Davis, ed., *Readings in Ancient History: Illustrative Extracts from the Sources*, 2 Vols. (Boston: Allyn and Bacon, 1912-13), *Vol. II: Rome and the West*. Scanned by: J. S. Arkenberg, Dept. of History, Cal. State Fullerton. Prof. Arkenberg has modernized the text.

> *Antoninus Pius (born 86, reigned 138-161 CE) had a singularly untroubled reign, although there is reason to believe that the forces which later ruined the Roman world were allowed by him to work unchecked. No one, however, has questioned the purity of his life and the simplicity and nobility of his character. His personality is described by his adopted son - the famous Marcus Aurelius. It is a high tribute to the ancient civilization and the Stoic philosophy that they could produce two such characters and bestow on them successively the government of the world.*

In my father [Antoninus Pius] I observed his meekness; his constancy without wavering in those things which, after due examination, he had determined. How free from all vanity he carried himself in matters of honor and dignity (as they are esteemed); his laboriousness and assiduity, his readiness to hear any man that had aught to say tending to any common good! how generally and impartially he would give every man his due: his skill and knowledge when rigor or extremity, when indulgence or moderation were in season. His moderate condescending to other men's occasions as an ordinary man, neither absolutely requiring his friends that they should wait on him at his ordinary meals, nor that they should of necessity accompany him in his journeys. His sociability, his gracious and delightful conversation never reached satiety, his care of his body was within bounds and measures, not as one who did not wish to live long, or overstudious of neatness and elegancy; yet not as one that did not regard it, so that through his own care of his health he seldom needed any medicine.

He was not easily moved and tossed up and down, but loved to be constant, both in the same places and businesses; and after his great fits of headache he would return fresh and vigorous to his wonted affairs. He was very discreet and moderate in exhibiting public sights and shows for the pleasure and pastime of the people; in public buildings, *congiaria*,[179] and the like. He did not use the baths at unseasonable hours. He was never curious or anxious about his food, or about the style or color of his clothes, or about any mere matter of external beauty. In all his conversation, he was far from all inhumanity, boldness, incivility, greediness, or impetuosity; never doing anything with such earnestness and intention that a man could say of him, that he flew into a heat about it, but contrariwise, all things distinctly, as at leisure, without trouble, orderly, soundly, and agreeably. A man, in short, might have applied to him what is recorded of Socrates.

Remember Antoninus Pius' constancy in things that were done by him in accordance with reason, his equability in all things; how he would never give over a matter until he understood the whole state of it fully and plainly; and how patiently and without any resentment he would bear with them that did unjustly condemn him; how he would never be overhasty in anything, nor give ear to slanders or false accusations, but examine and observe with the best diligence the several actions and dispositions of men. He would easily be content with a few things---mere lodgings, bedding, the ordinary food and attendance. He bore with those who opposed his opinions and even rejoiced if any man could better advise him, and finally he was exceedingly religious without superstition.

---

[179] General distribution of money or corn doles.

EUTROPIUS

The Reign of Marcus Aurelius

Source: Eutropius, *Compendium of Roman History* VIII.12-14. William Stearns Davis, ed., *Readings in Ancient History: Illustrative Extracts from the Sources*, 2 Vols. (Boston: Allyn and Bacon, 1912-13), *Vol. II: Rome and the West*. Scanned by: J. S. Arkenberg, Dept. of History, Cal. State Fullerton. Prof. Arkenberg has modernized the text.

Marcus Aurelius was Emperor from 161 to 180 CE. No ruler ever came to power with higher ideals and purposes, but the reign was not a very prosperous one. The philosopher in the purple was afflicted by the widespread pestilences in the Empire, and by the dangerous wars on the frontiers. He struggled against the difficulties manfully, and overcame most of them; but his reign marks the beginning of the long slow decline of the Empire.

Marcus Aurelius was trained in philosophy by Apollonius of Chalcedon: in the Greek language by Sextus of Chaeronea, the grandson of Plutarch, while the eminent orator Fronto instructed him in Latin literature. He conducted himself towards all men at Rome, as if he had been their equal, being moved by no arrogance by his elevation to the Empire. He exercised prompt liberality, and managed the provinces with the utmost kindness and indulgence.

Under his rule affairs were successfully conducted against the Germans. He himself carried on a war with the Marcomanni, which was greater than any in the memory of man (in the way of wars with the Germans)---so that it was compared to the Punic Wars, for it was exceedingly formidable, and in it whole armies were lost; especially as in this reign, after the victory over the Parthians there occurred a great pestilence so that at Rome, and throughout Italy and the provinces a large fraction of the population, and actually the bulk of the regular troops perished from the plague.

With the greatest labor and patience he persevered for three whole years at Carnutum [a strategically located fortress town in Pannonia], and brought the Marcomannic war to an end; a war in which the Quadi, Vandals, Sarmatians, Suevi and all the barbarians in that region, had joined the outbreak of the Marcomanni. He slew several thousand men, and having delivered the Pannonians from bondage held a triumph at Rome. As the treasury was drained by the war, and he had no money to give his soldiers; and as he would not lay any extra tax on the provinces or Senate, he sold off all his imperial furniture and decorations by an auction held in the Forum of Trajan, consisting of gold and cups of crystal and precious stone, silk garments belonging to his wife and to himself, embroidered---as they were---with gold, and numbers of jeweled ornaments. This sale was kept up through two successive months and a great deal of money was raised by it. After his victory, however, he refunded the money to such purchasers as were willing to restore what they had bought, but was by no means troublesome to those who wished to keep their purchase.

After his victory he was so magnificent in his display of games he is said to have exhibited in the arena one hundred lions at once. Having then at last rendered the state happy by his excellent management and gentleness of character, he died in the eighteenth year of his reign, in the sixty-first of his life. He was enrolled among the gods, all the Senate voting unanimously that he should have such honor.

HERODIAN

How Didius Julianus Bought the Empire at Auction

Source: Herodian of Syria (3rd Cent. CE): History of the Emperors II.6ff. From: William Stearns Davis, ed., Readings in Ancient History: Illustrative Extracts from the Sources, 2 Vols. (Boston: Allyn and Bacon, 1912-13), Vol. II: Rome and the West. Scanned by: J. S. Arkenberg, Dept. of History, Cal. State Fullerton. Prof. Arkenberg has modernized the text.

In 193 CE the Praetorian Guards murdered the Emperor Pertinax, who had striven to reduce them to discipline. The sale of the purple which followed forms one of the most fearful and dramatic incidents in the history of the Empire, illustrating: (1) how completely the guardsmen had lost all sense of decency, discipline, and patriotism; (2) how the idea that all things were purchasable for money had possessed the men of the Empire. It ought to be said that the Praetorians were an especially pampered corps, and probably the rest of the army was less corrupted. Didius Julianus held his ill-gotten power only from March 28th, 193 CE, to June 1st of the same year, being deposed and slain when Septimius Severus and the valiant Danube legions marched on Rome to avenge Pertinax. The ringleaders of the Praetorians were executed; the rest of the guardsmen dishonorably discharged and banished from Italy.

When the report of the murder of the Emperor Pertinax spread among the people, consternation and grief seized all minds, and men ran about beside themselves. An undirected effort possessed the people—they strove to hunt out the doers of the deed, yet could neither find nor punish them. But the Senators were the worst disturbed, for it seemed a public calamity that they had lost a kindly father and a righteous ruler. Also a reign of violence was dreaded, for one could guess that the soldiery would find that much to their liking. When the first and the ensuing days had passed, the people dispersed, each man fearing for himself; men of rank, however, fled to their estates outside the city, in order not to risk themselves in the dangers of a change on the throne. But at last when the soldiers were aware that the people were quiet, and that no one would try to avenge the blood of the Emperor, they nevertheless remained inside their barracks and barred the gates; yet they set such of their comrades as had the loudest voices upon the walls, and had them declare that the Empire was for sale at auction, and promise to him who bid highest that they would give him the power, and set him with the armed hand in the imperial palace.

When this proclamation was known, the more honorable and weighty Senators, and all persons of noble origin and property, would not approach the barracks to offer money in so vile a manner for a besmirched sovereignty. However, a certain Julianus—who had held the consulship, and was counted rich—was holding a drinking bout late that evening, at the time the news came of what the soldiers proposed. He was a man notorious for his evil living; and now it was that his wife and daughter and fellow feasters urged him to rise from his banqueting couch and hasten to the barracks, in order to find out what was going on. But on the way they pressed it on him that he might get the sovereignty for himself, and that he ought not to spare the money to outbid any competitors with great gifts to the soldiers.

When he came to the wall of the camp, he called out to the troops and promised to give them just as much as they desired, for he had ready money and a treasure room full of gold and silver. About the same time too came Sulpicianus, who had also been consul and was prefect of Rome and father-in-law of Pertinax, to try to buy the power also. But the soldiers did not receive him, because they feared lest his connection with Pertinax might lead him to avenge him by some treachery. So they lowered a ladder and brought Julianus into the fortified camp; for they would not open the gates, until they had made sure of the amount of the bounty they expected. When he was admitted he promised first to bring the memory of Commodus again into honor and restore his images in the Senate house, where they had been cast down; and to give the soldiers the same lax discipline they had enjoyed under Commodus. Also he promised the troops as large a sum of money as they could ever expect to require or receive. The payment should be immediate, and he would at once have the cash brought over from his residence. Captivated by such speeches, and with such vast hopes awakened, the soldiers hailed Julianus as Emperor, and demanded that along with his own name he should take that of Commodus. Next they took their standards, adorned them again with the likeness of Commodus and made ready to go with Julianus in procession.

The latter offered the customary imperial sacrifices in the camp; and then went out with a great escort of the guards. For it was against the will and intention of the populace, and with a shameful and unworthy stain upon the public honor that he had bought the Empire, and not

without reason did he fear the people might overthrow him. The guards therefore in full panoply surrounded him for protection. They were formed in a phalanx around him, ready to fight; they had "their Emperor" in their midst; while they swung their shields and lances over his head, so that no missile could hurt him during the march. Thus they brought him to the palace, with no man of the multitude daring to resist; but just as little was there any cheer of welcome, as was usual at the induction of a new Emperor. On the contrary the people stood at a distance and hooted and reviled him as having bought the throne with lucre at an auction.

VARIOUS

The Lives of Soldiers and Sailors

Sources: Valerius Maximus, *Memorable Deeds and Sayings* VII.vi.1; Livy 42.34; *Select Papyri I* (1932) #111, 112 (II. A.D.).

Valerius Maximus, *Memorable Deeds and Sayings* VII.vi.1

For during the Second Punic War [218-201 BCE] the Roman youth of military age having been drained by several unfavorable battles, the Senate, on the motion of the consul Tiberius Gracchus (consul in 215 and 213), decreed that slaves should be bought up out of public moneys for use in repulsing the enemy. After a plebiscite [[a vote of the Consilium Plebis] was passed on this matter by the people through the intervention of the Tribunes of the Plebs, a commission of three men was chosen to purchase 24,000 slaves, and having administered an oath to them that they would give zealous and courageous service and that they would bear arms as long as the Carthaginians were in Italy, they sent them to the camp. From Apulia and the Paediculi were also bought 270 slaves for replacements in the cavalry... The City, which up to this time had disdained to have as soldiers even free men without property added to its army as almost its chief support persons taken from slave lodgings and slaves gathered from shepherd huts.'

Livy 42.34

Citizens of Rome. I am Spurius Ligustinus, of the Tribe Crustumina, and I come of Sabine stock. My father left me half an acre of land and the little hut in which I was born and brought up. I am still living there today [171 BCE]. As soon as I came of age, my father gave me his brother's daughter to wife, who brought nothing with her save her free birth and her chastity, together with a fertility which would be enough even for a wealthy home. We have six sons, and two daughters (both already married). Four of my sons have taken the toga of manhood; two are still under age. I joined the army in the consulship of Publius Sulpicius and Gaius Aurelius (Cotta) [200 BCE], and I served two years in the ranks in the army which was taken across to Macedonia, in the campaign against King Philip [V, of Macedonia who died in 179]. In the third year Titus Quinctius Flamininus promoted me, for my bravery, to be centurion of the 10th maniple of hastati.

After the defeat of King Philip and the Macedonians, when we had been brought back to Italy and demobilized, I immediately left for Spain as a volunteer with the consul Marcus Porcius [CATO, consul in 195 BCE]. Of all the living generals, none has been a keener observer and judge of bravery than he, as is well known to those who through long military service have had experience of him and other commanders. This general judged me worthy to be appointed centurion of the 1st century of hastati. I enlisted for the third time, again as a volunteer, in the army sent against the Aetolians and King Antiochus. Manius Acilius [Glabrio, consul of 191] appointed me centurion of the first century of the principes. When King Antiochus had been driven out [Battle of Thermopylae] and the Aetolians had been crushed, we were brought back to Italy. And twice after that I took part in campaigns in which the legions served for a year. Thereafter I saw two campaigns in Spain, one with Quintus Fulvius Flaccus as Praetor [182, continued in office in 181 and 180], the other with Tiberius Sempronius Gracchus [father of the Gracchus brothers] in command [180].

I was brought back home by Flaccus with the others whom he brought back with him from the province for his Triumph, on account of their bravery. And I returned to Spain because I was asked to do so by Tiberius Gracchus. Four times in the course of a few years I held the rank of Chief Centurion. Thirty four times I was rewarded for bravery by the generals. I have been given six civic crowns. I have completed 22 years of service in the army, and I am now over 50 years old. But even if I had not completed my service, and if my age did not give me exemption, it would still be right for me to be descharged, Publius Licinius, since I could give your four soldiers as my substitutes...' There was an official vote of thanks, and the Military Tribunes, on account of his bravery appointed him First Centurion of the First Legion. The other centurions withdrew their appeal and obediently responded to the call for conscription.

Letter of a Recruit: Apollinarius

Apollinarius to Taesis, his mother and lady, many greetings!

Before all I pray for your health. I myself am well, and make supplication for you before the gods of this place. I wish you to know, mother, that I arrived in Rome in good health on the 20th of the month Pachon, and was posted to Misenum, though I have not let learned the name of my company (kenturian); for I had not gone to Misenum at the time of writing this letter. I beg you then, mother, look after yourself and do not worry about me; for I have come to a fine place. Please write me a letter about your welfare and that of my brothers and of all your folk. And whenever I find a messenger I will write to you; never will I be slow to write. Many salutations to my brothers and Apollinarius and his children, and Karalas and his children. I salute Ptolemaeus and Ptolemais and her children and Heraclous and her children. I salute all who love you, each by name. I pray for your health.

[Address:] Deliver at Karanis to Taesis, from her son Apollinarius of Misenum.

Letter of a Recruit: Apion

Apion to Epimachus, his father and lord, very many greetings.

Before all else I pray for your health and that you may always be well and prosperous, together with my sister and her daughter and my brother. I thank the Lord Serapis that when I was in danger at sea he straightway saved me. On arriving at Misenum, I received from Caesar three gold pieces for traveling expenses. And it is well with me.

Now I ask you, my lord and father, write me a letter, telling me first of your welfare, secondly of my brother's and sister's, and enabling me thirdly to make obeisance before your handwriting, because you educated me well and I hope thereby to have quick advancement, if the gods so will.

Give many salutations to Capiton and my brother and sister and Serenilla and my firends. I have sent you by Euctemon a portrait [eikonin]of myself. My name is Antonius Maximus, my company [kenturi(a)] is the Athenonica. I pray for your health.

[Postscript:] Serenus, son of Agathodaemon, salutes you, and..., and Turbo son of Gallonius, and....

[Addressed:] To Philadelphia, to Epimachus from Apion his son.

[Additional address:] Deliver at the camp of the first cohort of the Apameni to Julianus, vice-secretary [antiliblario] this letter from Apion to be forwarded to his father Epimachus.

Petition to the Emperor Philip Against Corruption (246 CE)

Most reverend and serene of all emperors, although in your most felicitous times all other persons enjoy an untroubled and calm existence, since all wickedness and oppression have ceased, we, alone experiencing a fortune most alien to these most fortunate times, present this supplication to you.

We are unreasonably oppressed and we suffer extortion by those persons whose duty it is to maintain the public welfare. For although we live remotely and are without military protection, we suffer afflictions alien to your most felicitous times. Generals and soldiers and lordlings of prominent offices in the city and your Caesarians, coming to us, traversing the Appian district, leaving the highway, taking us from our tasks, requisitioning our plowing oxen, make exactions that are by no means their due. And it happens thus that we are wronged by extortions. Our possessions are spent on them, and our fields are stripped and laid waste....

ZOSIMUS

Imperial Weakness Invites Barbarian Aggression

Source: Zosimus I.1.11–17. Translated by Anonymous. In *Arrian's History of Alexander's Expedition: Translated from the Greek : with Notes Historical, Geographical, and Critical.* London: Printed for R. Lea; J. Nunn; Lackington, Allen, and co.; White, Cochrane, and co.; J. Faulder; and J. Walker and co, 1814.

The army has confronted the emperor Alexander Severus (reigned 222–235) with disaffection and a challenger to his throne, which has the effect, says Zosimus, of making Alexander more avaricious for wealth and power.

While his affairs were thus unfortunately situated, the armies in Pannonia and Moesia, which were far from respecting him previously, now became more disposed to revolt, and being therefore determined on an innovation, raised to the empire Maximinus, the captain of a Pannonian troop. Having collected all his forces, he marched into Italy with the utmost speed, thinking it the safest to attack the emperor by surprise. But Alexander, who was then in the vicinity of the Rhine, having received intelligence of their intended revolt, proceeded to Rome without loss of time. He offered pardon to the soldiers and to Maximinus upon the condition that they would desist from their attempt; he could not however appease them, and therefore desperately exposed himself to death. Mamaea his mother, and the prefects, who issued from the palace to allay the tumult, were likewise murdered. Maximinus. thus became well established in the throne, but the people universally regretted the change of a moderate emperor for a cruel tyrant.[180] Maximinus was of obscure birth, and therefore on his exaltation to the imperial dignity, his excessive insolence in his new authority eclipsed those good

qualities with which nature had endowed him. He thus became intolerable to all men, not only doing injuries to those that were in honorable offices, but being guilty of the greatest cruelties in the exercise of his power, bestowing favors only upon sycophants who laid information against quiet persons, by charging them with being debtors to the imperial treasury. At length he went so far as to murder persons out of avarice, before he heard them plead in their own defense, seized on the towns as his own, and plundered the inhabitants.

The nations subject to the Romans being unable to endure his monstrous cruelty, and greatly distressed by the ravages he committed, the Africans proclaimed Gordianus and his son of the same name,[181] emperors, and sent ambassadors to Rome, one of whom was Valerianus, a man of consular rank, who afterwards himself became emperor. This was highly gratifying to the senate, which deliberated how to remove the tyrant, inciting the soldiers to revolt, and reminding the people of the injuries they sustained as well in their individual capacities, as in that of members of so mighty a state. Having thus agreed how to act, they selected out of the whole senate twenty persons who understood military discipline, and out of that number appointed two, Balbinus and Maximus, to hold the chief command, and proceeded towards Rome, being ready for an insurrection. But Maximinus, hearing of their intention, marched with great precipitation towards Rome, with the Moors and Gauls that were under his command, and on the way laid siege to the garrison of Aquileia, because they closed their gates against him. His own party, at length consulting the public benefit, with great reluctance consented to those who wished to put him to death, and he was thereby reduced to such extremity, as to be under the necessity of making his son a petitioner in his behalf, supposing that his tender age would abate their anger and incline them to compassion. But at this they became more enraged, and after they had murdered the boy in a most barbarous manner, they dispatched the father likewise; on which one of them cut off his head, and carried it to Rome, as an evidence and a trophy of their victory. Being thus delivered from all their apprehensions, they waited for the arrival of the two emperors from Africa.

These princes being wrecked in a storm, the senate conferred the supreme direction of affairs on Gordianus, the son of one of them.[182] In his reign, the Romans relaxed a little from their former melancholy, being treated by the emperor with plays and other amusements. But awaking as it were from a profound sleep, they formed a secret conspiracy against the emperor, instigated by the counsel of Balbinus and Maximus, who incited some of the soldiers against him.

---

[180] Maximinus Thrax or Maximinus I, was Roman Emperor from 235 to 238 CE. He was the first of the so-called barracks emperors.

[181] Gordian I and his son Gordian II, co-emperors in early 238.
[182] Gordian III, emperor 238–244.

This being detected, the heads of the conspiracy, and many of the accomplices, were put to death.

Soon after this, the Carthaginians became discontented with the emperor, and attempted to substitute Sabianus in his stead; but Gordianus raised a force in Africa, which quickly caused them to submit.[183] Upon this they delivered up the intended usurper, solicited pardon for their offences, and were freed from the danger that hung over them. Meantime Gordianus married the daughter of Timesicles, a man in high estimation for his learning, and appointed him prefect of the court; by which he seemed to supply the deficiency of his own youth in the administration of public affairs. Having secured the empire, he was in continual expectation that the Persians would make an attack on the eastern provinces, Sapores having succeeded in that kingdom to Artaxerxes, who had restored the government to the Persians from the Parthians. For after the death of Alexander the son of Philip,[184] and of his successors in the empire of the Macedonians, at the period when those provinces were under the authority of Antiochus, Arsaces a Parthian, being exasperated at an injury done to his brother Teridates, made war upon the satrap of Antiochus, and caused the Parthians to drive away the Macedonians, and form a government of their own. The emperor therefore made all possible preparations for marching against the Persians. Although he appeared in the first battle to have obtained the victory, yet the confidence of the emperor in the success of this enterprise was considerably diminished by the death of Timesicles, the prefect of the court. Philip being chosen in his place, the emperor's popularity in the army was gradually dissipated and. vanished.

Philip was a native of Arabia, a nation in bad repute, and had advanced his fortune by no very honorable means. As soon as he was fixed in his office, he aspired at the imperial dignity, and endeavored to seduce all the soldiers that were disposed to innovation. Observing that abundance of military provisions was supplied, while the emperor was staying about Carrae and Nisibis, he ordered the ships that brought those provisions to go further up the country, in order that the army, being oppressed with famine, might be provoked to mutiny. His design succeeded to his wish; for the soldiers, under pretence of want of necessaries, surrounded Gordianus in a violent manner, and having killed him, as the chief cause of so many perishing, conferred the purple on Philip according to their engagement.[185] He therefore made peace with Sapores, and marched towards Rome; and as he had bound the soldiers to him by large presents, he sent messengers to Rome to report that Gordianus had died of a disease. On his arrival at Rome, having made the senate his friends, he thought it most politic to confer the highest preferments on his near relations. From this motive he made his brother Priscus general of the army in Syria, and entrusted the forces in Moesia and Macedonia to his son-in-law Severianus.

Thinking that he had by these means established himself in the possession of the empire, he made an expedition against the Carpi, who had plundered all the country about the Ister. When an engagement took place, the Barbarians not being able to withstand the impetuous charge of the Romans, fled into a castle in which they were besieged. But finding that their troops, who were dispersed in various directions, had again rallied in a body, they resumed their courage, and sallying from the castle attacked the Roman army. Being unable to bear the brisk onset of the Moors, the army solicited for peace, to which Philip readily assented, and marched away. As there were at that time many disturbances in the empire, the eastern provinces, which were uneasy, partly, owing to the exactions of exorbitant tributes, and partly to their dislike of Priscus, their governor, who was a man of an intolerably evil disposition, wished for innovation, and set up Papianus for emperor, while the inhabitants of Moesia and Pannonia were more inclined to Marinus.

Philip, being disturbed by these events, desired the senate cither to assist him against such imminent dangers, or, if they were displeased with his government, to suffer him to lay it down and dismiss him quietly. No person making a reply to this, Decius, a person of illustrious birth and rank, and moreover gifted, with every virtue, observed, that he was unwise in being so much concerned at those events, for they would vanish of themselves, and could not possibly long subsist. And though the event corresponded with the conjecture of Decius, which long experience in the world had enabled him to make, Papianus and Marinus being taken off, yet Philip was still in fear, knowing how obnoxious, the officers in that country were to the army. He therefore desired Decius to assume the command of the legions in Moesia and Pannonia. As he refused this under the plea that it was inconvenient both for Philip and himself, Philip made use of the rhetoric of necessity, as the Thessalians term it, and compelled him to go to Pannonia to punish the accomplices of Marinus. The army in that country, finding that Decius punished all that had offended, thought it most politic, to avoid the present danger, and to set up a sovereign who would better consult the good of the state, and who, being more expert both in civil and military affairs, might without difficulty conquer Philip.

For this purpose they clothed Decius in purple, and notwithstanding all his apprehensions of future mischances, compelled him to assume the supreme authority. Philip therefore, on hearing that Decius was thus made emperor, collected all his forces to overpower him. The supporters of Decius, though they knew that

---

[183] Sabiunius's rebellion: 240 CE.
[184] I.e., Alexander III of Macedon, son of Philip II.
[185] Philip the Arab, emperor 244–249.

the enemy had greatly the advantage in numbers, still retained their confidence, trusting to the general skill and prudence of Decius in affairs. And when the two armies engaged, although the one was superior in number, yet the other so excelled it in discipline and conduct, that a great number of Philip's partisans were slain and he himself amongst them, together with his son, on whom he had conferred the title of Caesar. Decius thus acquired the empire.[186]

The Scythians, taking advantage of the disorder which every where prevailed through the negligence of Philip, crossed the Tanais, and pillaged the countries in the vicinity of Thrace. But Decius, marching against them, was not only victorious in every battle, but recovered the spoils they had taken, and endeavored to cut off their retreat to their own country, intending to destroy them all, to prevent their ever again, making a similar incursion. For this purpose he posted Gallus on the bank of the Tanais with a competent force, and led in person the remainder of his army against the enemy. This expedition exceeded to his utmost wish; but Gallus, who was disposed to innovation, sent agents to the Barbarians, requesting their concurrence in a conspiracy against Decius. To this they gave a willing assent, and Gallus retained his post on the bank of the Tanais, but the Barbarians divided themselves into three battalions, the first of which posted itself behind a marsh. Decius having destroyed a considerable number of the first battalion, the second advanced, which he likewise defeated, and discovered part of the third, which lay near the marsh. Gallus sent intelligence to him, that he might march against them across the fen. Proceeding therefore incautiously in an unknown place, he and his army became entangled in the mire, and under that disadvantage were so assailed by the missiles of the Barbarians, that not one of them escaped with life. Thus ended the life of the excellent emperor Decius.

To him succeeded Gallus;[187] who declared his son Volusianus his associate in the empire, and published an open declaration, that Decius and his army had perished by his contrivance. The Barbarians now became more prosperous than before. For Callus not only permitted them to return home with the plunder, but promised to pay them annually a sum of money, and allowed them to carry off all the noblest captives; most of whom had been taken at Philippopolis in Thrace.

Gallus, having made these regulations, came to Rome, priding himself on the peace he had made with the Barbarians. And though he at first spoke with approbation of Decius's mode of government, and adopted one of his sons, yet, after some time was elapsed, fearing that some of them who were fond of new projects might recur to a recapitulation of the princely virtues of Decius, and therefore might at some opportunity give the empire to his son, he concerted the young man's destruction, without regard either to his own adoption of him, or to common honor and justice.

Gallus was so supine in the administration of the empire, that the Scythians in the first place terrified all the neighboring nations, and then laid waste all the countries as far by degrees as the sea coast; not leaving one nation subject to the Romans unpillaged, and taking almost all the unfortified towns, and many that were fortified. Besides the war on every side, which was insupportably burdensome to them, the cities and villages were infested with a pestilence, which swept away the remainder of mankind in those regions; nor was so great a mortality ever known in any former period.

At this crisis, observing that the emperors were unable to defend the state, but neglected all without the walls of Rome, the Goths, the Borani, the Urugundi, and the Carpi once more plundered the cities of Europe of all that had been left in them; while in another quarter, the Persians invaded Asia, in which they acquired possession of Mesopotamia, and proceeded even as far as Antioch in Syria, took that city, which is the metropolis of all the east, destroyed many of the inhabitants, and carried the remainder into captivity, returning home with immense plunder, after they had destroyed all the buildings in the city, both public and private, without meeting with the least resistance. And indeed the Persians had a fair opportunity to have made themselves masters of all Asia, had they not been so overjoyed at their excessive spoils, as to be contented with keeping and carrying home what they had acquired.

Meantime the Scythians of Europe were in perfect security and went over into Asia, spoiling all the country as far as Cappadocia, Pesinus, and Ephesus, until Aemilianus, commander of the Pannonian legions, endeavoring as much as possible to encourage his troops, whom the prosperity of the Barbarians had so disheartened that they durst not face them, and reminding them of the renown of Roman courage, surprised the Barbarians that were in that neighborhood. Having destroyed great numbers of them, and led his forces into their country, removing every obstruction to his progress, and at length freeing the subjects of the Roman empire from their ferocity, he was appointed emperor by his army. On this he collected all the forces of that country, who were become more bold since his successes against the Barbarians, and directed his march towards Italy, with the design of fighting Gallus, who was as yet unprepared to contend with him. For Gallus had never heard of what had occurred in the east, and therefore made only what accidental preparations were in his reach, while Valerianus went to bring the Celtic and German legions. But Aemilianus

---

[186] Decius, emperor 249–251. His son Herennius Etruscus was co-emperor in 251, but was killed in battle.
[187] Trebonianus Gallus, emperor 251–253.

advanced with great speed into Italy, and the armies were very near to each other, when the soldiers of Gallus, reflecting that his force was much inferior to the enemy both in number and strength, and likewise that he was a negligent indolent man, put him and his son to death, and going over to the party of Aemilianus, appeared to establish his authority.[188]

EUSEBIUS

The Persecution under Decius

Source: Eusebius *Eccl. Hist.* 6.39–41. Translated by Arthur Cushman McGiffert. From *Nicene and Post-Nicene Fathers, Second Series*, Vol. 1. Edited by Philip Schaff and Henry Wace. Buffalo, NY: Christian Literature Publishing Co., 1890.

> *Eusebius, Bishop of Caesarea from 314 CE, wrote both church history and studies of the Gospel and other Christian texts.*

After a reign of seven years Philip was succeeded by Decius. [189] On account of his hatred of Philip, he commenced a persecution of the churches,[190] in which Fabianus suffered martyrdom at Rome, and Cornelius succeeded him in the episcopate.

In Palestine, Alexander, bishop of the church of Jerusalem, was brought again on Christ's account before the governor's judgment seat in Cæsarea, and having acquitted himself nobly in a second confession was cast into prison, crowned with the hoary locks of venerable age.

And after his honorable and illustrious confession at the tribunal of the governor, he fell asleep in prison, and Mazabanes became his successor in the bishopric of Jerusalem.

Babylas in Antioch, having like Alexander passed away in prison after his confession, was succeeded by Fabius in the episcopate of that church.

But how many and how great things came upon Origen in the persecution, and what was their final result—as the demon of evil marshaled all his forces, and fought against the man with his utmost craft and power, assaulting him beyond all others against whom he contended at that time,—and what and how many things he endured for the word of Christ, bonds and bodily tortures and torments under the iron collar and in the dungeon; and how for many days with his feet stretched four spaces in the stocks he bore patiently the threats of fire and whatever other things were inflicted by his enemies; and how his sufferings terminated, as his judge strove eagerly with all his might not to end his life;

and what words he left after these things, full of comfort to those needing aid, a great many of his epistles show with truth and accuracy.

I shall quote from the epistle of Dionysius to Germanus an account of what befell the former. Speaking of himself, he writes as follows: I speak before God, and he knows that I do not lie. I did not flee on my own impulse nor without divine direction.

But even before this, at the very hour when the Decian persecution was commanded, Sabinus sent a frumentarius to search for me, and I remained at home four days awaiting his arrival.

But he went about examining all places—roads, rivers, and fields—where he thought I might be concealed or on the way. But he was smitten with blindness, and did not find the house, for he did not suppose, that being pursued, I would remain at home. And after the fourth day God commanded me to depart, and made a way for me in a wonderful manner; and I and my attendants and many of the brethren went away together. And that this occurred through the providence of God was made manifest by what followed, in which perhaps we were useful to some.

Farther on he relates in this manner what happened to him after his flight:

"For about sunset, having been seized with those that were with me, I was taken by the soldiers to Taposiris, but in the providence of God, Timothy was not present and was not captured. But coming later, he found the house deserted and guarded by soldiers, and ourselves reduced to slavery."

After a little he says:

And what was the manner of his admirable management? For the truth shall be told. One of the country people met Timothy fleeing and disturbed, and inquired the cause of his haste. And he told him the truth.

And when the man heard it (he was on his way to a marriage feast, for it was customary to spend the entire night in such gatherings), he entered and announced it to those at the table. And they, as if on a preconcerted signal, arose with one impulse, and rushed out quickly and came and burst in upon us with a shout. Immediately the soldiers who were guarding us fled, and they came to us lying as we were upon the bare couches.

But I, God knows, thought at first that they were robbers who had come for spoil and plunder. So I remained upon the bed on which I was, clothed only in a linen garment, and offered them the rest of my clothing which was lying beside me. But they directed me to rise and come away quickly.

Then I understood why they had come, and I cried out, beseeching and entreating them to depart and leave us alone. And I requested them, if they desired to benefit me in any way, to anticipate those who were carrying

---

[188] Aemelian, emperor Aug.–Oct. 253.
[189] Decius, emperor 249–251.
[190] Philip the Arab had been tolerant toward Christians; Eusebius suggests Philip was himself a secret Christian, but there is no support for this in other sources.

Page 116

me off, and cut off my head themselves. And when I had cried out in this manner, as my companions and partners in everything know, they raised me by force. But I threw myself on my back on the ground; and they seized me by the hands and feet and dragged me away.

And the witnesses of all these occurrences followed: Gaius, Faustus, Peter, and Paul. But they who had seized me carried me out of the village hastily, and placing me on an ass without a saddle, bore me away.

Dionysius relates these things respecting himself.

The same writer, in an epistle to Fabius, bishop of Antioch, relates as follows the sufferings of the martyrs in Alexandria under Decius:

The persecution among us did not begin with the royal decree, but preceded it an entire year. The prophet and author of evils to this city, whoever he was, previously moved and aroused against us the masses of the heathen, rekindling among them the superstition of their country.

And being thus excited by him and finding full opportunity for any wickedness, they considered this the only pious service of their demons, that they should slay us.

They seized first an old man named Metras, and commanded him to utter impious words. But as he would not obey, they beat him with clubs, and tore his face and eyes with sharp sticks, and dragged him out of the city and stoned him.

Then they carried to their idol temple a faithful woman, named Quinta, that they might force her to worship. And as she turned away in detestation, they bound her feet and dragged her through the entire city over the stone-paved streets, and dashed her against the millstones, and at the same time scourged her; then, taking her to the same place, they stoned her to death.

Then all with one impulse rushed to the homes of the pious, and they dragged forth whomsoever any one knew as a neighbor, and despoiled and plundered them. They took for themselves the more valuable property; but the poorer articles and those made of wood they scattered about and burned in the streets, so that the city appeared as if taken by an enemy.

But the brethren withdrew and went away, and 'took joyfully the spoiling of their goods,' like those to whom Paul bore witness. I know of no one unless possibly some one who fell into their hands, who, up to this time, denied the Lord.

Then they seized also that most admirable virgin, Apollonia, an old woman, and, smiting her on the jaws, broke out all her teeth. And they made a fire outside the city and threatened to burn her alive if she would not join with them in their impious cries. And she, supplicating a little, was released, when she leaped eagerly into the fire and was consumed.

Then they seized Serapion in his own house, and tortured him with harsh cruelties, and having broken all his limbs, they threw him headlong from an upper story. And there was no street, nor public road, nor lane open to us, by night or day; for always and everywhere, all of them cried out that if any one would not repeat their impious words, he should immediately be dragged away and burned.

And matters continued thus for a considerable time. But a sedition and civil war came upon the wretched people and turned their cruelty toward us against one another. So we breathed for a little while as they ceased from their rage against us. But presently the change from that milder reign was announced to us, and great fear of what was threatened seized us.

For the decree arrived, almost like that most terrible time foretold by our Lord, which if it were possible would offend even the elect.

All truly were affrighted. And many of the more eminent in their fear came forward immediately; others who were in the public service were drawn on by their official duties; others were urged on by their acquaintances. And as their names were called they approached the impure and impious sacrifices. Some of them were pale and trembled as if they were not about to sacrifice, but to be themselves sacrifices and offerings to the idols; so that they were jeered at by the multitude who stood around, as it was plain to every one that they were afraid either to die or to sacrifice.

But some advanced to the altars more readily, declaring boldly that they had never been Christians. Of these the prediction of our Lord is most true that they shall 'hardly' be saved. Of the rest some followed the one, others the other of these classes, some fled and some were seized.

And of the latter some continued faithful until bonds and imprisonment, and some who had even been imprisoned for many days yet abjured the faith before they were brought to trial. Others having for a time endured great tortures finally retracted.

But the firm and blessed pillars of the Lord being strengthened by him, and having received vigor and might suitable and appropriate to the strong faith which they possessed, became admirable witnesses of his kingdom.

The first of these was Julian, a man who suffered so much with the gout that he was unable to stand or walk. They brought him forward with two others who carried him. One of these immediately denied. But the other, whose name was Cronion, and whose surname was Eunus, and the old man Julian himself, both of them having confessed the Lord, were carried on camels through the entire city, which, as you know, is a very large one, and in this elevated position were beaten and finally burned in a fierce fire, surrounded by all the populace.

But a soldier, named Besas, who stood by them as they were led away rebuked those who insulted them. And they cried out against him, and this most manly warrior of God was arraigned, and having done nobly in the great contest for piety, was beheaded.

A certain other one, a Libyan by birth, but in name and blessedness a true Macar, was strongly urged by the judge to recant; but as he would not yield he was burned alive. After them Epimachus and Alexander, having remained in bonds for a long time, and endured countless agonies from scrapers and scourges, were also consumed in a fierce fire.

And with them there were four women. Ammonarium, a holy virgin, the judge tortured relentlessly and excessively, because she declared from the first that she would utter none of those things which he commanded; and having kept her promise truly, she was dragged away. The others were Mercuria, a very remarkable old woman, and Dionysia, the mother of many children, who did not love her own children above the Lord. As the governor was ashamed of torturing thus ineffectually, and being always defeated by women, they were put to death by the sword, without the trial of tortures. For the champion, Ammonarium, endured these in behalf of all.

The Egyptians, Heron and Ater and Isidorus, and with them Dioscorus, a boy about fifteen years old, were delivered up. At first the judge attempted to deceive the lad by fair words, as if he could be brought over easily, and then to force him by tortures, as one who would readily yield. But Dioscorus was neither persuaded nor constrained.

As the others remained firm, he scourged them cruelly and then delivered them to the fire. But admiring the manner in which Dioscorus had distinguished himself publicly, and his wise answers to his persuasions, he dismissed him, saying that on account of his youth he would give him time for repentance. And this most godly Dioscorus is among us now, awaiting a longer conflict and more severe contest.

But a certain Nemesion, who also was an Egyptian, was accused as an associate of robbers; but when he had cleared himself before the centurion of this charge most foreign to the truth, he was informed against as a Christian, and taken in bonds before the governor. And the most unrighteous magistrate inflicted on him tortures and scourgings double those which he executed on the robbers, and then burned him between the robbers, thus honoring the blessed man by the likeness to Christ.

A band of soldiers, Ammon and Zeno and Ptolemy and Ingenes, and with them an old man, Theophilus, were standing close together before the tribunal. And as a certain person who was being tried as a Christian, seemed inclined to deny, they standing by gnashed their teeth, and made signs with their faces and stretched out their hands, and gestured with their bodies. And when the attention of all was turned to them, before any one else could seize them, they rushed up to the tribunal saying that they were Christians, so that the governor and his council were affrighted. And those who were on trial appeared most courageous in prospect of their sufferings, while their judges trembled. And they went exultingly from the tribunal rejoicing in their testimony; God himself having caused them to triumph gloriously.

VOPISCUS

Aurelian's Conquest of Palmyra

Source: Vopiscus: Life of Aurelian. From: William Stearns Davis, ed., Readings in Ancient History: Illustrative Extracts from the Sources, 2 Vols. (Boston: Allyn and Bacon, 1912-13), Vol. II: Rome and the West. Scanned by: J. S. Arkenberg, Dept. of History, Cal. State Fullerton. Prof. Arkenberg has modernized the text.

During the disasters of the middle of the third century CE the Asiatic provinces of the Empire were nearly torn away, first by the Persians, then by the rulers of Palmyra, a thriving and powerful city situated upon an oasis in the Syrian desert. From 266 to 273 CE. the sovereign of this city and the "Queen of the East" was Zenobia, a woman of courage and energy, who almost founded an Oriental empire to the detriment of Rome. From this dismemberment the Roman world was saved by the Emperor Aurelian, who among his other conquests overcame Zenobia and destroyed Palmyra (273 CE), after no puny struggle.

After taking Tyana and winning a small battle near Daphne, Aurelian took possession of Antioch, having promised to grant pardon to all the inhabitants, and—acting on the counsel of the venerable Apollonius—he showed himself most humane and merciful. Next, close by Emesa,[191] he gave battle to Zenobia and to her ally Zaba—a great battle in which the very fate of the Empire hung in the issue. Already the cavalry of Aurelian were weary, wavering, and about to take flight, when, by divine assistance, a kind of celestial apparition renewed their courage, and the infantry coming to the aid of the cavalry, they rallied stoutly. Zenobia and Zaba were defeated, and the victory was complete. Aurelian, thus made master of the East, entered Emesa as conqueror. First of all he presented himself in the temple of Elagabalus, as if to discharge himself of an ordinary vow—but there he beheld the same divine figure which he had seen come to succor him during the battle. Therefore in that same place he consecrated some

---

[191] A very sacred city, and the great seat of the worship of the Syrian sun god Elagabalus.

temples, with splendid presents; he also erected in Rome a temple to the Sun, and consecrated it with great pomp.

Afterward he marched on Palmyra, to end his labors by the taking of that city. The robber bands of Syria, however, made constant attacks while his army was on the march; and during the siege he was in great danger by being wounded by an arrow. Finally, wearied and discouraged by his losses, Aurelian undertook to write to Zenobia, pledging her—if she would surrender, to preserve her life—in the following letter: "Aurelian, Emperor of Rome and Restorer of the Orient to Zenobia and those waging war on her side. You should have done what I commanded you in my [former] letter. I promise you life if you surrender. You, O Zenobia, can live with your family in the place which I will assign you upon the advice of the venerable Senate. You must deliver to the treasury of Rome your jewels, your silver, your gold, your robes of silk, your horses and your camels. The Palmyrenes, however, shall preserve their local rights."

Zenobia replied to this letter with a pride and boldness, not at all in accord with her fortune. For she imagined that she could intimidate him. "Zenobia, Queen of the East, to Aurelian Augustus. No one, saving you, has ever required of me what you have in your letter. One ought in war to harken only to the voice of courage. You demand that I surrender myself, as if you did not know that the Queen Cleopatra preferred to die rather than to live in any other save her station. The Persians do not abandon us, and we will wait their succors. The Saracens and the Armenians are on our side. The brigands of Syria have defeated your army, O Aurelian; what will it be when we have received the reinforcements which come to us from all sides? You will lower then that tone with which you—as if already full conqueror—now bid me to surrender."

On the reading of this letter the Emperor did not blush, yet he was angered, and at once assembling his army with his generals, and surrounding Palmyra on all sides, the great Emperor devoted his attention to everything; for he cut off the succors from the Persians, and corrupted the hordes of Saracens and Armenians, winning them over sometimes by his severity, sometimes by his adroitness; in brief, after many attacks, the valiant Queen was vanquished. Although she fled on camels by which she strove to reach the Persians, the cavalrymen sent in pursuit captured her, and brought her to Aurelian.

The tumult of the soldiers—requiring that Zenobia be given up for punishment—was very violent; but Aurelian conceived that it would be shameful to put to death a woman, so he contented himself with executing most of those men who had fomented, prepared, and conducted this war, reserving Zenobia to adorn his triumph and to feast the eye of the Roman People. It is grievous that he must need place in the number of those massacred the philosopher Longinus, who was—it is said—the master of Zenobia in the Greek tongue. It is alleged that Aurelian consented to his death because there was attributed to him that aforenamed letter so full of offensive pride.

It is seldom and even difficult that Syrians remain faithful. The Palmyrenes, who had been defeated and conquered, seeing that Aurelian had gone away and was busy with the affairs of Europe, wished to give the power to one Achilleus, a kinsman of Zenobia, and stirred up a great revolt. They slew six hundred archers and Sandrion, whom Aurelian had left as governor in their region; but the Emperor, ever in arms, hastened back from Europe, and destroyed Palmyra, even as it deserved.

In his magnificent triumph, celebrated in Rome after Aurelian had conquered Tetricius, the usurping "Emperor of Gaul," and other enemies, Zenobia was led in procession exposed to public view, adorned with jewels, and loaded with chains of gold so heavy that some of her guards had to hold them up for her. Later, however, she was treated with great humanity, granted a palace near Rome, and spent her last days in peace and luxury.

DIOCLETIAN AND CONSTANTINE
Efforts to Stabilize the Economy

Source: Bruce Bartlett, "How Excessive Government Killed Ancient Rome", *Cato Institute Journal* 14: 2, Fall 1994.

The third century crisis in Roman government took a number of forms—political, military, and economic. By the reign of Claudius II Gothicus (268-270 A.D.) the silver content of the denarius was down to just 0.02%. As a consequence, prices skyrocketed. A measure of Egyptian wheat, for example, which sold for seven to eight drachmas in the second century now cost 120,000 drachmas. This suggests an inflation of 15,000 percent during the third century. As part of their efforts to make the empire secure, Diocletian and Constantine I both instituted economic polices with the goal of stabilizing prices and ensuring social stability. These tasks have proved beyond the means of modern governments with millions of employees available to implement policy: it is certain that the very small corps of administrators in the Roman Empire could have had chance of imposing such rules. At all events, these regulations do not seem to have worked..

Diocletian: Prices Edict, 301, Preamble

For who is so hard and so devoid of human feeling that he cannot, or rather has not perceived, that in the commerce carried on in the markets or involved in the daily life of cities immoderate prices are so widespread that the unbridled passion for gain is lessened neither by abundant supplies nor by fruitful years; so that without a doubt men who are busied in these affairs constantly plan to control the very winds and weather from the movements of the stars, and, evil that they are, they cannot endure the watering of the fertile fields by the rains from above which bring the hope of future harvests, since they reckon it their own loss if abundance comes through the moderation of the weather.

Constantine: Edict on Employment

Any person in whose possession a tenant that belongs to another is found not only shall restore the aforesaid tenant to his place of origin but also shall assume the capitation tax for this man for the time that he was with him. Tenants also who meditate flight may be bound with chains and reduced to a servile condition, so that by virtue of a servile condemnation they shall be compelled to fulfill the duties that befit free men.

EUSEBIUS

The Conversion of Constantine

Source: From the *Library of Nicene and Post Nicene Fathers*, 2nd series, Chapters 27–32. (New York: Christian Literature, 1990), Vol I, 489-91.

The conversion of the emperor Constantine to Christianity was remembered by the Church as the triumph of the sacred over the secular.

Being convinced, however, that he needed some more powerful aid than his military forces could afford him, on account of the wicked and magical enchantments which were so diligently practiced by the tyrant, he sought Divine assistance, deeming the possession of arms and a numerous soldiery of secondary importance, but believing the co-operating power of Deity invincible and not to be shaken. He considered, therefore, on what God he might rely for protection and assistance. While engaged in this enquiry, the thought occurred to him, that, of the many emperors who had preceded him, those who had rested their hopes in a multitude of gods, and served them with sacrifices and offerings, had in the first place been deceived by flattering predictions, and oracles which promised them all prosperity, and at last had met with an unhappy end, while not one of their gods had stood by to warn them of the impending wrath of heaven; while one alone who had pursued an entirely opposite course, who had condemned their error, and honored the one Supreme God during his whole life, had formal I him to be the Savior and Protector of his empire, and the Giver of every good thing. Reflecting on

this, and well weighing the fact that they who had trusted in many gods had also fallen by manifold forms of death, without leaving behind them either family or offspring, stock, name, or memorial among men: while the God of his father had given to him, on the other hand, manifestations of his power and very many tokens: and considering farther that those who had already taken arms against the tyrant, and had marched to the battle-field under the protection of a multitude of gods, had met with a dishonorable end (for one of them had shamefully retreated from the contest without a blow, and the other, being slain in the midst of his own troops, became, as it were, the mere sport of death (4)); reviewing, I say, all these considerations, he judged it to be folly indeed to join in the idle worship of those who were no gods, and, after such convincing evidence, to err from the truth; and therefore felt it incumbent on him to honor his father's God alone.

ACCORDINGLY he called on him with earnest prayer and supplications that he would reveal to him who he was, and stretch forth his right hand to help him in his present difficulties. And while he was thus praying with fervent entreaty, a most marvelous sign appeared to him from heaven, the account of which it might have been hard to believe had it been related by any other person. But since the victorious emperor himself long afterwards declared it to the writer of this history, when he was honored with his acquaintance and society, and confirmed his statement by an oath, who could hesitate to accredit the relation, especially since the testimony of after-time has established its truth? He said that about noon, when the day was already beginning to decline, he saw with his own eyes the trophy of a cross of light in the heavens, above the sun, and bearing the inscription, CONQUER BY THIS. At this sight he himself was struck with amazement, and his whole army also, which followed him on this expedition, and witnessed the miracle.

He said, moreover, that he doubted within himself what the import of this apparition could be. And while he continued to ponder and reason on its meaning, night suddenly came on ; then in his sleep the Christ of God appeared to him with the same sign which he had seen in the heavens, and commanded him to make a likeness of that sign which he had seen in the heavens, and to use it as a safeguard in all engagements with his enemies.

AT dawn of day he arose, and communicated the marvel to his friends: and then, calling together the workers in gold and precious stones, he sat in the midst of them, and described to them the figure of the sign he had seen, bidding them represent it in gold and precious stones. And this representation I myself have had an opportunity of seeing.

Now it was made in the following manner. A long spear, overlaid with gold, formed the figure of the cross by means of a transverse bar laid over it. On the top of the whole was fixed a wreath of gold and precious stones; and within this, the symbol of the Savior's name, two letters indicating the name of Christ by means of its initial characters, the letter P being intersected by X in its centre: and these letters the emperor was in the habit of wearing on his helmet at a later period. From the cross-bar of the spear was suspended a cloth, a royal piece, covered with a profuse embroidery of most brilliant precious stones; and which, being also richly interlaced with gold, presented an indescribable degree of beauty to the beholder. This banner was of a square form, and the upright staff, whose lower section was of great length, bore a golden half-length portrait of the pious emperor and his children on its upper part, beneath the trophy of the cross, and immediately above the embroidered banner.

The emperor constantly made use of this sign of salvation as a safeguard against every adverse and hostile power, and commanded that others similar to it should be carried at the head of all his armies.

These things were done shortly afterwards. But at the time above specified, being struck with amazement at the extraordinary vision, and resolving to worship no other God save Him who had appeared to him, he sent for those who were acquainted with the mysteries of His doctrines, and enquired who that God was, and what was intended by the sign of the vision he had seen. They affirmed that He was God, the only begotten Son of the one and only God: that the sign which had appeared was the symbol of immortality, and the trophy of that victory over death which He had gained in time past when sojourning on earth. They taught him also the causes of His advent, and explained to him the true account of His incarnation. Thus he was instructed in these matters, and was impressed with wonder at the divine manifestation which had been presented to his sight. Comparing, therefore, the heavenly vision with the interpretation given, he found his judgment confirmed; and, in the persuasion that the knowledge of these things had been imparted to him by Divine teaching, he determined thenceforth to devote himself to the reading of the Inspired writings.

Moreover, he made the priests of God his counselors, and deemed it incumbent on him to honor the God who had appeared to him with all devotion. And after this, being fortified by well-grounded hopes in Him, he hastened to quench the threatening fire of tyranny.

CONSTANTINE

The Edict of Milan

Source: Lactantius, *De Mort. Pers.*, ch. 48. opera, ed. 0. F. Fritzsche, II, p 288 sq. (Bibl Patr. Ecc. Lat. XI). Translated in University of Pennsylvania. Dept. of History: Translations and Reprints from the Original Sources of European history, (Philadelphia, University of Pennsylvania Press [1897?-1907?]), Vol 4:, 1, pp. 28-30.

The persecution of Christians ended in 313 CE when Constantine of the West and Licinius of the East proclaimed the Edict of Milan, which established a policy of religious freedom for all. This is an English translation of the edict.

When I, Constantine Augustus, as well as I, Licinius Augustus, fortunately met near Mediolanurn (Milan), and were considering everything that pertained to the public welfare and security, we thought, among other things which we saw would be for the good of many, those regulations pertaining to the reverence of the Divinity ought certainly to be made first, so that we might grant to the Christians and others full authority to observe that religion which each preferred; whence any Divinity whatsoever in the seat of the heavens may be propitious and kindly disposed to us and all who are placed under our rule. And thus by this wholesome counsel and most upright provision we thought to arrange that no one whatsoever should be denied the opportunity to give his heart to the observance of the Christian religion, of that religion which he should think best for himself, so that the Supreme Deity, to whose worship we freely yield our hearts) may show in all things His usual favor and benevolence. Therefore, your Worship should know that it has pleased us to remove all conditions whatsoever, which were in the rescripts formerly given to you officially, concerning the Christians and now any one of these who wishes to observe Christian religion may do so freely and openly, without molestation. We thought it fit to commend these things most fully to your care that you may know that we have given to those Christians free and unrestricted opportunity of religious worship. When you see that this has been granted to them by us, your Worship will know that we have also conceded to other religions the right of open and free observance of their worship for the sake of the peace of our times, that each one may have the free opportunity to worship as he pleases; this regulation is made we that we may not seem to detract from any dignity or any religion.

Moreover, in the case of the Christians especially we esteemed it best to order that if it happens anyone heretofore has bought from our treasury from anyone whatsoever, those places where they were previously accustomed to assemble, concerning which a certain decree had been made and a letter sent to you officially, the same shall be restored to the Christians without payment or any claim of recompense and without any kind of fraud or deception, Those, moreover, who have obtained the same by gift, are likewise to return them at once to the Christians. Besides, both those who have purchased and those who have secured them by gift, are to appeal to the vicar if they seek any recompense from our bounty, that they may be cared for through our clemency. All this property ought to be delivered at once to the community of the Christians through your intercession, and without delay. And since these Christians are known to have possessed not only those places in which they were accustomed to assemble, but also other property, namely the churches, belonging to them as a corporation and not as individuals, all these things which we have included under the above law, you will order to be restored, without any hesitation or controversy at all, to these Christians, that is to say to the corporations and their conventicles: providing, of course, that the above arrangements be followed so that those who return the same without payment, as we have said, may hope for an indemnity from our bounty. In all these circumstances you ought to tender your most efficacious intervention to the community of the Christians, that our command may be carried into effect as quickly as possible, whereby, moreover, through our clemency, public order may be secured. Let this be done so that, as we have said above, Divine favor towards us, which, under the most important circumstances we have already experienced, may, for all time, preserve and prosper our successes together with the good of the state. Moreover, in order that the statement of this decree of our good will may come to the notice of all, this rescript, published by your decree, shall be announced everywhere and brought to the knowledge of all, so that the decree of this, our benevolence, cannot be concealed.

SOZOMEN

Constantine Founds Constantinople

Source: Sozomen *Ecclesiastical History*, II.3. From: William Stearns Davis, ed., Readings in Ancient History: Illustrative Extracts from the Sources, 2 Vols. (Boston: Allyn and Bacon, 1912-13), Vol. II: Rome and the West, 295-296

Nothing that Constantine the Great did shows his ability more clearly than his seizing upon the site of old Byzantium for the location for his new capital [324 CE]. The place was admirably sited for an imperial residence, being over against Asia which the Persians were threatening, and in easy touch with the Danube, where the Northern Barbarians were always swarming. Constantinople was from the outset a Christian city; as contrasted with old Rome, where paganism still kept a firm grip, at least on much of the population, for nearly a century.

The Emperor [Constantine] always intent on the advancement of religion erected splendid Christian temples to God in every place—especially in great cities such as Nicomedia in Bithynia, Antioch on the Orontes, and Byzantium. He greatly improved this latter city, and made it equal to Rome in power and influence; for when he had settled his empire as he was minded, and had freed himself from foreign foes, he resolved on founding a city which should be called by his own name, and should equal in fame even Rome. With this intent he went to the plain at the foot of Troy on the Hellespont... and here he laid out the plan of a large and beautiful city, and built gates on a high spot of ground, whence they are still visible from the sea to sailors. But when he had proceeded thus far, God appeared to him by night and bade him seek another site for his city.

Led by the divine hand, he came to Byzantium in Thrace, beyond Chalcedon in Bithynia, and here he desired to build his city, and render it worthy of the name of Constantine. In obedience to the command of God, he therefore enlarged the city formerly called Byzantium, and surrounded it with high walls; likewise he built splendid dwelling houses; and being aware that the former population was not enough for so great a city, he peopled it with men of rank and their families, whom he summoned from Rome and from other countries. He imposed special taxes to cover the expenses of building and adorning the city, and of supplying the inhabitants with food. He erected all the needed edifices for a great capital—a hippodrome, fountains, porticoes and other beautiful adornments. He named it Constantinople and New Rome—and established it as the Roman capital for all the inhabitants of the North, the South, the East, and the shores of the Mediterranean, from the cities on the Danube and from Epidamnus and the Ionian Gulf to Cyrene and Libya.

He created another Senate which he endowed with the same honors and privileges as that of Rome, and he strove to render the city of his name equal in every way to Rome in Italy; nor were his wishes in vain, for by the favor of God, it became the most populous and wealthy of cities. As this city became the capital of the Empire during the period of religious prosperity, it was not polluted by altars, Grecian temples, nor pagan sacrifices. Constantine also honored this new city of Christ by adorning it with many and splendid houses of prayer, in which the Deity vouchsafed to bless the efforts of the Emperor by giving sensible manifestations of his presence.

Letter to Arsacius

Based in part on the translation of Edward J. Chinnock, A Few Notes on Julian and a Translation of His Public Letters (London: David Nutt, 1901) pp. 75-78 as quoted in D. Brendan Nagle and Stanley M. Burstein, The Ancient World: Readings in Social and Cultural History (Englewood Cliffs, NJ; Prentice Hall, 1995) pp. 314-315.

The Emperor Julian, who reigned around the year 360, like all Emperors, was Pontifex Maximus, Chief Priest of the State Religion. He became known as Julian the Apostate for abandoning Christianity in favor of traditional Roman paganism.

The religion of the Greeks does not yet prosper as I would wish, on account of those who profess it. But the gifts of the gods are great and splendid, better than any prayer or any hope ... Indeed, a little while ago no one would have dared even to pray for a such change, and so complete a one in so short a space of time.[192] Why then do we think that this is sufficient and do not observe how the kindness of Christians to strangers, their care for the burial of their dead, and the sobriety of their lifestyle has done the most to advance their cause?

Each of these things, I think, ought really to be practiced by us. It is not sufficient for you alone to practice them, but so must all the priests in Galatia[193] without exception. Either make these men good by shaming them, persuade them to become so or fire them ... Secondly, exhort the priests neither to approach a theater nor to drink in a tavern, nor to profess any base or infamous trade. Honor those who obey and expel those who disobey.

Erect many hostels, one in each city, in order that strangers may enjoy my kindness, not only those of our own faith but also of others whosoever is in want of money. I have just been devising a plan by which you will be able to get supplies. For I have ordered that every year throughout all Galatia 30,000 modii of grain and 60,000 pints of wine shall be provided. The fifth part of these I order to be expended on the poor who serve the priests, and the rest must be distributed from me to strangers and beggars. For it is disgraceful when no Jew is a beggar and the impious Galileans[194] support our poor in addition to their own; everyone is able to see that our coreligionists are in want of aid from us. Teach also those who profess the Greek religion to contribute to such services, and the villages of the Greek religion to offer the first-fruits to the gods. Accustom those of the Greek religion to such benevolence, teaching them that this has been our work from ancient times. Homer, at any rate, made Eumaeus say: "O Stranger, it is not lawful for me, even if one poorer than you should come, to

dishonor a stranger. For all strangers and beggars are from Zeus. The gift is small, but it is precious."[195] Do not therefore let others outdo us in good deeds while we ourselves are disgraced by laziness; rather, let us not quite abandon our piety toward the gods ...

While proper behavior in accordance with the laws of the city will obviously be the concern of the governors of the cities, you for your part [as a priest] must take care to encourage people not to violate the laws of the gods since they are holy ... Above all you must exercise philanthropy. From it result many other goods, and indeed that which is the greatest blessing of all, the goodwill of the gods ...

We ought to share our goods with all men, but most of all with the respectable, the helpless, and the poor, so that they have at least the essentials of life. I claim, even though it may seem paradoxical, that it is a holy deed to share our clothes and food with the wicked: we give, not to their moral character but to their human character. Therefore I believe that even prisoners deserve the same kind of care. This type of kindness will not interfere with the process of justice, for among the many imprisoned and awaiting trial some will be found guilty, some innocent. It would be cruel indeed if out of consideration for the innocent we should not allow some pity for the guilty, or on account of the guilty we should behave without mercy and humanity to those who have done no wrong ... How can the man who, while worshipping Zeus the God of Companions, sees his neighbors in need and does not give them a dime—how can he think he is worshipping Zeus properly? ...

Priests ought to make a point of not doing impure or shameful deeds or saying words or hearing talk of this type. We must therefore get rid of all offensive jokes and licentious associations. What I mean is this: no priest is to read Archilochus or Hipponax or anyone else who writes poetry as they do. They should stay away from the same kind of stuff in Old Comedy. Philosophy alone is appropriate for us priests. Of the philosophers, however, only those who put the gods before them as guides of their intellectual life are acceptable, like Pythagoras, Plato, Aristotle, and the Stoics ... only those who make people reverent ... not the works of Pyrrho and Epicurus ... We ought to pray often to the gods in private and in public, about three times a day, but if not that often, at least in the morning and at night.

No priest is anywhere to attend shameful theatrical shows or to have one performed at his own house; it is in no way appropriate. Indeed, if it were possible to get rid of such shows altogether from the theater and restore the theaters, purified, to Dionysus as in the olden days, I would certainly have tried to bring this about. But since I thought that this was out of the question, and even if possible would for other reasons be inexpedient,

---

[192] I.e., the arrival of Julian himself, a reforming traditionalist, on the throne.
[193] A region in Asia Minor, modern Turkey.
[194] The name given by Julian to Christians.

[195] Julian is quoting from the Odyssey, 14-531.

I did not even try. But I do insist that priests stay away from the licentiousness of the theaters and leave them to the people. No priest is to enter a theater, have an actor or a chariot driver as a friend, or allow a dancer or mime into his house. I allow to attend the sacred games those who want to, that is, they may attend only those games from which women are forbidden to attend not only as participants but even as spectators.

AMMIANUS MARCELLINUS

The Luxury of the Rich in Rome

Source: Ammianus Marcellinus, History, XIV.16. From: William Stearns Davis, ed., Readings in Ancient History: Illustrative Extracts from the Sources, 2 Vols. (Boston: Allyn and Bacon, 1912-13), Vol. II: Rome and the West, pp. 224-225, 239-244, 247-258, 260-265, 305-309.

The following was written only about a generation before Alaric plundered Rome in 410 CE. Ammianus Marcellinus, who observed Rome on a visit, saw the city as full of emptiness, shallowness, and as lacking of all real culture.

Rome is still looked upon as the queen of the earth, and the name of the Roman people is respected and venerated. But the magnificence of Rome is defaced by the inconsiderate levity of a few, who never recollect where they are born, but fall away into error and licentiousness as if a perfect immunity were granted to vice. Of these men, some, thinking that they can be handed down to immortality by means of statues, are eager after them, as if they would obtain a higher reward from brazen figures unendowed with sense than from a consciousness of upright and honorable actions; and they are even anxious to have them plated over with gold!

Others place the summit of glory in having a couch higher than usual, or splendid apparel; and so toil and sweat under a vast burden of cloaks which are fastened to their necks by many clasps, and blow about by the excessive fineness of the material, showing a desire by the continual wriggling of their bodies, and especially by the waving of the left hand, to make more conspicuous their long fringes and tunics, which are embroidered in multiform figures of animals with threads of divers colors.

Others again, put on a feigned severity of countenance, and extol their patrimonial estates in a boundless degree, exaggerating the yearly produce of their fruitful fields, which they boast of possessing in numbers, from east and west, being forsooth ignorant that their ancestors, who won greatness for Rome, were not eminent in riches; but through many a direful war overpowered their foes by valor, though little above the common privates in riches, or luxury, or costliness of garments.

If now you, as an honorable stranger, should enter the house of any passing rich man, you will be hospitably received, as though you were very welcome; and after having had many questions put to you, and having been forced to tell a number of lies, you will wonder—since the gentleman has never seen you before—that a person of high rank should pay such attention to a humble individual like yourself, so that you become exceeding happy, and begin to repent not having come to Rome ten years before. When, however, relying on this affability you do the same thing the next day, you will stand waiting as one utterly unknown and unexpected, while he who yesterday urged you to "come again," counts upon his fingers who you can be, marveling for a long time whence you came, and what you can want. But when at last you are recognized and admitted to his acquaintance, if you should devote yourself to him for three years running, and after that cease with your visits for the same stretch of time, then at last begin them again, you will never be asked about your absence any more than if you had been dead, and you will waste your whole life trying to court the humors of this blockhead.

But when those long and unwholesome banquets, which are indulged in at periodic intervals, begin to be prepared, or the distribution of the usual dole baskets takes place, then it is discussed with anxious care, whether, when those to whom a return is due are to be entertained, it is also proper to ask in a stranger; and if after the question has been duly sifted, it is determined that this may be done, the person preferred is one who hangs around all night before the houses of charioteers, or one who claims to be an expert with dice, or affects to possess some peculiar secrets. For hosts of this stamp avoid all learned and sober men as unprofitable and useless—with this addition, that the nomenclators also, who usually make a market of these invitations and such favors, selling them for bribes, often for a fee thrust into these dinners mean and obscure creatures indeed.

The whirlpool of banquets, and divers other allurements of luxury I omit, lest I grow too prolix. Many people drive on their horses recklessly, as if they were post horses, with a legal right of way, straight down the boulevards of the city, and over the flint-paved streets, dragging behind them huge bodies of slaves, like bands of robbers. And many matrons, imitating these men, gallop over every quarter of the city, with their heads covered, and in closed carriages. And so the stewards of these city households make careful arrangement of the cortege; the stewards themselves being conspicuous by the wands in their right hands. First of all before the master's carriage march all his slaves concerned with spinning and working; next come the blackened crew employed in the kitchen; then the whole body of slaves promiscuously mixed with a gang of idle plebeians; and last of all, the multitude of eunuchs, beginning with the old men and ending with the boys, pale and unsightly from the deformity of their features.

Those few mansions which were once celebrated for the serious cultivation of liberal studies, now are filled with ridiculous amusements of torpid indolence, reechoing with the sound of singing, and the tinkle of flutes and lyres. You find a singer instead of a philosopher; a teacher of silly arts is summoned in place of an orator, the libraries are shut up like tombs, organs played by waterpower are built, and lyres so big that they look like wagons! and flutes, and huge machines suitable for the theater. The Romans have even sunk so far, that not long ago, when a dearth was apprehended, and the foreigners were driven from the city, those who practiced liberal accomplishments were expelled instantly, yet the followers of actresses and all their ilk were suffered to stay; and three thousand dancing girls were not even questioned, but remained unmolested along with the members of their choruses, and a corresponding number of dancing masters.

On account of the frequency of epidemics in Rome, rich men take absurd precautions to avoid contagion, but even when these rules are observed thus stringently, some persons, if they be invited to a wedding, though the vigor of their limbs be vastly diminished, yet when gold is pressed in their palm they will go with all activity as far as Spoletum! So much for the nobles. As for the lower and poorer classes some spend the whole night in the wine shops, some lie concealed in the shady arcades of the theaters. They play at dice so eagerly as to quarrel over them, snuffing up their nostrils, and making unseemly noises by drawing back their breath into their noses:—or (and this is their favorite amusement by far) from sunrise till evening, through sunshine or rain, they stay gaping and examining the charioteers and their horses; and their good and bad qualities. Wonderful indeed it is to see an innumerable multitude of people, with prodigious eagerness, intent upon the events of the chariot race!

PROCOPIUS OF CAESAREA

Alaric's Sack of Rome, 410 CE

Source: History of the Wars [written c. 550 CE], III.ii.7-39. From: Procopius, History of the Wars, 7 vols., trans. H. B. Dewing (Cambridge, Mass., and London: Harvard University Press & Wm. Heinemann, 1914; reprint ed., 1953-54), II.11-23. Scanned by: J. S. Arkenberg, Dept. of History, Cal. State Fullerton. Prof. Arkenberg has modernized the text.

The Visigoths' attack on Rome had the side effect of ending Roman rule in Britain, symbolic of the empire's contraction.

But the Visigoths, separating from the others, removed from there and at first entered into an alliance with the Emperor Arcadius, but at a later time (for faith with the Romans cannot dwell in barbarians), under the leadership of Alaric, they became hostile to both emperors, and, beginning with Thrace, treated all Europe as an enemy's land. Now the emperor Honorius had before this time been sitting in Rome, with never a thought of war in his mind, but glad, I think, if men allowed him to remain quiet in his palace. But when word was brought that the barbarians with a great army were not far off, but somewhere among the Taulantii (in Illyricum), he abandoned the palace and fled in disorderly fashion to Ravenna, a strong city lying just about at the end of the Ionian Gulf, while some say that he brought in the barbarians himself, because an uprising had been started against him among his subjects; but this does not seem to me trustworthy, as far, at least, as one can judge of the character of the man. And the barbarians, finding that they had no hostile force to encounter them, became the most cruel of all men. For they destroyed all the cities which they captured, especially those south of the Ionian Gulf, so completely that nothing has been left to my time to know them by, unless, indeed, it might be one tower or one gate or some such thing which chanced to remain. And they killed all the people, as many as came in their way, both old and young alike, sparing neither women nor children. Wherefore, even up to the present time Italy is sparsely populated. They also gathered as plunder all the money out of all Europe, and, most important of all, they left in Rome nothing whatever of public or private wealth when they moved on to Gaul. But I shall now tell how Alaric captured Rome.

After much time had been spent by him in the siege, and he had not been able either by force or by any other device to capture the place, he formed the following plan. Among the youths in the army whose beards had not yet grown, but who had just come of age, he chose out three hundred whom he knew to be of good birth and possessed of valor beyond their years, and told them secretly that he was about to make a present of them to certain of the patricians in Rome, pretending that they were slaves. And he instructed them that, as soon as they got inside the houses of those men, they should display much gentleness and moderation and serve them eagerly in whatever tasks should be laid upon them by their owners; and he further directed them that not long afterwards, on an appointed day at midday, when all those who were to be their masters would most likely be already asleep after their meal, they should all come to the gate called Salarian and with a sudden rush kill the guards, who would have no previous knowledge of the plot, and open the gates as quickly as possible. After giving these orders to the youths, Alaric straightway sent ambassadors to the members of the senate, stating that he admired them for their loyalty toward their emperor, and that he would trouble them no longer, because of their valor and faithfulness, with which it was plain that they were endowed to a remarkable degree, and in order that tokens of himself might be preserved among men both noble and brave, he wished to present each one of them with some domestics.

After making this declaration and sending the youths no long afterwards, he commanded the barbarians to make preparations for the departure, and he let this be known to the Romans. And they heard his words gladly, and receiving the gifts began to be exceedingly happy, since they were completely ignorant of the plot of the barbarians. For the youths, by being unusually obedient to their owners, averted suspicion, and in the camp some were already seen moving from their positions and raising the siege, while it seemed that the others were just on the point of doing the very same thing. But when the appointed day had come, Alaric armed his whole force for the attack and was holding them in readiness close by the Salarian Gate; for it happened that he had encamped there at the beginning of the siege. And all the youths at the time of the day agreed upon came to this gate, and, assailing the guards suddenly, put them to death; then they opened the gates and received Alaric and the army into the city at their leisure. And they set fire to the houses which were next to the gate, among which was also the house of Sallust, who in ancient times wrote the history of the Romans, and the greater part of this house has stood half-burned up to my time; and after plundering the whole city and destroying the most of the Romans, they moved on.

At that time they say that the Emperor Honorius in Ravenna received the message from one of the eunuchs, evidently a keeper of the poultry, that Rome had perished. And he cried out and said, "And yet it has just eaten from my hands!" For he had a very large cock, Roma by name; and the eunuch comprehending his words said that it was the city of Rome which had perished at the hands of Alaric, and the emperor with a sigh of relief answered quickly, "But I, my good fellow, thought that my fowl Roma had perished." So great, they say, was the folly with which this emperor was possessed. But some say that Rome was not captured in this way by Alaric, but that Proba, a woman of very unusual eminence in wealth and in fame among the Roman senatorial class, felt pity for the Romans who were being destroyed by hunger and the other suffering they endured; for they were already even tasting each other's flesh; and seeing that every good hope had left them, since both the river and the harbor were held by the enemy, she commanded her domestics, they say, to open the gates by night.

Now when Alaric was about to depart from Rome, he declared Attalus, one of their nobles, emperor of the Romans, investing him with the diadem and the purple and whatever else pertains to the imperial dignity. And he did this with the intention of removing Honorius from his throne and of giving over the whole power in the

West to Attalus. With such a purpose, then, both Attalus and Alaric were going with a great army against Ravenna. But this Attalus was neither able to think wisely by himself, nor to be persuaded by one who had wisdom to offer. So while Alaric did not by any means approve the plan, Attalus sent commanders to Libya without an army. Thus then, were these things going on.

And the island of Britannia revolted from the Romans, and the soldiers there chose as their emperor Constantinus, a man of no mean station. And he straightway gathered a fleet of ships and a formidable army and invaded both Spain and Gaul with a great force, thinking to enslave these countries. But Honorius was holding ships in readiness and waiting to see what would happen in Libya, in order that, if those sent by Attalus were repulsed, he might himself sail for Libya and keep some portion of his own kingdom, while if matters there should go against him, he might reach Theodosius[196] and remain with him....

But while Honorius was thus anxiously awaiting the outcome of these events and tossed amid the billows of uncertain fortune, it so chanced that some wonderful pieces of good fortune befell him. For God is accustomed to succor those who are neither clever nor able to devise anything of themselves, and to lend them assistance, if they be not wicked, when they are in the last extremity of despair; such a thing, indeed, befell this emperor. For it was suddenly reported from Libya that the commanders of Attalus had been destroyed, and that a host of ships was at hand from Byzantium with a very great number of soldiers who had come to assist him, though he had not expected them, and that Alaric, having quarreled with Attalus, had stripped him of the emperor's garb and was now keeping him under guard as a private citizen.

And afterwards Alaric died of disease, and the army of the Visigoths under the leadership of Adaulphus proceeded into Gaul, and Constantinus, defeated in battle, died with his sons. However, the Romans never succeeded in recovering Britannia, but it remained from that time on under tyrants.

---

[196] Theodosius II, Emperor in the East, 408-450 CE.

RUTILIUS NAMATIANUS

The Greatness of Rome in the Days of Ruin, 413CE

Source: William Stearns Davis, ed., Readings in Ancient History: Illustrative Extracts from the Sources, 2 Vols. (Boston: Allyn and Bacon, 1912-13), Vol. II: Rome and the West, pp. 322-325. Scanned in and modernized by Dr. Jerome S. Arkenberg, Cal. State Fullerton.

Rutilius Namatianus, a native of Gaul but in ca. 413 CE the City Prefect of Rome, wrote this poem in praise of the city that he had seen plundered by Alaric. He was a pagan, one of the circle of literary men who fixed their eyes on the glorious past, and had no pleasure in Christianity. His tribute to the greatness of Rome is clear evidence that even the awful calamities of Honorius' reign did not shatter men's faith in the abiding majesty of the Eternal City.

Give ear to me, Queen of the world which you rule,
O Rome, whose place is amongst the stars!
Give ear to me, mother of men, and mother of gods!
Through your temples we draw near to the very heaven.
You do we sing, yea and while the Fates give us life,
You we will sing.
For who can live and forget you?
Before your image my soul is abased—
Graceless and sacrilegious,
It were better for me to forget the sun,
For your beneficent influence shines
Even as his light
To the limits of the habitable world.
Yea the sun himself, in his vast course,
Seems only to turn in your behalf.
He rises upon your domains;
And on your domains, it is again that he sets.
As far as from one pole to the other spreads the vital
power of nature, so far your virtue has penetrated over
the earth.
For all the scattered nations you created one common
country.
Those that struggle against you are constrained to bend
to your yoke;
For you proffer to the conquered the partnership in your
just laws;
You have made one city what was aforetime the wide
world!
O! Queen, the remotest regions of the universe join in a
hymn to your glory!
Our heads are raised freely under your peaceful yoke.
For you to reign, is less than to have so deserved to
reign;
The grandeur of your deeds surpasses even your mighty
destinies.

JORDANES

The Battle of Chalôns, 451 CE

Source: Jordanes, *The History and Deeds of the Goths*. William Stearns Davis, ed., Readings in Ancient History: Illustrative Extracts from the Sources, 2 Vols. (Boston: Allyn and Bacon, 1912-13), Vol. II: Rome and the West, pp. 322-325. Scanned in and modernized by Dr. Jerome S. Arkenberg, Dept. of History, Cal. State Fullerton.

In 451 CE. Attila the Hun with his horsemen, after having been repulsed before Orleans in Gaul, was brought to bay by Aetius, the Roman general, and his allies, the Germanic Visigoths, Burgundians, and Franks. It should be remembered in this connection that the Huns were, if possible, more hated by the Germans than by the Romans.

The armies met in the Catalaunian Plains. The battlefield was a plain rising by a sharp slope to a ridge which both armies sought to gain; for advantage of position is a great help. The Huns with their forces seized the right side, the Romans, the Visigoths and their allies the left, and then began a struggle for the yet untaken crest. Now Theodoric with his Visigoths held the right wing, and Aetius with the Romans the left [of the line against Attila]. On the other side, the battle line of the Huns was so arranged that Attila and his bravest followers were stationed in the center. In arranging them thus the king had chiefly his own safety in view, since by his position in the very midst of his race, he would be kept out of the way of threatened danger. The innumerable peoples of divers tribes, which he had subjected to his sway, formed the wings. Now the crowd of kings—if we may call them so—and the leaders of various nations hung upon Attila's nod like slaves, and when he gave a sign even by a glance, without a murmur each stood forth in fear and trembling, or at all events did as he was bid. Attila alone was king of kings over all and concerned for all.

So then the struggle began for the advantage of position we have mentioned. Attila sent his men to take the summit of the mountain, but was outstripped by Thorismud[197] and Aetius, who in their effort to gain the top of the hill reached higher ground, and through this advantage easily routed the Huns as they came up. When Attila saw his army was thrown into confusion by the event he [urged them on with a fiery harangue and . . .] inflamed by his words they all dashed into the battle.

And although the situation was itself fearful, yet the presence of the king dispelled anxiety and hesitation. Hand to hand they clashed in battle, and the fight grew fierce, confused, monstrous, unrelenting—a fight whose like no ancient time has ever recorded. There were such deeds done that a brave man who missed this marvelous spectacle could not hope to see anything so wonderful all his life long. For if we may believe our elders a brook

---

[197] Crown prince of the Visigoths.

flowing between low banks through the plain was greatly increased by blood from the wounds of the slain. Those whose wounds drove them to slake their parching thirst drank water mingled with gore. In their wretched plight they were forced to drink what they thought was the blood they had poured out from their own wounds.

Here King Theodoric [the Visigoth] while riding by to encourage his army, was thrown from his horse and trampled underfoot by his own men, thus ending his days at a ripe old age. But others say he was slain by the spear of Andag of the host of the Ostrogoths who were then under the sway of Attila. Then the Visigoths fell on the horde of the Huns and nearly slew Attila. But he prudently took flight and straightway shut himself and his companions within the barriers of the camp which he had fortified with wagons. [The battle now became confused: chieftains became separated from their forces: night fell with the Roman-Gothic army holding the field of combat.]

At dawn on the next day the Romans saw that the fields were piled high with corpses, and that the Huns did not venture forth; they thought that the victory was theirs, but knew that Attila would not flee from battle unless overwhelmed by a great disaster. Yet he did nothing cowardly, like one that is overcome, but with clash of arms sounded the trumpets and threatened an attack. [His enemies] determined to wear him out by a siege. It is said that the king remained supremely brave even in this extremity and had heaped up a funeral pyre of horse trappings, so that if the enemy should attack him he was determined to cast himself into the flames; that none might have the joy of wounding him, and that the lord of so many races might not fall into the hands of his foes. However, owing to dissensions between the Romans and Goths he was allowed to escape to his home land, and in this most famous war of the bravest tribes, 160,000 men are said to have been slain on both sides.

Roman Praenomina

The Roman first name, or *praenomen*, was chosen from a very short list; often those selection was conditioned by a family tradition, such as the firstborn being named M., the second son Sex., and so on. The most common *praenomina* had standardized abbreviations that sometimes reflected archaic spellings. The number of names in used shrank over the course of the Republic.

- ▶ Appius (Ap.)
- ▶ Aulus (A.)
- ▶ Caeso (K.)
- ▶ Decimus (D.)
- ▶ Gaius (C.)
- ▶ Gnaeus (Cn.)
- ▶ Lucius (L.)
- ▶ Mamercus (Mam.)
- ▶ Manius (M'.)
- ▶ Marcus (M.)
- ▶ Numerius (N.)
- ▶ Postumus (Post.)[198]
- ▶ Proculus (Pro.)
- ▶ Publius (P.)
- ▶ Quintus (Q.)
- ▶ Servius (Ser.)
- ▶ Sextus (Sex.)
- ▶ Spurius (S.)
- ▶ Tiberius (Ti.)
- ▶ Titus (T.)
- ▶ Vibius (V.)

Other praenomina:

- ▶ Agrippa
- ▶ Faustus
- ▶ Hostus
- ▶ Mettius
- ▶ Nonus
- ▶ Octavius
- ▶ Opiter
- ▶ Paullus
- ▶ Septimus
- ▶ Sertor
- ▶ Statius
- ▶ Tullus
- ▶ Volesus
- ▶ Vopiscus

---

[198] Normally reserved for boys born after their fathers' deaths.

Made in the USA
Middletown, DE
05 February 2020